SONIA LAWSON

Passions and Alarms

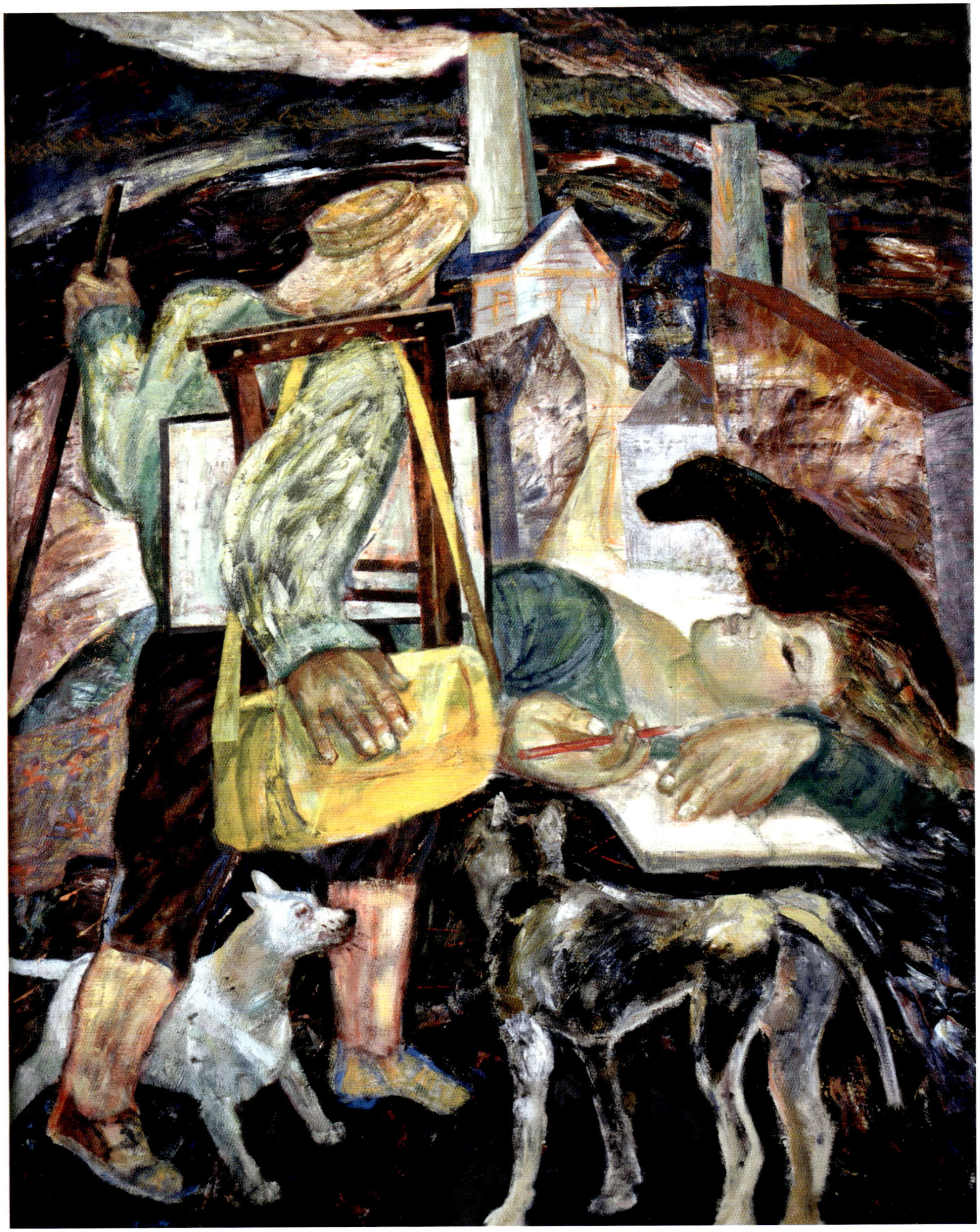

SONIA LAWSON
Passions and Alarms

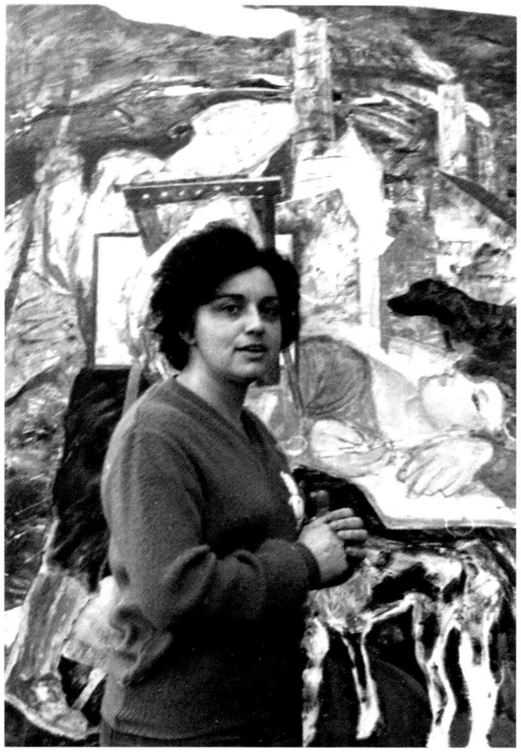

Nicholas Usherwood

Sansom & Company

First published in 2014 by Sansom & Co,
an imprint of Redcliffe Press Ltd.
81g Pembroke Road, Bristol BS8 3EA

www.sansomandcompany.co.uk
info@sansomandcompany.co.uk

www.sonialawson.co.uk

ISBN 978 1 908326 62 1

British Library Cataloguing-in-Publication Data
A catalogue record for this book is available from the British Library

Image layout: Z Congo
Design and typesetting: Nick Newton Design

Printed via Akcent Media

Front cover: **Exercising Dogs on Watling Street**. Collection: Arts Council of England
Back cover: **French Connection** (detail)
Frontispiece: **Pilgrimage to the Ridings, Homage to my Family** 1981–2, oil on canvas, 153 x 122 cm
Title page: Sonia Lawson, 1982, photographed in front of **Pilgrimage to the Ridings, Homage to my Family**

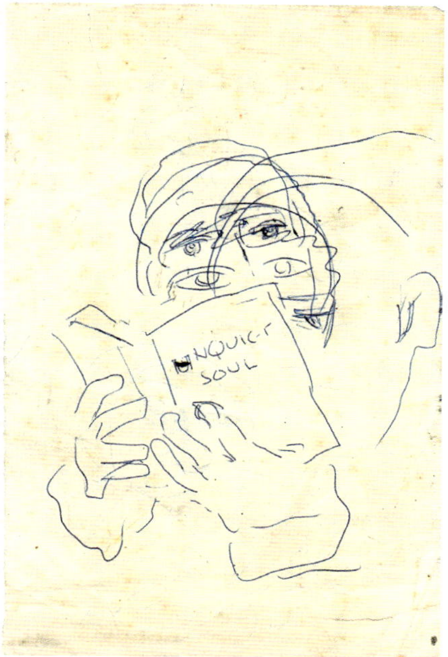

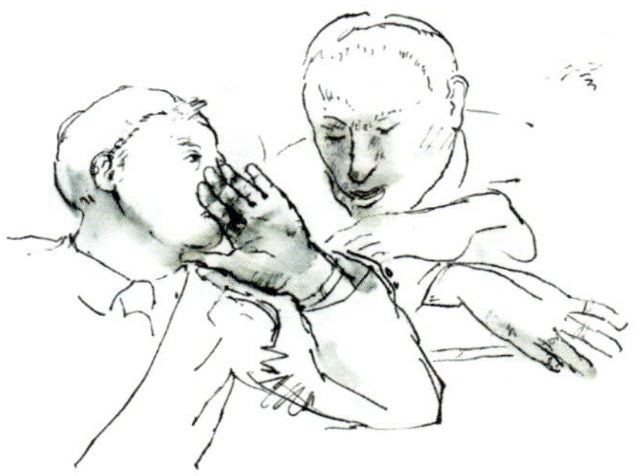

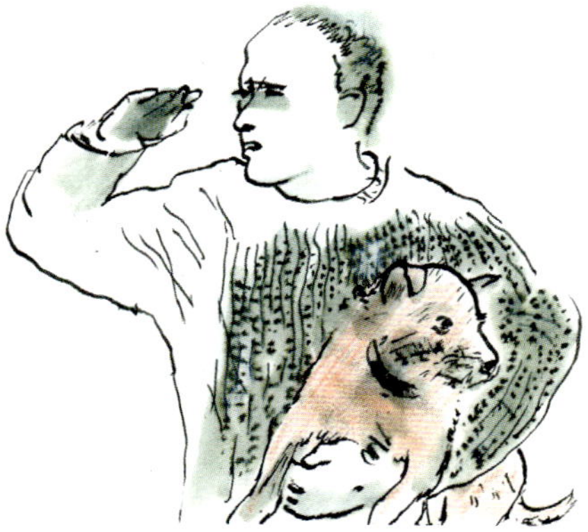

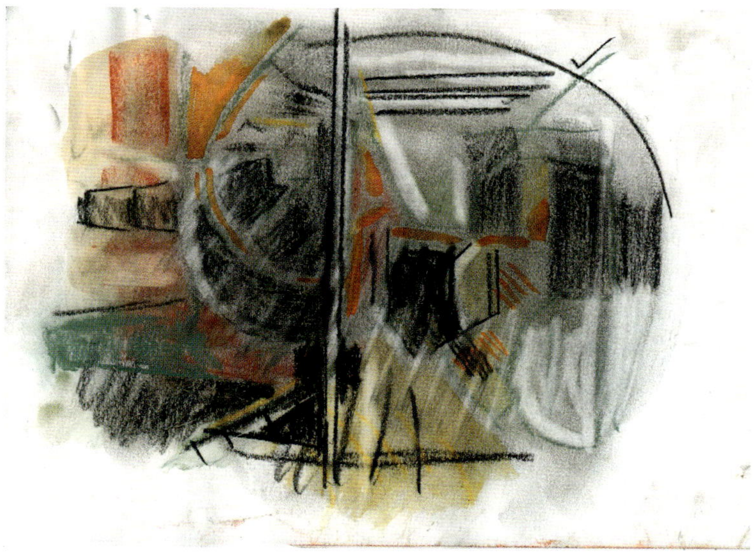

Selection of images from Sonia Lawson's sketchbooks

Contents

Foreword

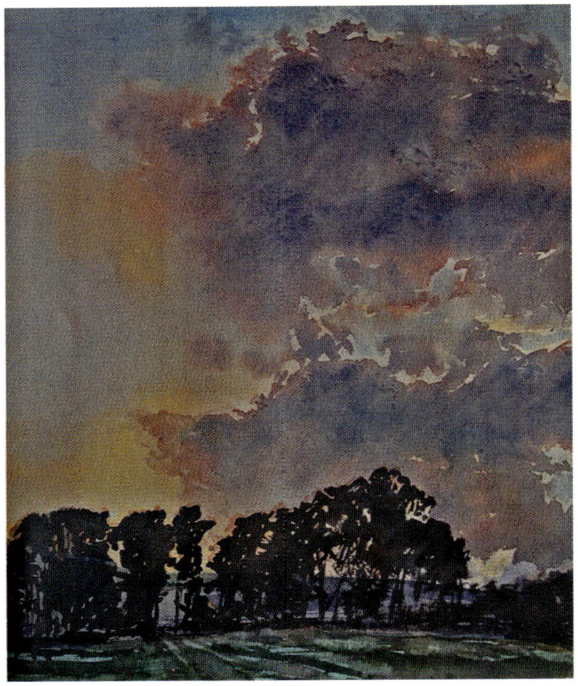

Western Sky, Castle Bolton, Wensleydale 1973, watercolour, 44 x 38 cm

This country has a rich twentieth-century tradition of producing profoundly idiosyncratic and intensely poetic figurative artists, the only problem being it also has a long-standing national curatorial and institutional habit either of totally ignoring them or consigning their work almost immediately to gallery and museum basements and storerooms, only rarely, if ever, to be seen again. Witness Richard Eurich, Algernon Newton, Evelyn Williams, Carel Weight, Julian Trevelyan, who are among a long list of names to have endured this neglect and it has been my privilege and delight, to have had the opportunity over the last 35 years to write about them all at some point, often at length and, in many cases, curated exhibitions of their art. There are hopeful signs too that in doing so it may have helped in the often maddeningly slow process of re-introducing their work to a new, wider and more appreciative audience, maybe even to museum curators!

Now, after many years of admiring her work, I have finally been given this opportunity to write about Sonia Lawson, another quite remarkable artist who seems to me to belong very clearly in this same tradition, her expressive and intensely feminine art, at the same time intensely autobiographical and rooted in a provincial (North Yorkshire) experience and yet speaking to a much wider and quite profound European sensibility, somehow evading the kind of broader curatorial and critical attention they unquestionably deserve. This is not to say that she is, in any respect, an unknown artist – regular showings at the Royal Academy Summer Exhibitions since the late 60s have kept her work in public view (she has also been an RA since 1982) as have public gallery shows at reasonably regular intervals over the years. She has, too, always had a steady flow of private patrons and public commissions and some distinguished critics writing about her work – Norbert Lynton, Edward Lucie-Smith, Julian Spalding and Waldemar Januszczak among them. Yet, for some reason, she has still never had a work bought by Tate, never had a major retrospective show in London and, apart from a decade of representation at the Boundary Gallery in the 1990s, never enjoyed the support of a regular commercial gallery. At least some of the reasons for this will, hopefully, emerge in the text that follows though the ever deepening and enriching intellect and emotion she has brought to her art over some eight decades and so apparent in the images that accompany the text, still makes this state of affairs puzzlingly inexplicable.

It is usual at this point to produce a whole string of names and acknowledgements of help given in the process of writing and producing the book. In this instance however this is unusually short given that, apart from the thoughts, ideas and information emerging from the various catalogue essays and longer reviews on her work that have appeared over the years, the basis for much of the text has largely emerged out of a series of interviews conducted with Sonia over the last eighteen months or so. However, given the fact that Sonia has been suffering severe illness over this same period as these interviews were conducted, these would not have been remotely feasible without the remarkable help given by Sonia's art-history trained daughter Zoe acting as a go-between, with me firing in questions by e-mail and Zoe then putting them to Sonia at good moments and e-mailing me back with her answers. It was a collaboration between the three of us of a kind I never encountered in 40 years of writing and one which has resulted in a whole body of entirely new information about her life and work. Without Zoe's patience, accuracy and forbearing however the whole enterprise would have been near impossible. Zoe is also Sonia's archivist and her presence has, in fact, been the lynchpin of the whole book, co-ordinating my writing and the photographic scans of Sonia's work, almost all of which have been provided by Sonia's husband Charlie with efficiency and good humour. Vital too in the whole process has been the support of my dear wife Jilly, a painter herself and long-time admirer of Sonia's work also, whose acute eye, has, over numerous visits to Sonia's studio, made me see many things I might so easily have overlooked. Above all though, thank you Sonia for letting me write about paintings which, in these forgetful times, remind us of our humanity and the wholeness of our sensuous experience of the world.

Nicholas Usherwood
30th August 2014

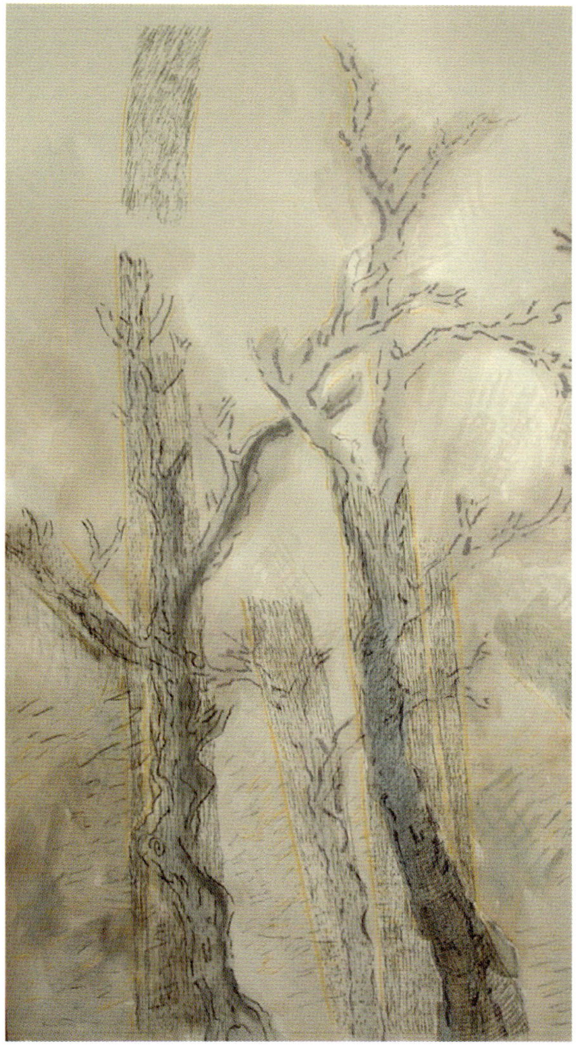

Bare Winter (detail) 2004, watercolour and conté on paper, 100 x 90 cm

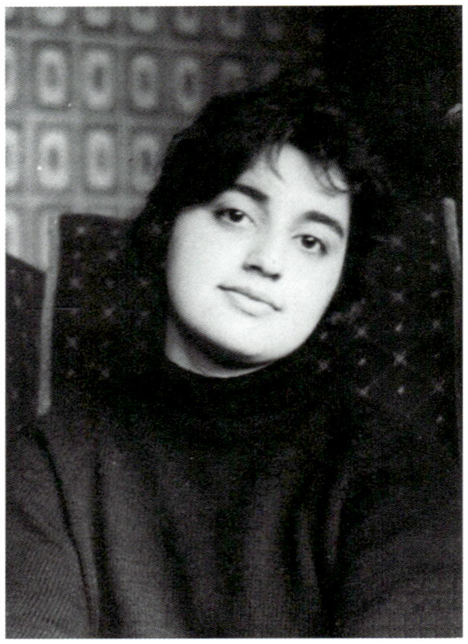

Sonia Lawson, 1956

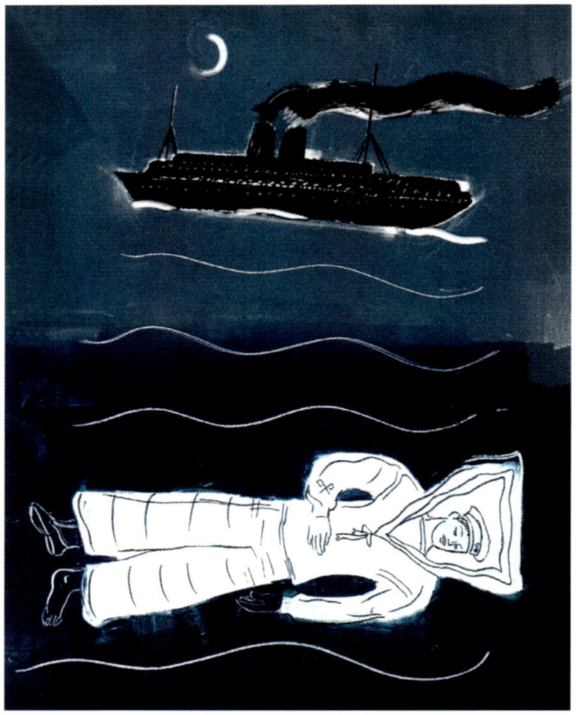

The Dream, monoprint, 29 x 21 cm, illustration to *Look at it This Way*, Collection of Kirkup's Poems published 1994

Introduction

My parents rise out of their thrones
Into the milky rooms of clouds. How can I sing?
Time tells me what I am. I change and I am the same.
I empty myself of my life and my life remains.

From *The Remains* by Mark Strand

Writing to Sonia Lawson, in 1995, in exasperation at the 'flat prose' of the catalogue text for her latest solo show at the Boundary Gallery, the distinguished poet, and family friend, James Kirkup, asks why the writer 'should want to tie you like an old tin can to the mangy tail of all those names? Can't we see you just as you are, unique and unclassable?' 'In desperation,' Kirkup answers his own rhetorical question by enclosing some 13 poems, each taking as its subject one of the paintings in the exhibition, concluding his note with the words 'yours is the kind of painting that can only be "explained" by poetry.'

In an emotional sense, what Kirkup is getting at goes absolutely to the heart of the matter. Critics and art-historians have tried valiantly but never really succeeded in fitting her work into any neat stylistic pigeonholes or artistic groupings while Lawson herself, from the moment she left the Royal College of Art in 1960, has pursued a fiercely independent path, living for the most part outside London, in Bedfordshire and North Yorkshire. Her art, similarly, has taken distinctly unpredictable and idiosyncratic twists and turns, from the landscape abstraction she practised while a student at the RCA via the intense and often harrowing political and socially oriented paintings of the late 1960s and 1970s and the more autobiographical, literary and historical themes of the 1980s to the increasingly monumental abstract landscape and figurative compositions that have marked the last two decades or so.

It is an often puzzling arc at first sight until one realises, with Kirkup, that the impulses behind these often radical shifts of direction are, fundamentally, directed less by stylistic and artistic considerations and have everything to do with the emotional, the personal and indeed, her intense sense of the feminine. Thus, if asked to name the three human qualities that most characterise the sensibility that emanates from Sonia Lawson's work, the words that most immediately come to (my) mind are tenderness, empathy and pity. Unusual terms to apply to a contemporary visual artist perhaps, and more usually found in discussions of the work of poets, writers and dramatists. This is emphatically not to say that Lawson was ever uninterested in the work of other artists – if anything she was rather better informed, for example, about what was going on in German twentieth-century and contemporary and European art generally than many of her generation, with Beckmann, Baselitz and Paladino among them, all important at quite an early stage in her career – but rather that the impulses to make work were largely driven by the need to give expression to the particular subjects and themes that were concerning her at various stages of her life. In this she bears a striking resemblance to another great, essentially Expressionist painter, Sidney Nolan, whose urge to make art was driven by his voracious lifetime of reading, and above all, like Lawson, of poetry. In Lawson's case, this, at times, almost obsessive habit, itself became a substantial subject of her art in itself – all those 'Night Reading' paintings and watercolours of the 1980s and early 1990s – encompassing everything from Kafka to John Clare, William Blake to the Brontë sisters, Mary Wollstonecraft to Sappho and Mary Pankhurst. And, like Nolan too, it was out of this reading that she found a way to give shape to the things she was thinking about and feeling, both

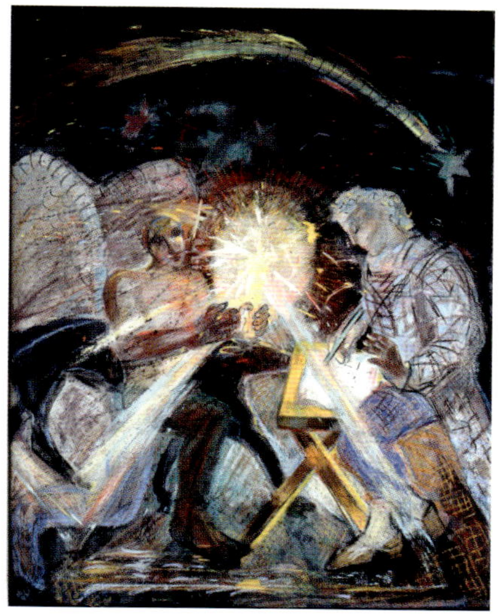

Night Writing Series

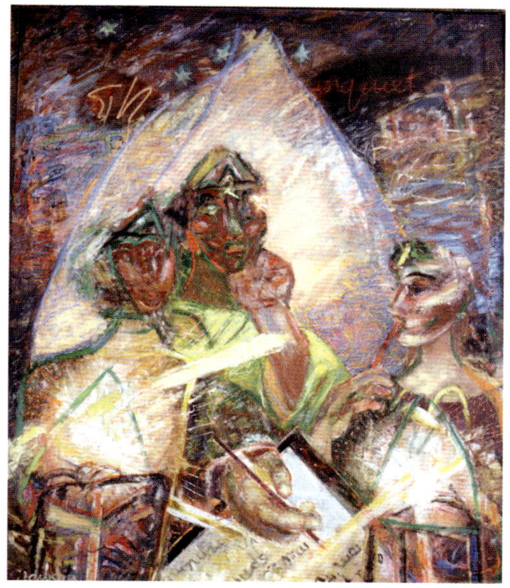

Night Writing, The Brontës

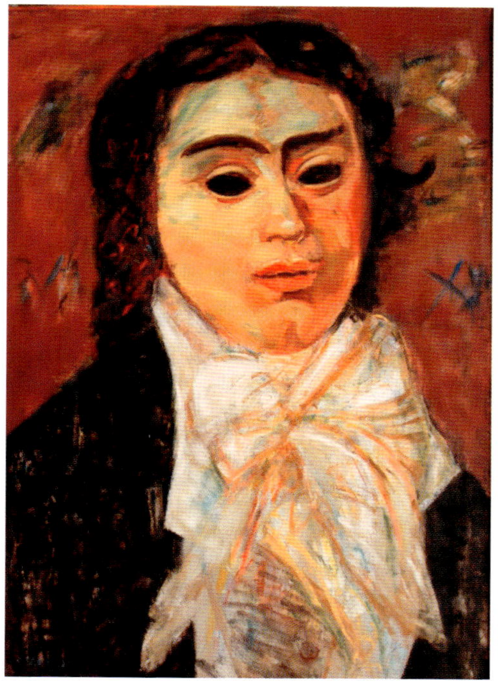

Coleridge 1994, oil on canvas, 122 x 92 cm

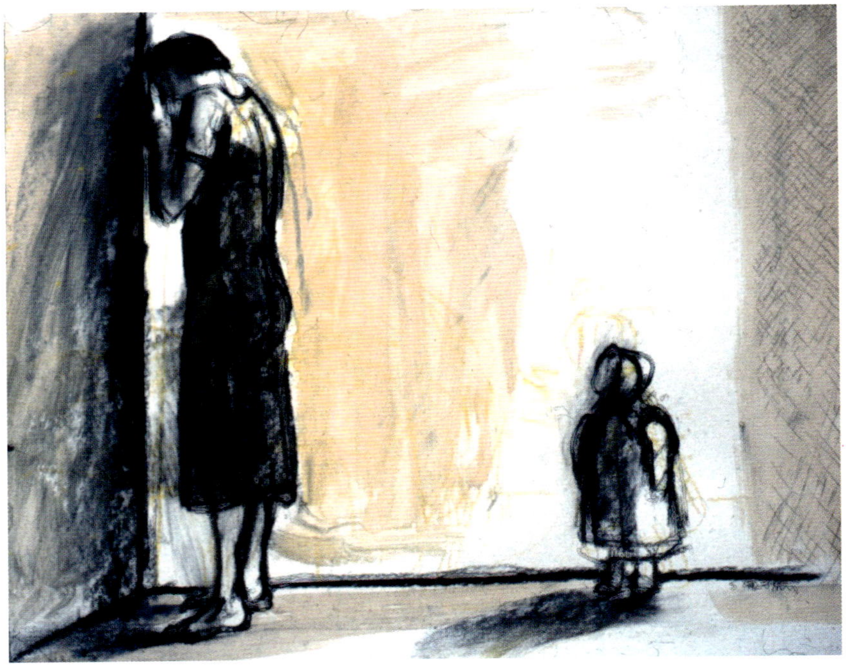

The Troubled Mother 1984, charcoal and watercolour, 42 x 59 cm

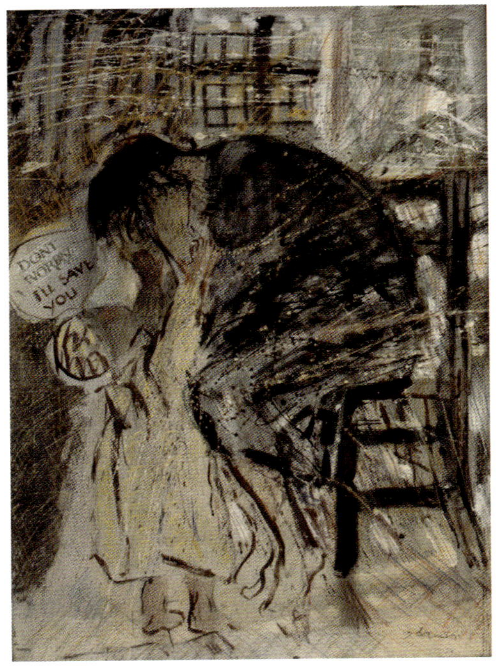

Gallant Child 1983, oil on canvas, 120 x 92 cm

at the personal and autobiographical level and, in a more conscious public way out of her intellectual curiosity about the world, the sparks that set a new series of paintings in motion. In this approach to making art, the way you paint is shaped by the kind of things you want to be painting, at that point in your life, with other painters and paintings providing the formal ways and means of realising them. She once observed of herself that 'I am in painting like a fisherman is part of the sea', paint being the means by which to land her 'catch', her imagery, which lives in the element in which it is discovered and is brought out with all the attendant physical risks that implies. It is not a way of working likely to endear yourself to critics or dealers who tend to want to know what to expect next, as Lawson has found out, but it does make for the most exhilarating kind of painting imaginable, as this book will make plain. In a catalogue note from 1973 Sonia herself showed she understood this about herself when she remarked 'I hope to retain a rawness that is like young blood, that is eager and unlaboured depending on my realisation, vision and feeling over the tyranny of appearances … I like to turn things up, one sees more, be like the seasons, flexible but with order. Rouault said he would like to have changed a bit but could not because one sort of thing was expected of him. Poor man.'

In terms of starting to understand the states of being and emotion that lie at the very heart of her work, two substantial charcoal and watercolour drawings that Lawson made in 1983/4, when she was just turning 50, seem to me key. The first, entitled

The Troubled Mother, shows a little girl pleading silently with her mother across the seemingly yawning space of a bare room interior, while the second, *Gallant Child*, shows the same child reaching up to comfort her huddled, bare-foot, weeping mother with the words 'I'll save you' inscribed in a bubble that lies between their two yearning heads. Neither is the expression of any imaginary childhood fantasy nor literary illustration, nor even a reaction to something reported in the media but, in reality, the visual recollection of the central emotional event of her early childhood, her own life-threatening illness at the age of three and her artist-mother's chronic illness with Graves' Disease, possibly exacerbated by anxiety over her child's condition. An illness deriving from thyroid excess, its implications for Lawson had been profound, above all in the fact that her mother had, as a consequence, been largely unable to bring her up. Instead she was cared for initially by grandparents but after they died, when she was still young, a maternal aunt and uncle, also in Wensleydale, had looked after her. Lawson's childhood recollections of time spent on their farm in the Yorkshire Dales are, at one level, still remarkably happy ones. At the same time she adored both her artist-parents – but, as she has recently observed to me, it still shook her confidence in the permanence of things.

Indeed it gradually becomes apparent that in these formative experiences lies the spiritual and intellectual core of her work, above all, in a desire to make an art of continuity and wholeness with time past and time present fixed in a timeless poetic moment. In short she was to gain from this complex of experiences that very strong sense of 'self' that gives to the work, for all its shifts of themes and styles, its remarkable emotional coherence and artistic unity. And, as the great twentieth-century American scientific and ecological thinker, Gregory Bateson, has written 'The poets of every generation have known these things all through the ages but the rest of us have gone astray into all sorts false reifications of the "self" and experience.' William Blake, one of Lawson's particular passions, knew that the Poetic Imagination is the only reality and that, in those terms, 'A tear is an intellectual thing.'

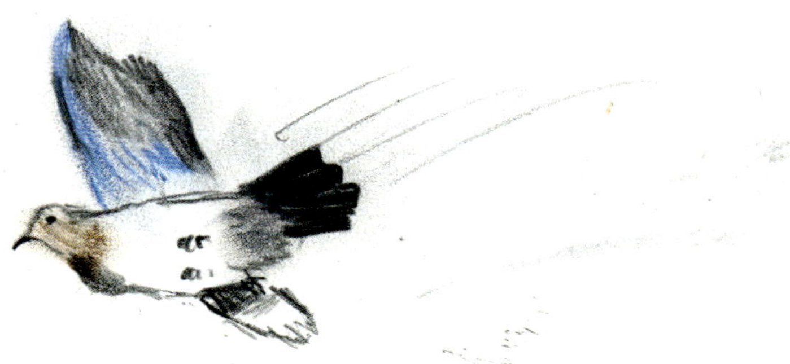

Free, charcoal and gouache, from Lawson's sketchbooks

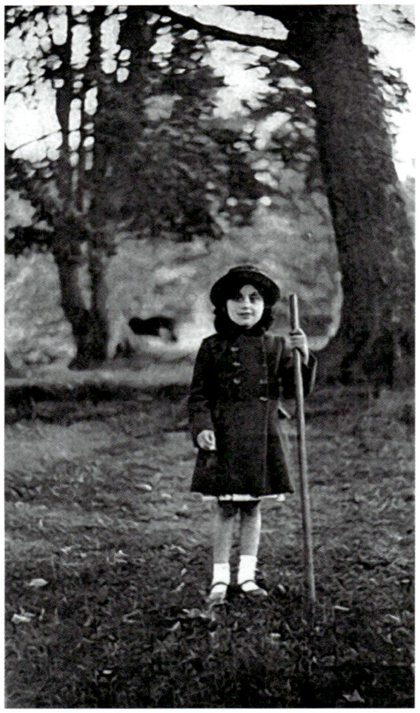

Sonia on a walk in Wensleydale, c.1941

Chapter 1

... When I read Neruda's
we are approaching a great and common tenderness
my mind startles and connects to this
all but obsolete small scene above the river
where unspectacular people secure
their bulky loads and drive away at dusk.
Allegiance to the land is tenderness ...

From *Hay* by Maxine Kumin

We like to think we shape the landscape – in superficial ways that is true – but very often it can be that a landscape and an environment can come to shape us, our minds and senses as well as in physical terms. Painting, with its innate and unique physicality, is among the most apt of media, a metaphorical equivalent for that raft of sensual experiences which, from earliest childhood builds itself into the fabric of an artist's visual imagination. At the heart of Sonia Lawson's art, there is always Wensleydale, its landscape and its people.

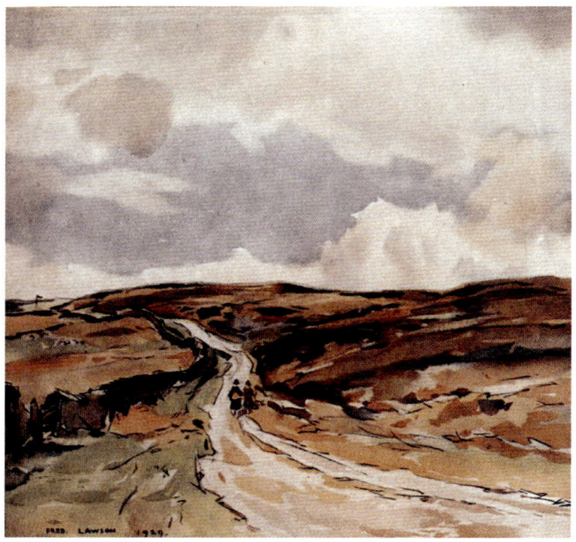

Fred Lawson, **Moorland Road to Reeth** 1929, watercolour, 35 x 45 cm

As has already been suggested in the introduction, Lawson's childhood was, for all its emotional difficulties, remarkably rich and enthralling in terms of the wealth of experiences – people, places, events, intellectual stimulation – that it provided. She was born in Darlington on June 2nd, 1934, and the family home was in the remote Wensleydale village of Castle Bolton, where her father, Leeds-born Fred Lawson, now in his mid-40s, was a well-established and very well-regarded painter of the Yorkshire Dales landscape while her mother, Muriel Metcalfe, some 20 years younger and brought up in the nearby market town of Leyburn, had been something of a child-prodigy, winning a scholarship to Newcastle University in her early teens. It was, or should have been, an idyllic life. Fred Lawson had studied at Leeds Art School, in its heyday before the Great War, when he had also been a member of the Leeds Art Society, the radical modernist organization that had counted Herbert Read among

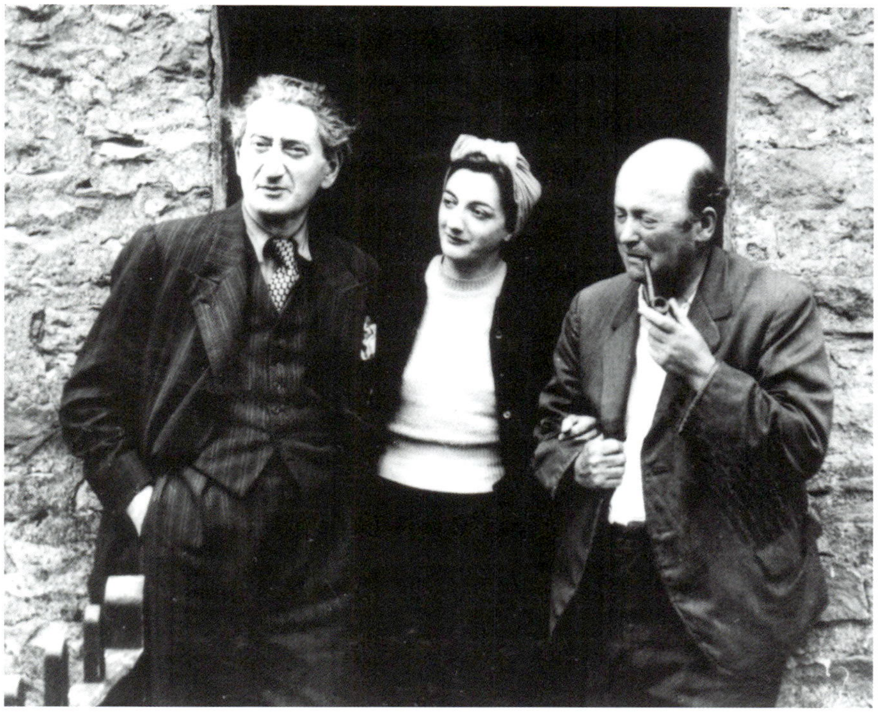

From right to left: Fred Lawson (with pipe) and Muriel Lawson (née Metcalfe) outside their cottage in Castle Bolton with Jacob Kramer, 1950s

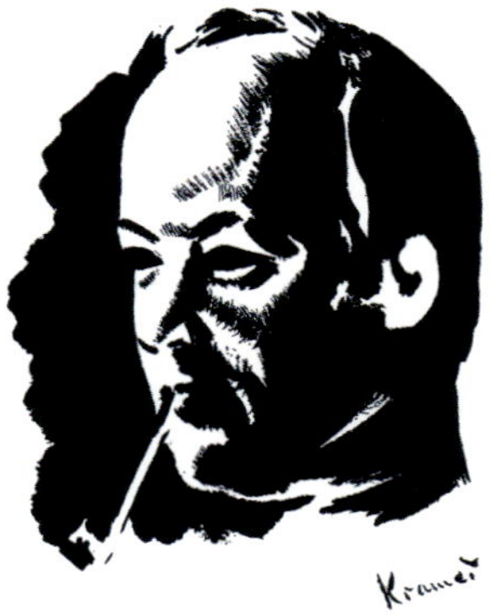

Jacob Kramer, **Fred Lawson** c.1950, ink drawing. Estate of John David Roberts. By permission of the William Roberts Society

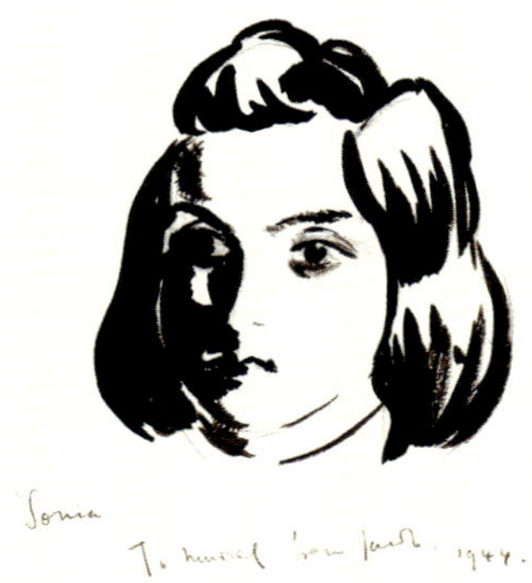

Jacob Kramer, **Sonia Lawson**, ink drawing inscribed *Sonia, to Muriel from Jacob, 1944*. Estate of John David Roberts. By permission of the William Roberts Society

its membership along with the great Jewish Expressionist painter Jacob Kramer. Both became lifelong friends of Lawson and along with a wide circle of Leeds and London intelligentsia, the poet James Kirkup, the writer J.B. Priestley, the painters Philip Naviasky and William Roberts (Jacob Kramer's brother-in-law) among them, they still used to visit her parents' Castle Bolton cottage when Sonia was a young child. She remembers the place with huge affection – 'the oil lamps and the gentle radiant warmth that bathed the room' and, above all, the gifted artistic social circle that gathered there.

Her mother was very much at home in this company, with Herbert Read particularly an active promoter and admirer of her work, and the years before and during the early part of her marriage (1933) were a highly creative time for her as she and Fred travelled about the country together. Indeed by this time Muriel had begun to achieve a new confidence and fluidity in her work, her watercolours of Northern harbours and landscapes, with their slashed, exuberant brushstrokes and interlacing of vibrant colour and intense light, suggesting an almost Fauvist and expressionistic quality akin to the earlier work of Vlaminck and Derain. It belied the fact that her creativity was already being severely undermined by serious long-term illness, Graves' Disease, a form of hyperthyroidism that would hamper her work on and off throughout her life.

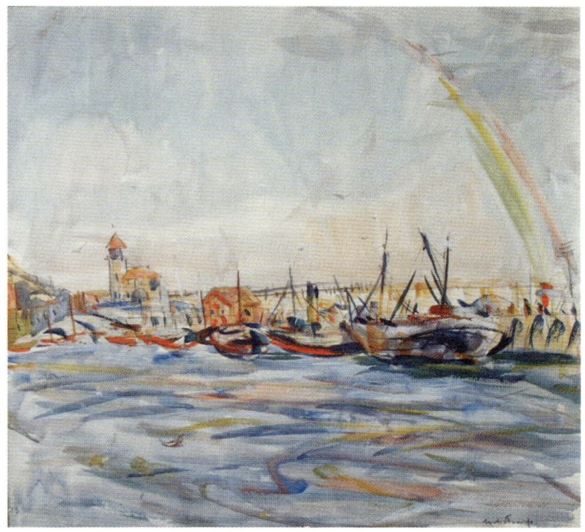

Muriel Metcalfe, **A Rainbow. Scarborough Harbour** 1930, watercolour, 35 x 38 cm

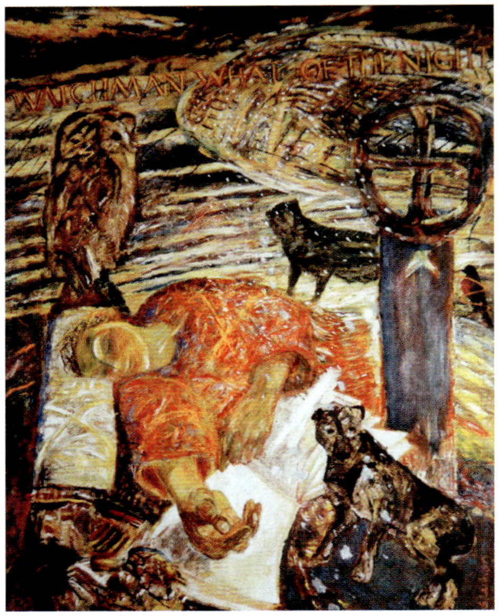

Watchman, What of the Night?

For Sonia, as has already been indicated in the introduction, her mother's illness had huge practical and emotional consequences in the fact that she was quite unable to take proper care of her daughter for much of the time, even after a radical operation in 1938 (paid for by friends) had considerably improved her condition. As a consequence, Sonia had gone to live, first with her maternal grandparents, who ran a painting and decorating business in Leyburn and then, after they died in the early 1940s, with her aunt Marjorie and uncle Archie Walker who lived next door and ran both the post office and a small working farm close by in the Dales. This was, in one sense, a good practical solution also, as Sonia herself has pointed out, saving herself the long winter walks to school from her parents' remotely situated cottage in Castle Bolton. It also, more importantly perhaps, meant a more sociable and less isolated way of life – her grandparents' business providing a steady flow of visitors for her to observe closely while, when she was slightly older and at school in the town, she was to find the people there and their lives intriguing. 'Children in a small town tend to know things,' she observed in a recent conversation with her daughter Zoe, remembering 'how they used to peek through windows in the winter evenings. People would have their curtains drawn but didn't seem to think that a chink in the curtains meant we could spy from the outside on the cosy front room. Viewing secret tableaux!' Immediately one's mind thinks forward to one of those complex, brilliantly lit compositions from the 1980s particularly, a work like *Watchman, What of the Night?* (1982).

Another, absolutely seminal experience from early childhood was the time she spent on her uncle's and aunt's small farm in the Dales with fields to explore, chickens providing eggs, milk from the cows. As she puts it 'there was plenty and enough!' In the introduction to an exhibition of recent work at Manchester Art Gallery in 1987 she wrote how 'If there were troubles it was to the animals I went. Their sculptural form and their warmth was amazing. They were warm, silent guardians – a comfort to be with. Miraculous, divine beings with a hide covered in wondrous patterns, multi-coloured hair going round their form as water round rocks, or with the ewes, wool so deep you couldn't find the base of it. Today, should the 4-minute warning sound, my close family not near, I'll lie down with the passive, baffled ruminants.' Indeed it is perhaps fair to say that it was between these twin poles of her childhood, of 'life among the artists and on the farm, situated in a Shangri-La of the rural north' and loved, as she came to realize, by two mothers, that lay the deeper, creative seeds of her lifetime's work, the 'constant jubilee' out of which, once she had found her voice, the paintings would burst forth over half a century of work.

If these were the immediate social and familial constants of Sonia's childhood, the overarching circumstances were, of course, the war itself, her primary memory of

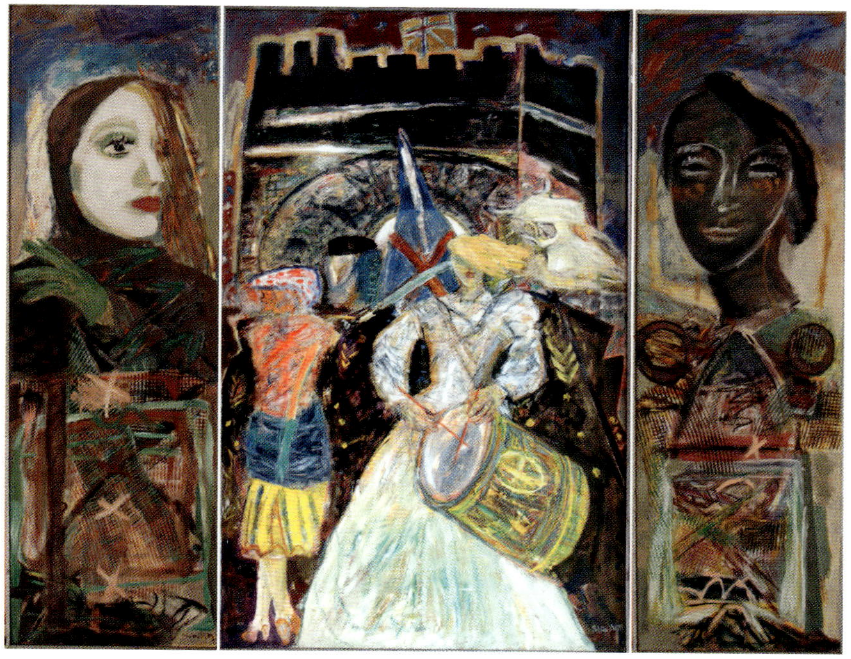

Garrison Town

it being one of intense excitement. For while the worst effects of the war were not obvious in Wensleydale (though a scatter of bombs did fall once on Leyburn, she recalls), the town itself was in fact not far from the larger centre of Richmond, very much a garrison town with the then huge Catterick army camp close by, and which itself lay alongside the then very important (and very ancient) arterial road, the A1, once known as Ermine Street. Allied soldiers, 'smart Canadians and Americans', were often in Leyburn itself 'seeming to breeze in bringing chocolates for the children and nylons for the young women – a sense of daring, sexy, romantic, and a certain heroism' while the area around Bellerby in the valley was used then, as now, for army training and manoeuvres. Sonia recalls vividly the tremendous sense of bustling, urgent activity about the wartime town, 'a different pace – dances, talks of war, victory/defeat and a sense of camaraderie between the grown ups, pulling against a common enemy for a communal cause'. These were qualities with which, much later, she was to infuse many of her great historically biased figure compositions of the early 1980s particularly, for example, *Garrison Town* and *Northern Garrison.* At the same time too, she also has strong memories of 'the newness and excitement of billeting prisoners of war. The Italian prisoners made many little artifacts and toys that they gave to children while the Germans were very well-dressed in fine smart tailored long coats. I remember a bitterly cold day when I and my aunt gave some delicate thin slices of Christmas cake to two German prisoners who were very polite and grateful.'

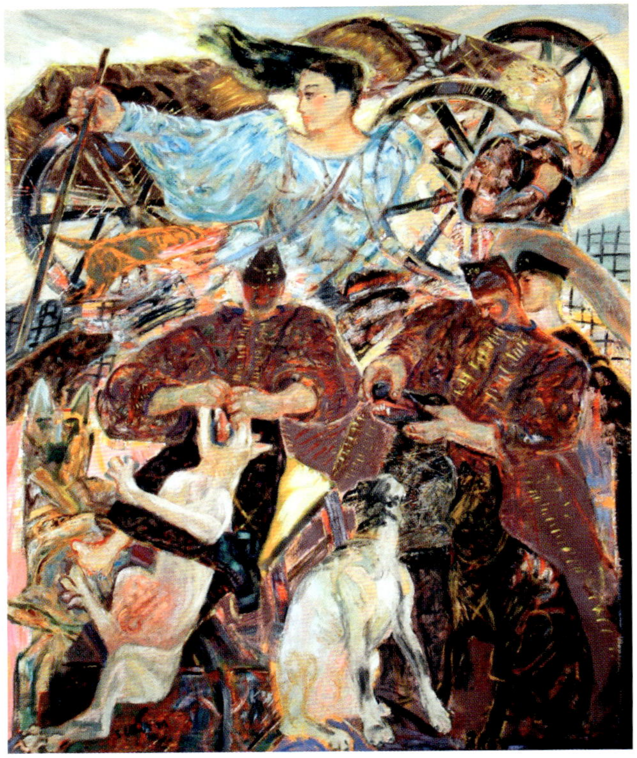

Northern Garrison

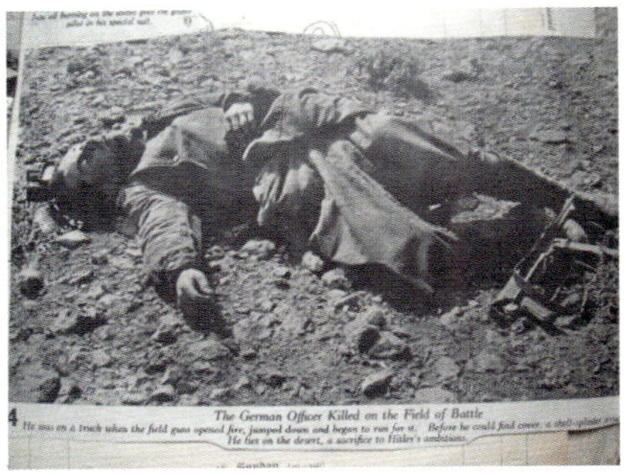

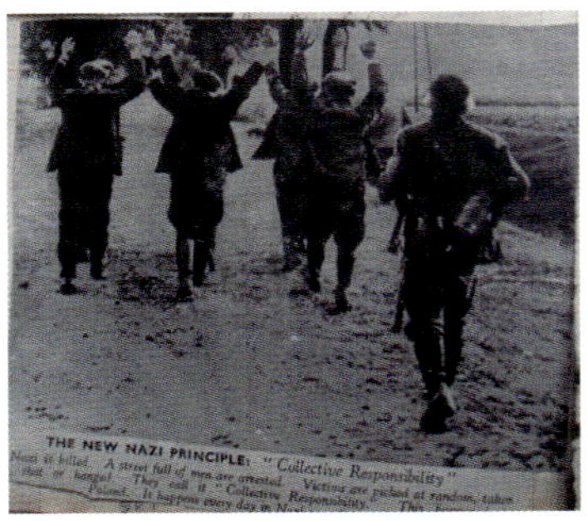

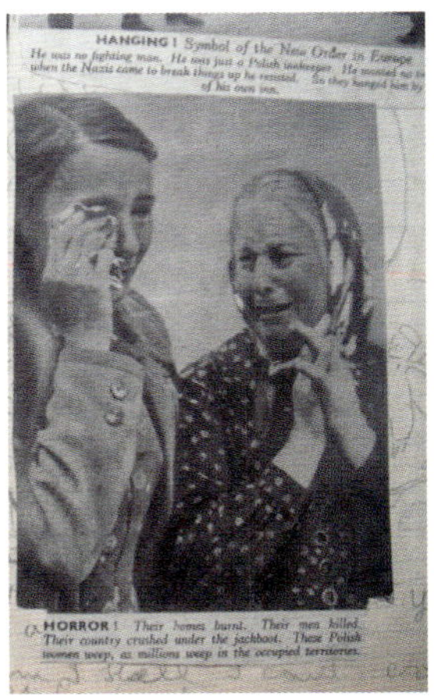

Pages from Sonia's scrapbooks made when she was 12 years old

The war, or rather the end of the war, was to have a more internalized, and also perhaps more revealing, impact on Sonia Lawson's general artistic direction when, in the course of the liberation, the full scale of the horrors the Nazi regime had been inflicting on Europe, became publicly apparent. As a 10-11 year old – a distinctly unusual activity for a young child perhaps – she started making extensive scrapbooks of items gleaned from newspapers and magazines of the photographs taken in concentration camps and at the Nuremberg trials (the habit of collecting such items has in fact continued through the rest of her life as her art has drawn on images from newspapers and current events). As she later recalled, the idea now first hit her that 'such inhumanity was not an accident but a systematic and prolonged exercise, deliberate and methodical, and the realization that these horrors had happened while she was growing up free and happy in the Yorkshire Dales'. They were complex feelings that were to become important drivers for her future painting. It reveals too, in more general terms, that remarkable tenderness and openness of heart that was to become consistently apparent in her work throughout the course of her later career.

In terms of her eventual career as an artist, Sonia has always maintained that the local schools she went to in Yorkshire were not vital to her choice, rather it was her mother and father that she learnt from. Certainly she never seems to have doubted she'd do anything other than become an artist herself and this seems to have been maintained as she grew into her early teens, by which time (1948) she had gone to live in Shoreham-by-Sea in Sussex where her aunt and uncle had gone to live, her uncle by now General Secretary of the National Federation of Sub Postmasters. He had always admired her wit and intelligence but he certainly never encouraged Lawson, saying he thought all artists were mad, a comment touching on her mother's ongoing illness and the fact that it had recently led to a depression in which Muriel had destroyed a lot of her own work. Lawson however never seems to have been deterred from her ambition by any such considerations, spending some six months at Worthing Art School and enjoying the South Down landscape where chalk replaced the limestone and moorland of the Dales for a time.

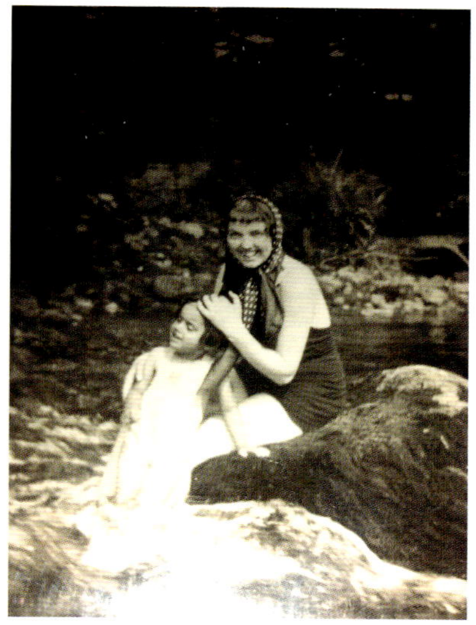

Happy summer's day by the river in Wensleydale, Sonia and Auntie Marjorie, c.1937

It was an interim period however and she never considered she had really started 'work' as an artist until she went on to Doncaster Art School in 1951, a sensible enough choice given that she was again living with her aunt and uncle who had recently moved there. In her four years at Doncaster she gained her national diploma (DipAD) and immediately applied to the Royal College of Art for further study. Her first attempt though was a miserable failure – with depressing lodgings in a Kensington flat so cold the water in the water jug froze – so it says much for her tenacity that she went back to Yorkshire seemingly undeterred and took a job as a post-lady near Doncaster. Signing in at 5.55 a.m. every morning and cycling 13 miles on her daily round across the flat fenland landscape only seems to have increased her determination – crossing the main railway line to London every day she found herself thinking as the trains roared by 'I'll be on one of you one of these days!' It taught her an interesting lesson too about female inequality when, instructing a new man on the post round, she found she was being paid under half what the new man would be getting. Without ever being an active feminist Sonia has, nonetheless, both in her life and through her art, always followed a quietly determined path in promoting ideas about the strength and resourcefulness of women in society.

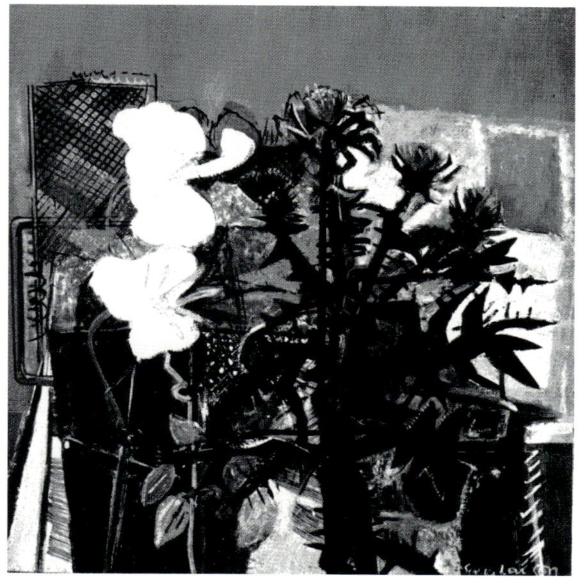

Landscape c.1958, oil on canvas, 60 x 60 cm, Sloane Street Gallery

At the same time, she had continued to paint a great deal in her spare time, reapplying to the RCA in 1955. Learning her lessons from the year before, she stayed at a small hotel recommended by the College which had all mod cons, including running hot water. Not frozen and not harassed, the interview went a great deal better and, afterwards, when she met Professor Carel Weight, the head of the Painting School in the corridor, he remarked 'That wasn't so bad, was it?' She knew then that things had gone well and that she had been accepted.

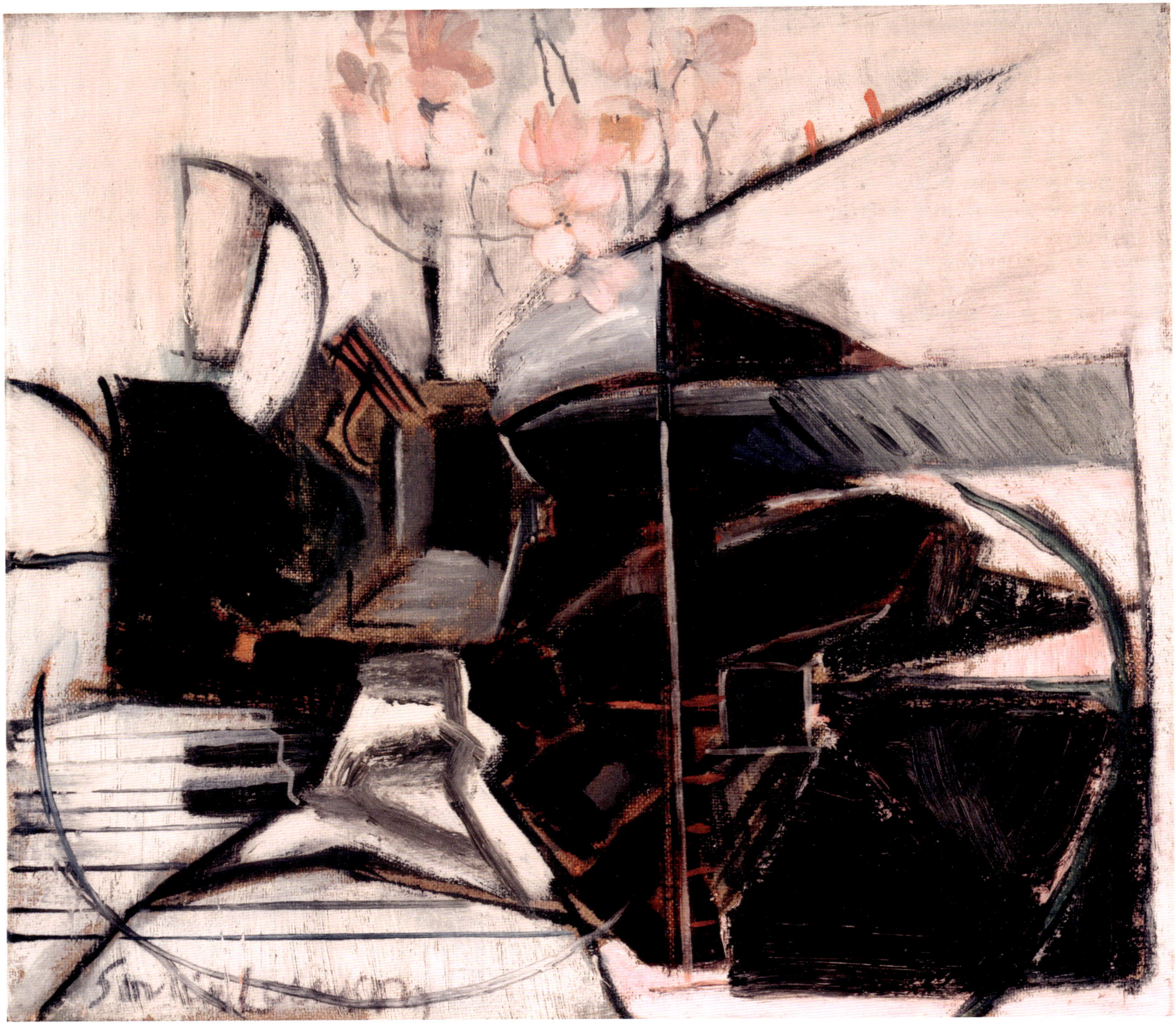

Entrance to a Garden 1959, oil on canvas, 34 x 39.1 cm
Collection: Late Professor Carel Weight bequest to Royal Academy of Arts in 1999

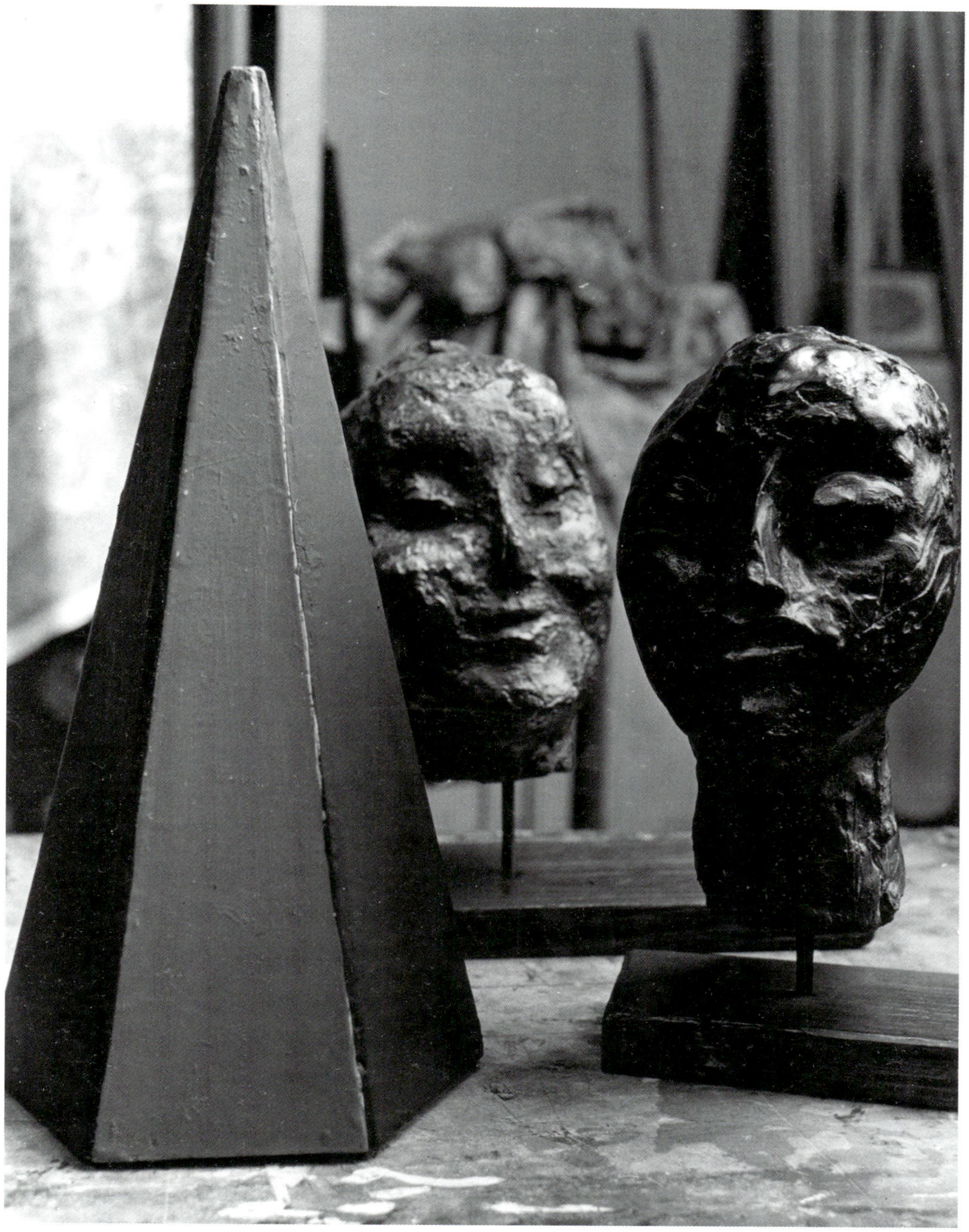

Photograph: **Heads** 1960, *ciment fondu* (now lost)

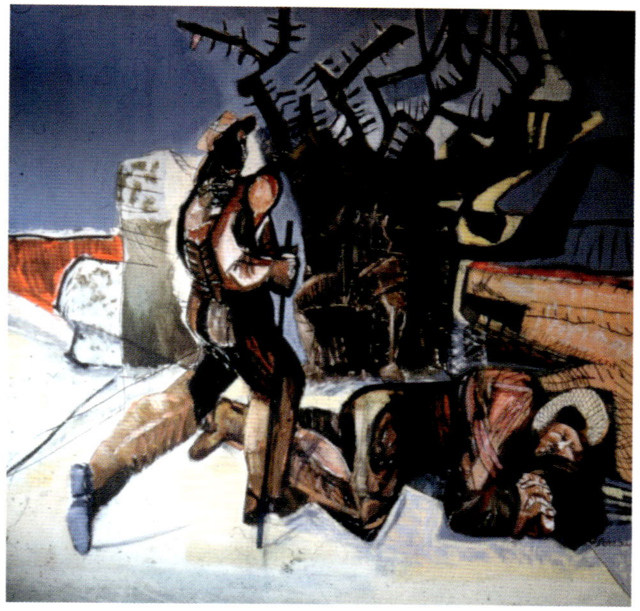

Rendezvous 1960, oil on canvas, 120 x 120 cm

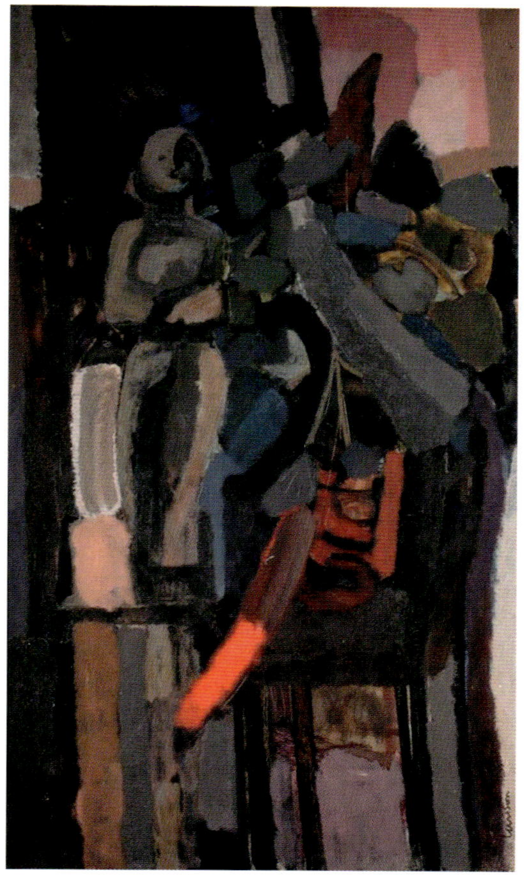

Still Life 1958, oil on hardboard, 121.5 x 73.3 cm
Collection: Royal College of Art

Chapter 2

> And it is not yet enough to have memories. You must be able to forget them when they are many, and you must have the immense patience to wait until they return. For the memories themselves are not important. Only when they have changed into our very blood, into glance and gesture, and are nameless, no longer to be distinguished from ourselves – only then can it happen that in some very rare hour the first word of a poem arises in their midst and goes forth from them.
>
> 'For the Sake of a Single Poem'
> from *The Notebooks of Malte Laurids Brigge*
> by Rainer Maria Rilke

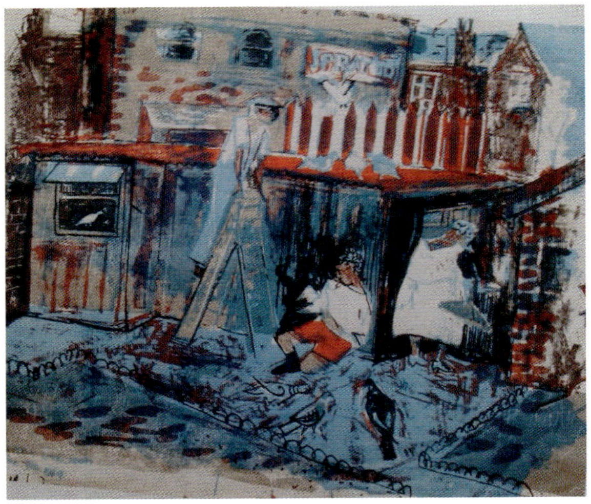

From Sonia Lawson's 1950s sketchbook, **Pigeon Fanciers**, mixed media, 29 x 39 cm

If the material and the horrors that were embedded in the scrapbooks that Sonia Lawson had kept as 10-11 year old at the end of the war were to act as a crucial spur to the work she was to undertake in her early 30s, they were, when she was a teenager and young art-school student, put very much to one side as she steadily learnt her craft. She seems to have been aware intuitively too that her artistic language and skills as well as her intellectual maturity meant she was still some way from being able to realise what she really wanted to say about that early moment of realisation concerning the tragedy of the human condition. The work Lawson had done as a teenager at Worthing and then at Doncaster School of Art, and which had got her scholarship into the Royal College of Art, derived very much from the numerous sketchbook drawings she was always making of the things she observed around her in her community. In Doncaster this included numerous industrial scenes – dramatic gouache and pencil studies of iron-works in full action, coal-miners coming out of work and painters and decorators at work – as well as the colourful hustle and bustle of markets, shoppers gossiping and the market stallholders encouraging them to buy, children shouting, dogs barking. Everyday life, full-on, acutely and sympathetically observed … her youthful drawings possess an already remarkably strong and innate understanding of human form, a quality that was to become, in time, absolutely

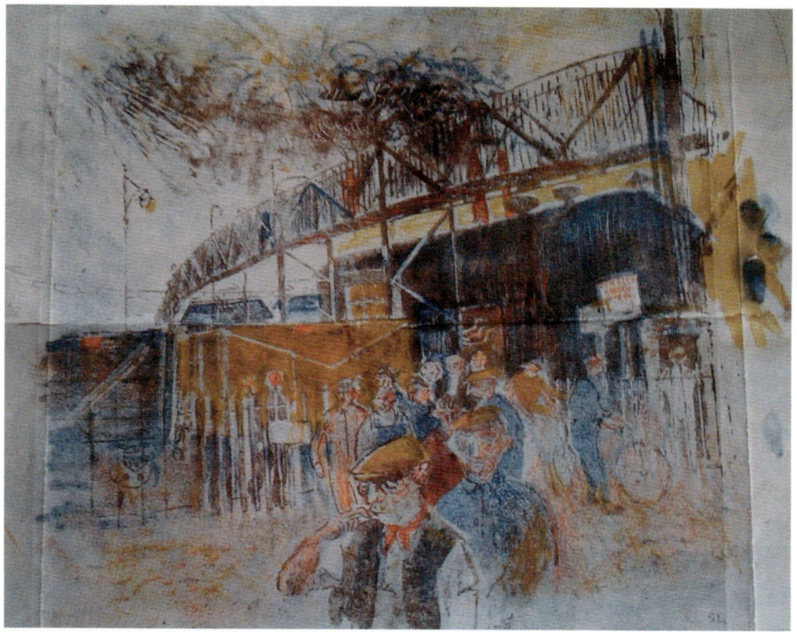

Coalite Works. Askern c.1954, lithograph, 30 x 38 cm

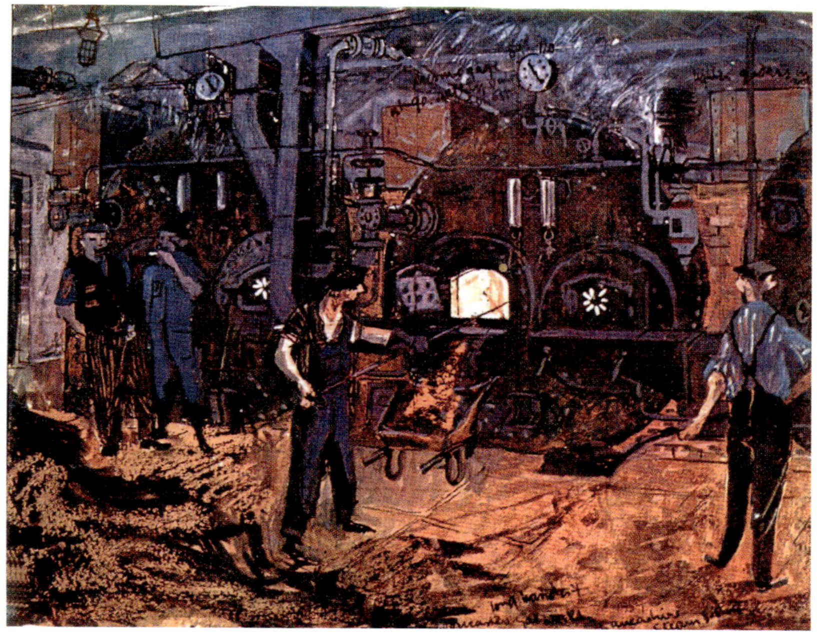

Gas Works. Doncaster c.1954, gouache on paper, 30 x 38 cm

central to her mature achievement. In this Sonia feels the example of her parents' work was absolutely paramount still; her father Fred Lawson, with his quick and intensely atmospheric watercolours and drawings of Dales life and landscape, her mother, Muriel Metcalfe, with her more modernistic sense of the abstract form beneath everyday appearance that came from her understandings of Cézanne, Picasso, Matisse and the Fauvists.

Meanwhile at the Royal College of Art in the mid- to late 1950s, a more progressive and adventurous spirit was abroad than she would have ever encountered at Doncaster School of Art. Peter Blake, Frank Auerbach and Leon Kossoff were in their last year when she arrived, David Hockney came the year before she left. Sonia tells a nice story of how she came across Hockney at one of the sinks where they cleaned their brushes dying his dark hair blond and asked him 'Why?' to which he replied 'gentlemen prefer blonds!' 'We laughed,' she remembers. She found London, and the College, both exciting and a shock – exhilarating, with skirts getting shorter even if it was still pre-King's Road hype. There were also meetings with her parents' old friend, the poet James Kirkup, who lived in Swiss Cottage and where she not only heard Billie Holiday's *Strange Fruit* for the first time (always a favourite singer thereafter) but once also met a Spanish dancer friend of his, Fernando, who demonstrated flamenco dancing to her and promptly drew furious complaints from the neighbours below for all the heel rapping on the floor!

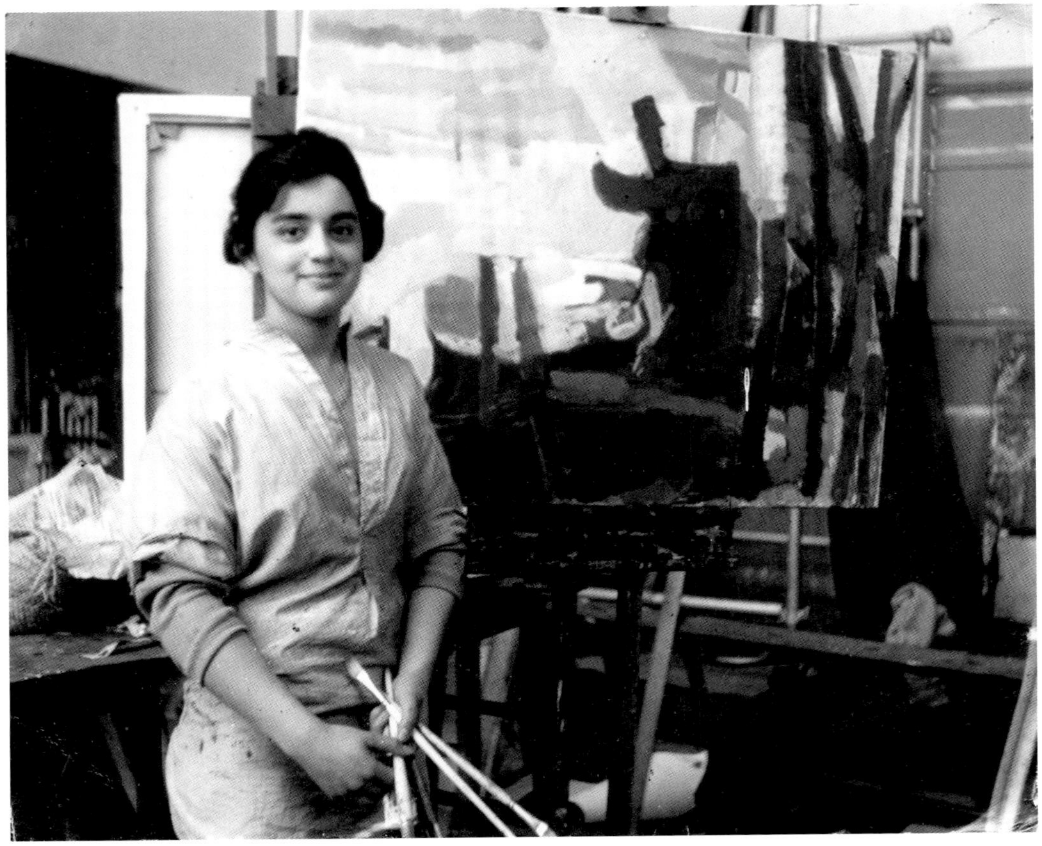

Sonia at the Royal College of Art, October 1958

Student life at the College was lively too with jive dances in the College canteen on Exhibition Road (where the studios were also situated at that date) where she remembers Ken Howard as a particularly good dancer. They also showed European films there too – Eisenstein's *Battleship Potemkin* among others – as well as French art-house movies and on occasion she went to the BFI cinema on the South Bank as well. It was to mark the beginning of a lifelong love of film which was to become such an important influence on her work throughout her life. Ingmar Bergman's *The Seventh Seal* (1957), for example, also seen around this time, she 'always looked upon … shot in black and white, as holding all the weight of passionate colour' – a significant observation in the light of the powerfully constructed 'political' compositions that were to follow over the next decade or more, with their often strongly contrasting compositions and dramatic contrasts of light and shade. There was the excellent College library too – where she first read the Letters of Heloise and Abelard, very appropriate, as she later observed, 'when you are in love!' which she was, with a fellow student – 'we liked each other's work and he was from Yorkshire!' As money was short there was not much going out to eat, apart from grotty cafés around South Kensington

Station, but there was, above all, London. 'Like Wordsworth I loved the limestone uplands but I also loved London' she observed to me recently, his great sonnet 'Upon Westminster Bridge' encapsulating her feelings exactly about the city.

It was not, even so, always quite as blithe and carefree a time at the College as it has sometimes been portrayed subsequently. One of the tutors, John Minton committed suicide while she was there while three fellow students died from illness of one kind or another. 'I think these things affected me,' she has remarked, as did the fact that London was still quite a gloomy, fog-bound, post-war place at this time, making trying to invent a new way of being hard. With the never-had-it-so good, swinging 60s still some distance off, it was not so easy either for a young woman from Yorkshire in a still very male dominated art-school set up. With the exception of Mary Fedden, the tutors at the College were all men and it is significant in this context that Lawson should remember the Professor there at that time, Carel Weight, and very much not a misogynist, (also to become Sonia's very good friend and supporter) once asking her 'Do you think women can be good painters?' Her answer was, of course, yes and she thought that he believed that too, but it does illustrate, nonetheless, the element of prejudice still hugely prevalent, even in avant-garde circles, that a young professional woman artist had to overcome, even at this comparatively late date.

In teaching terms too the College still retained a fairly patrician approach to things and Lawson felt that, again, it was only really Carel Weight who would talk to students as equals though Donald Hamilton Fraser, Roger de Grey and Leonard Rosoman were always very approachable and supportive as well. Yet, as is so often still the case with the senior London art schools, some of the strongest influences came through the example of fellow students themselves. Kossoff and Auerbach, even in their last year, were still spending much of their time in the Life Room and Lawson felt 'their bold charcoal drawings and approach, vigorous and embracing' as important influences – 'it had impact as a solidity in monochrome.'

The other great 'teachers' were of course the London galleries and for Sonia this, above all, meant the British Museum where she was, perhaps somewhat surprisingly, most particularly drawn to Egyptian sculpture which she loved above all for its stillness and sense of permanence. In a BBC TV documentary, directed by John Schlesinger, for the prestige BBC arts programme of the day, Monitor (where Lawson is shown as one of three up-and-coming young art students starting out on their career), she talks particularly about her admiration for the great carved Egyptian stone heads and their links to the landscape of her childhood – 'I am able to look at the colossal head of an Egyptian king and I find the same serenity and monumental quality that I do in the Yorkshire landscape, the rocks and the rock formations up there.' Interestingly, in view

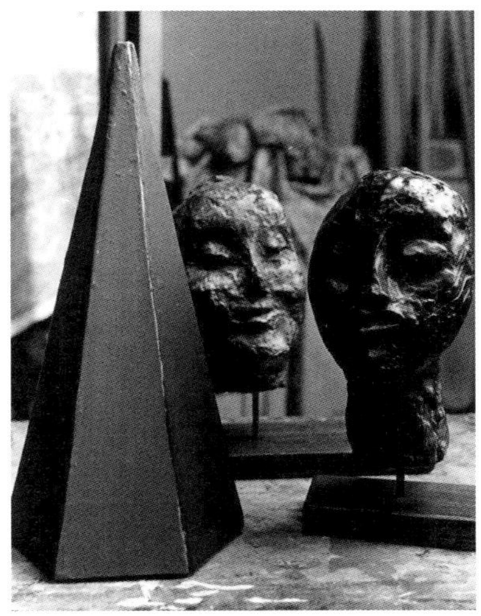

Heads

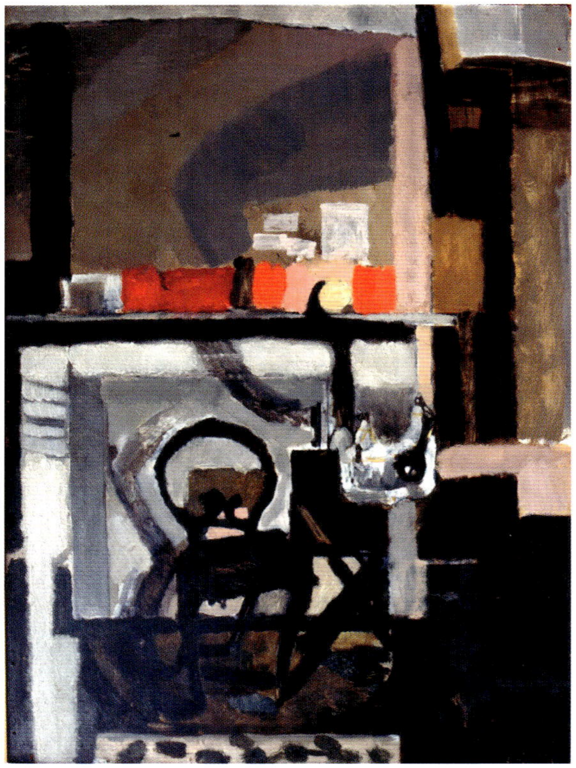

Interior, 1958, oil on canvas, 153 x 122 cm

of the work she has been doing over the last fifteen years or so since 2000, with its thick, heavily incised, almost rock-like surfaces, such sculptural qualities in both her painting and drawing seem in fact to have been something of a preoccupation right from her time at the College, as the group of three powerfully modelled *ciment fondu* heads of c.1960 (no longer extant) illustrated here emphasises very clearly.

In terms of the kind of paintings Lawson now started to make as a student there is a quite emphatic shift, both in terms of her subject matter – a clear move away from landscape and figure towards the still-life and interior – and her style, which goes very firmly in the direction of a bold semi-abstraction. Picasso was an unavoidable influence at that time as was Ecole de Paris painting in general and it is tempting to suggest Nicholas de Stael's Tachiste technique with its bold slabs of pure strong colour must have played its part in a work like *Interior* (1958) (private collection). If this was not a direct influence, then possibly it may have been at the suggestion or example of one of her favoured tutors, Donald Hamilton Fraser, then at the height of his youthful reputation as the leading exponent of a broadly tachiste semi-abstract style in this country.

In retrospect Lawson came to see the move towards abstraction during her time at the College as a 'means of disconnecting form and function, a sense of release into colour, abstract shapes, timeless forms outside the here and now' that would give her the freedom and space to tackle the wider range of subjects and themes she was just beginning to realise she was wanting to bring into her future work. Abstraction gave her a metaphorical as well as an actual, pictorial means of doing just that. Another good example of these experimental directions evident in her work during her time

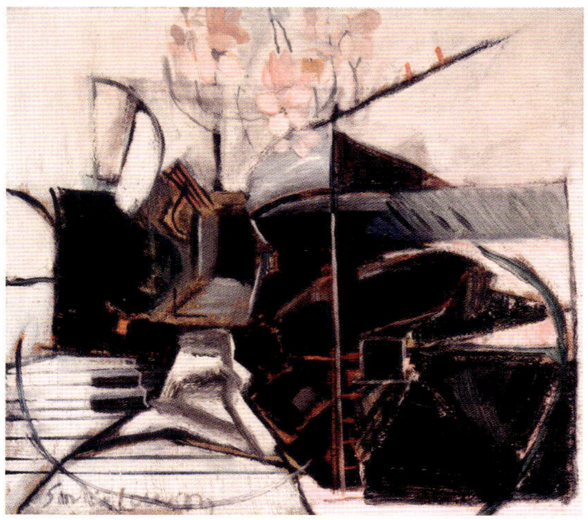

Entrance to a Garden

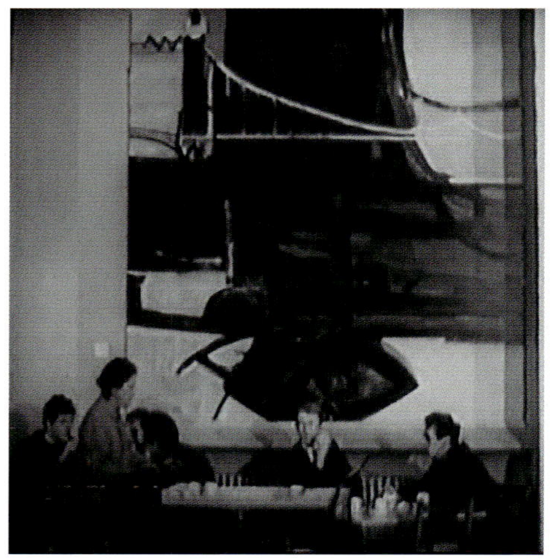

London Mural 1958
V&A café

at the Royal College of Art is the very different piece, *Entrance to a Garden* c.1960 (Royal Academy Collection via Carel Weight Bequest) which, with its austere, almost monochromatic colour and clear spatial delineation of forms in space has an intensely sculptural, architectonic form, and is the most abstract piece of work she would undertake until her monumental paintings of the late 1990s.

Sonia Lawson became something of a star of her year: she did two murals for the Victoria & Albert Museum café (massive and dramatically powerful abstractions as the contemporary photograph makes clear), while at the end of her third year (1958) she gained a 1st Class Diploma and was awarded a two-month travelling scholarship followed by a further post-graduate year at the RCA. She chose to take the travelling scholarship in the South of France, working in Marseille, Aix-en-Provence, Arles and Antibes and visiting the great Matisse chapel at Vence. Meanwhile her work had already been seen in regional exhibitions in Leeds, Bradford and an Arts Council Touring exhibition before her first show (shared with Olwyn Bowey) at the well-regarded Zwemmer Gallery at the end of 1960. In the same year she had already featured in the major John Schlesinger Monitor documentary referred to earlier and been bought for collections in the UK and America. In short her career was up and running and with part-time teaching jobs first at Harrow School of Art (1960–65) and then at West Surrey College of Art Farnham and St. Martin's, she had an element of financial security too.

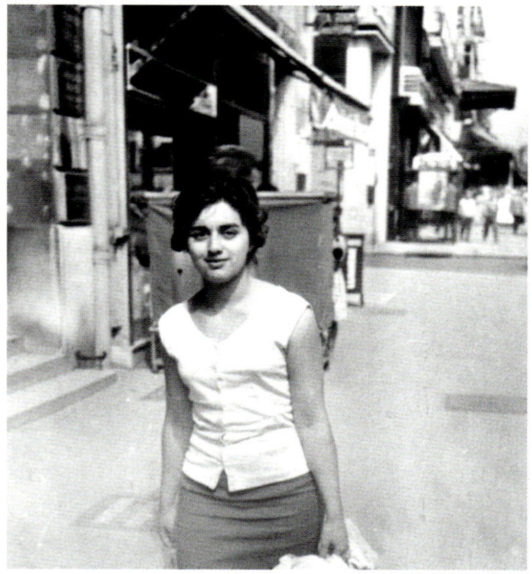

Sonia Lawson, 1959, Marseille

The period immediately after the RCA was, nonetheless, a difficult time for her personally, as indeed that particular moment often can be for any young artist. She began to find London increasingly oppressive and felt herself to be socially very isolated and lacking in a sense of the community she had grown so accustomed to in a small Dales town. At the same time, quite apart from her mother's ongoing illness, her father was now also seriously ill and any spare time she had was spent travelling to the Dales to help look after him up until his death in 1968. Lawson remained nonetheless very active as a painter and the Zwemmer show was followed by further exhibitions at Cheltenham Art Gallery (1962) alongside Peter Blake, Euan Uglow and John Hoyland among the five others, the prestigious New Art Centre London (1963) and the Queen's Square Gallery in Leeds (1964), while in the same year Richard Buckle commissioned a picture from her for the major show celebrating 400 years of Shakespeare that was being held at Stratford-upon-Avon.

Given that a good deal of the work from these years immediately after leaving the RCA is now untraceable or known only from rather grainy black and white images, it is hard to form a really clear picture of the development of her work after leaving art-school. There does seem to have been a steady darkening of mood, with a spiky

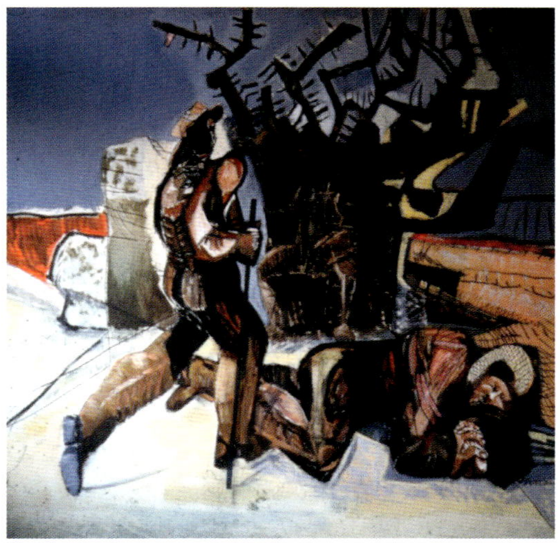

Rendezvous

Sutherland-like landscape and landscape with figures theme for her 1963 New Art Centre show – *Rendezvous* (c.1963), which was sold at the exhibition, is an example. Then her work seems to shift to a rather more complex 'figures in a landscape' composition, for example, *The Dark Tower*, a sombre semi-abstraction, for her Leeds exhibition the following year – 1964. She herself talks now about her pent-up misery at this mid-point in the 60s – alone and drifting is how she puts it now and acutely aware through the press and newspapers of the constant presence of war somewhere on the globe – this was the moment of Vietnam after all. Even so nothing quite prepares us for the quite astonishing sequence of political prisoner and war-based paintings that were now to suddenly burst out in her work from 1967. She herself can point to no single trigger for them but the sense is that the appalling memories of those latent feelings of a loss of innocence, guilt and anger that she had first felt at the end of the war, as a child putting together those scrapbooks of human atrocity in Europe, had for her, as for Rilke, finally 'changed into our very blood … and are nameless, no longer to be distinguished from ourselves.'

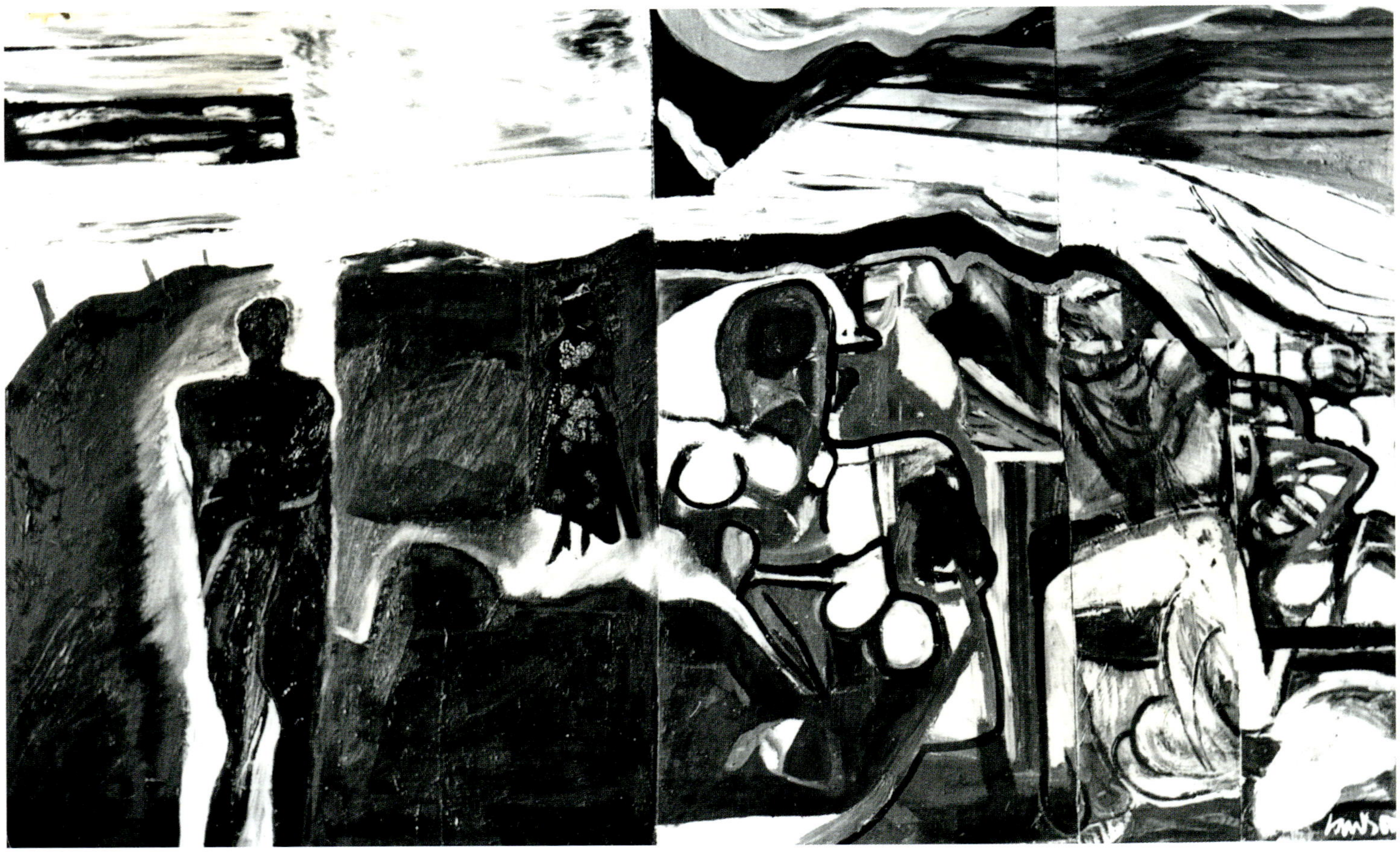

The Dark Tower 1964, oil on canvas. Exhibited at the Queen Square Gallery, Leeds

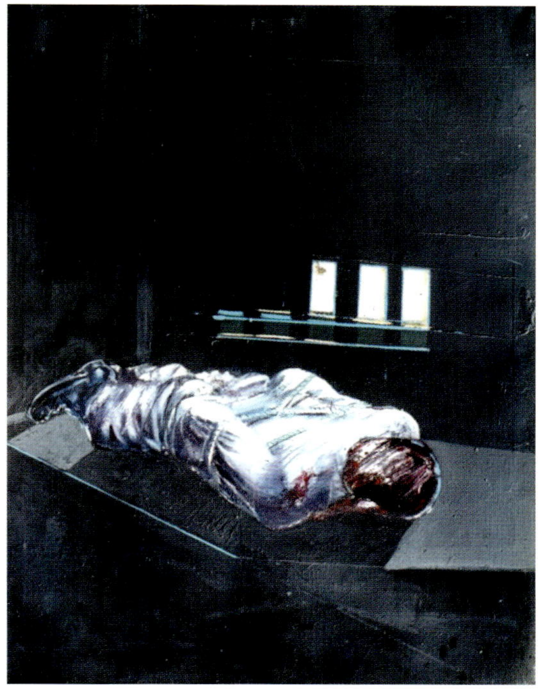

Bound Figure 1966, oil on canvas, 91 × 71 cm

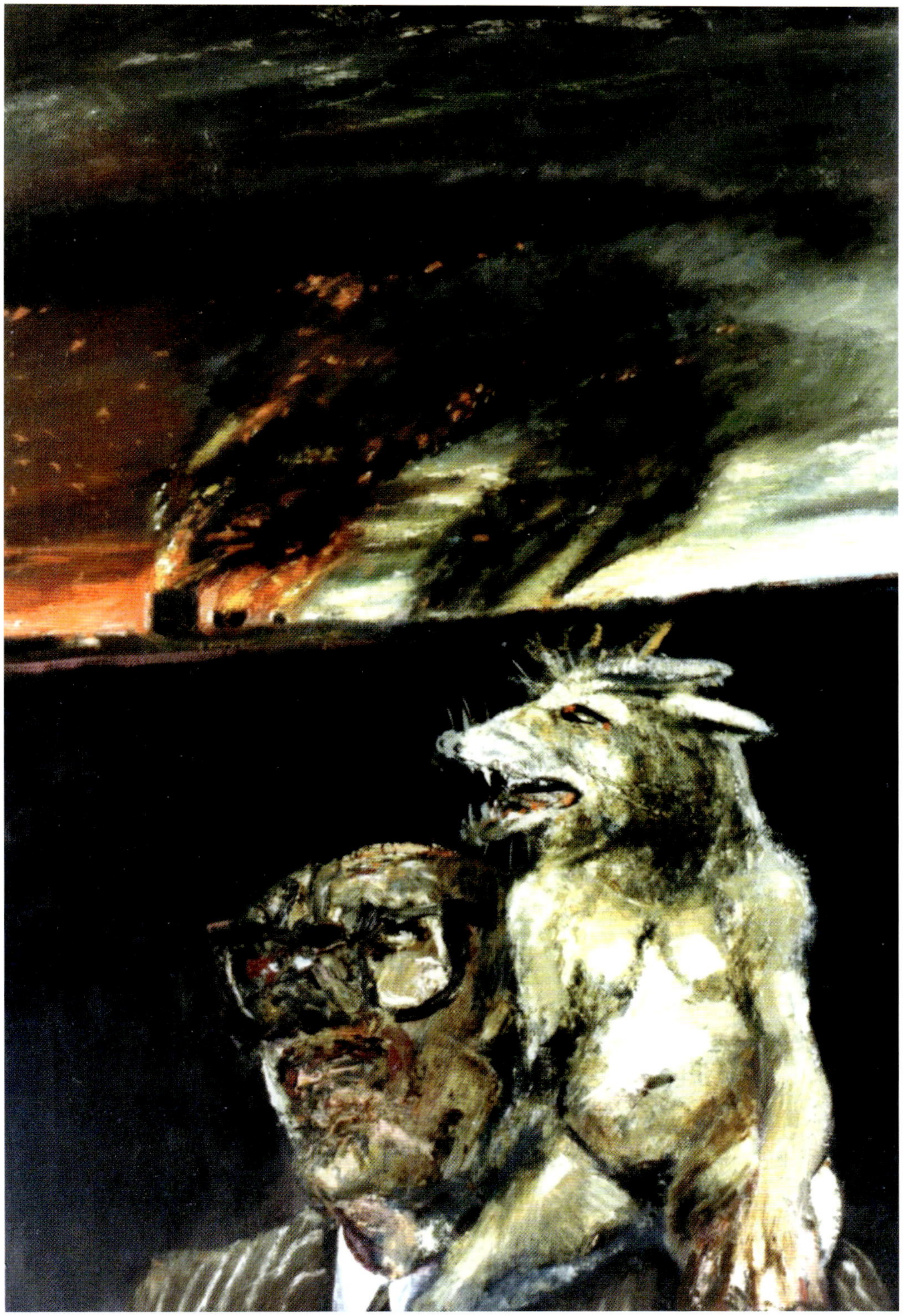

Warlock 1967, oil on canvas, 77 × 56 cm

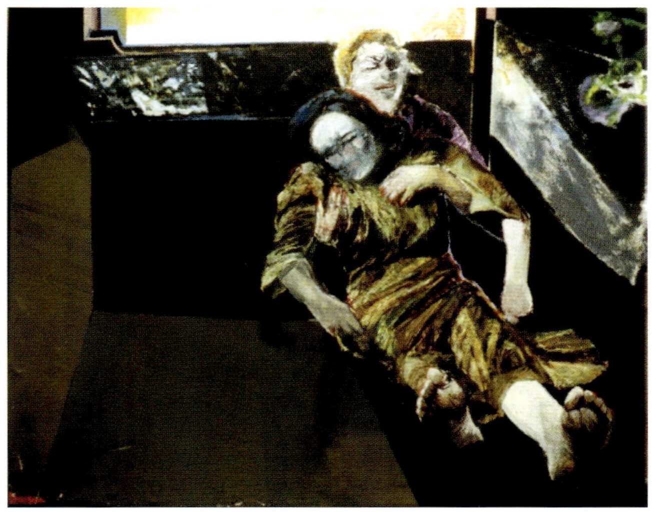

Rescue II 1968, oil on canvas, 122 × 153 cm

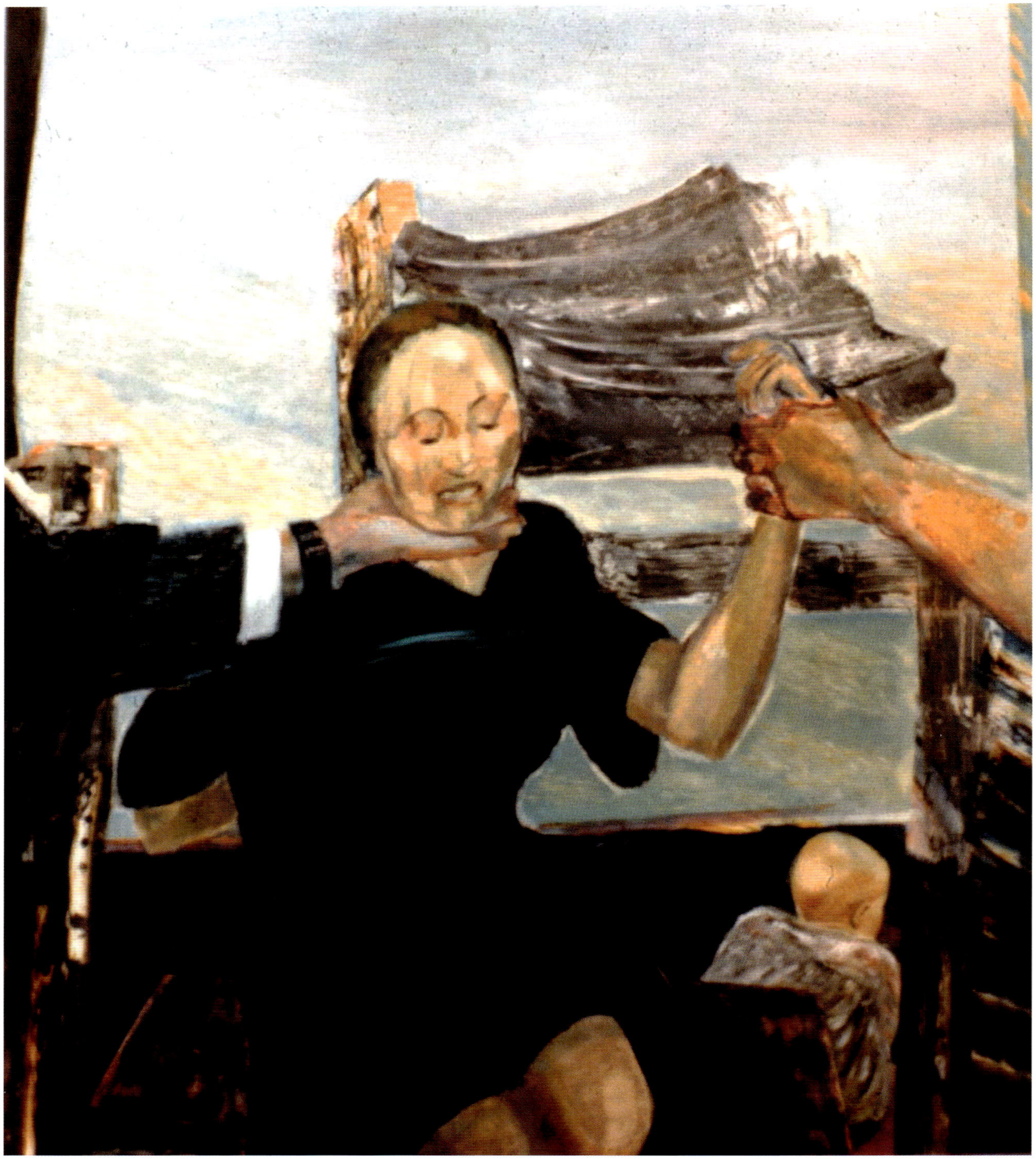

Separation at Dawn 1970, oil on canvas, 153 x 122 cm

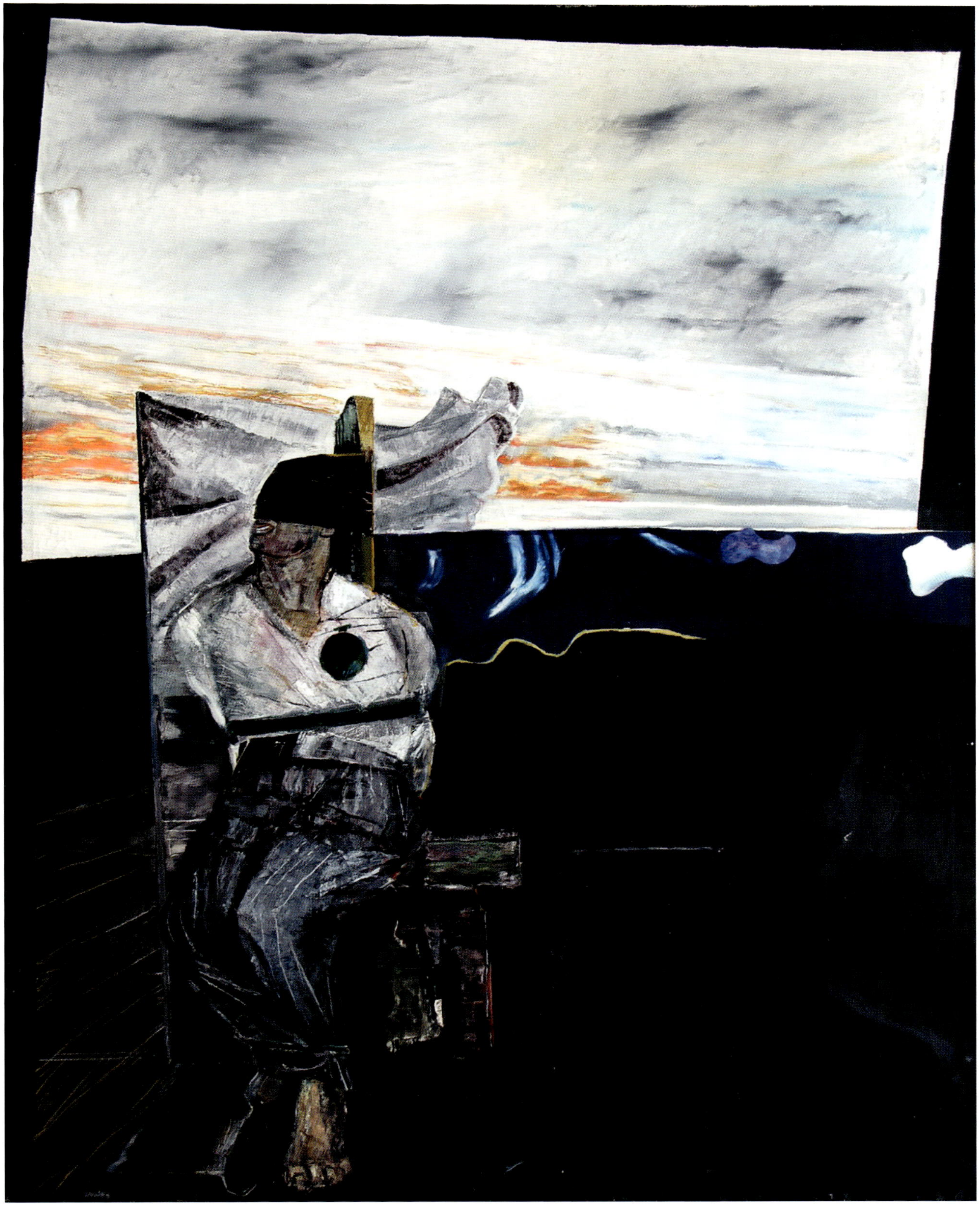

Figure at Dawn c.1966–67, oil on canvas, 183 x 153 cm

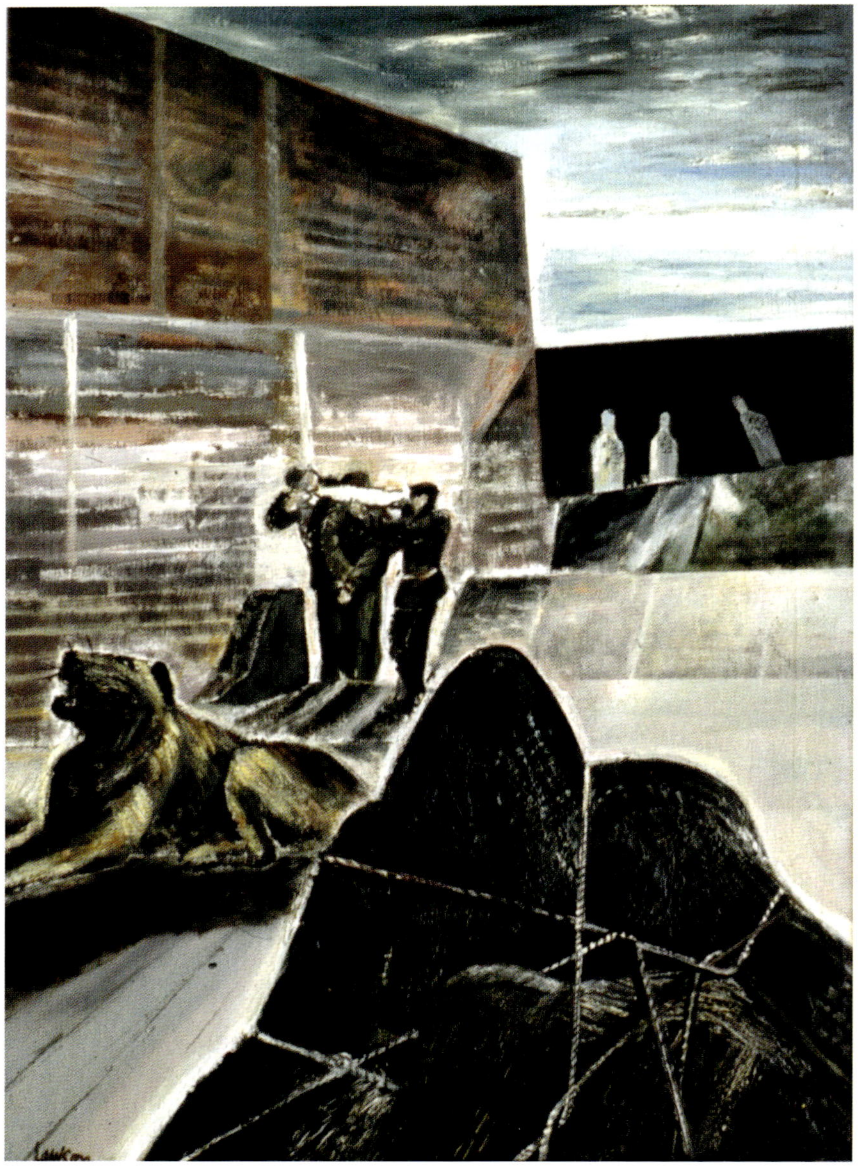

Execution at Daybreak 1967, oil on canvas, 77 x 56 cm

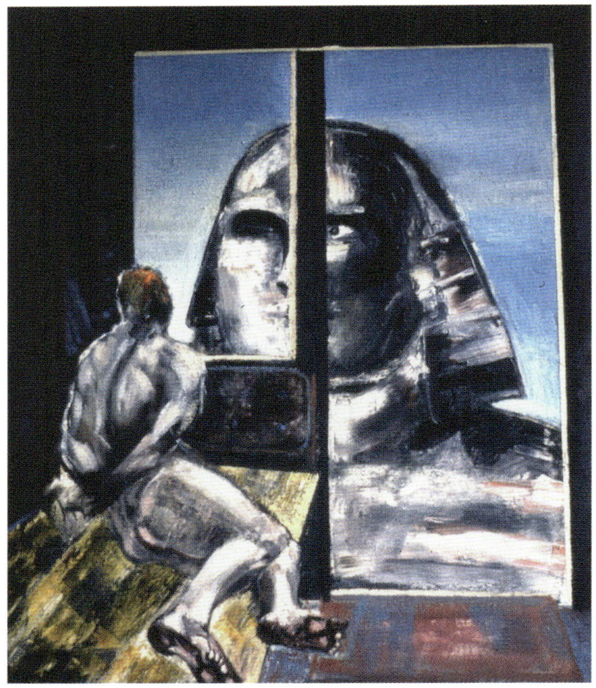

Interrogation Enigma 1967, oil on canvas, 61 x 56 cm

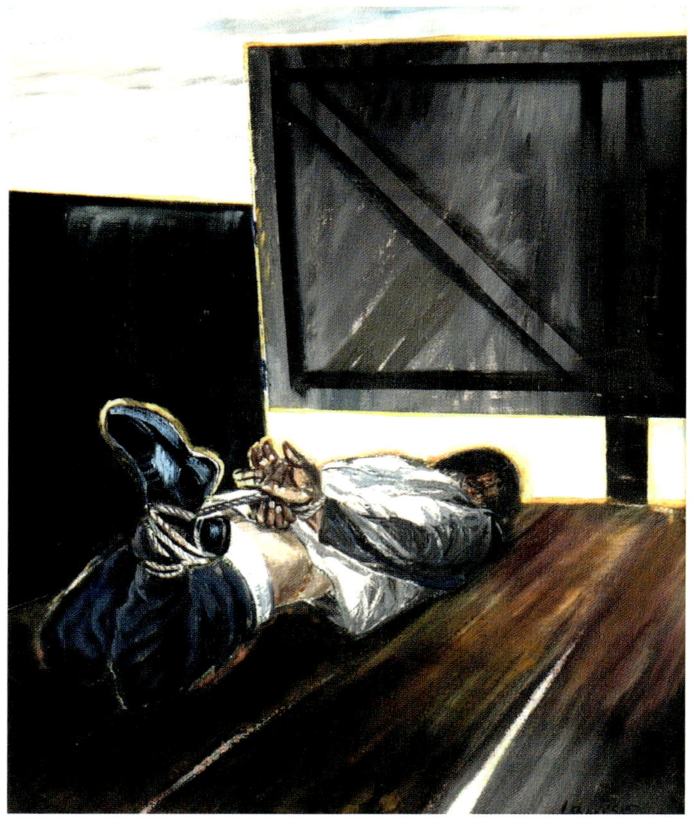

Prisoner 1967, oil on canvas, 153 x 122 cm. Collection: Royal West of England Academy, Bristol

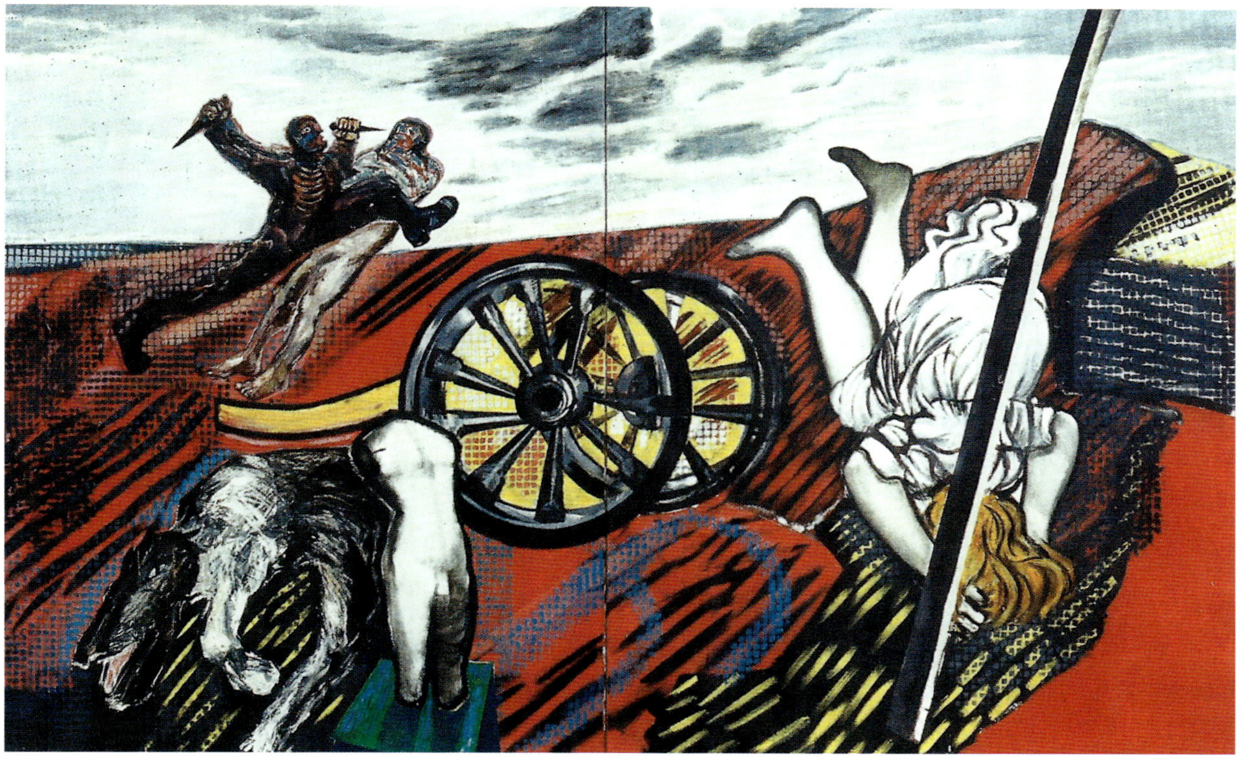

Untitled Anti War I 1967, oil on canvas, 156 × 244 cm

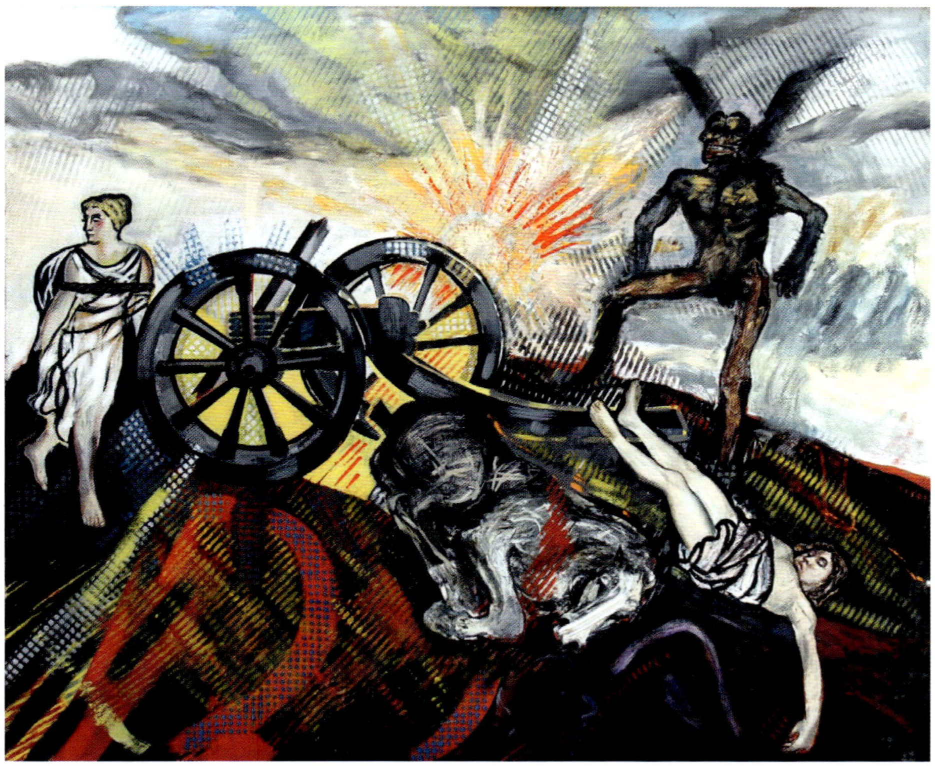

Untitled Anti War II 1968, oil on canvas, 152 × 185 cm

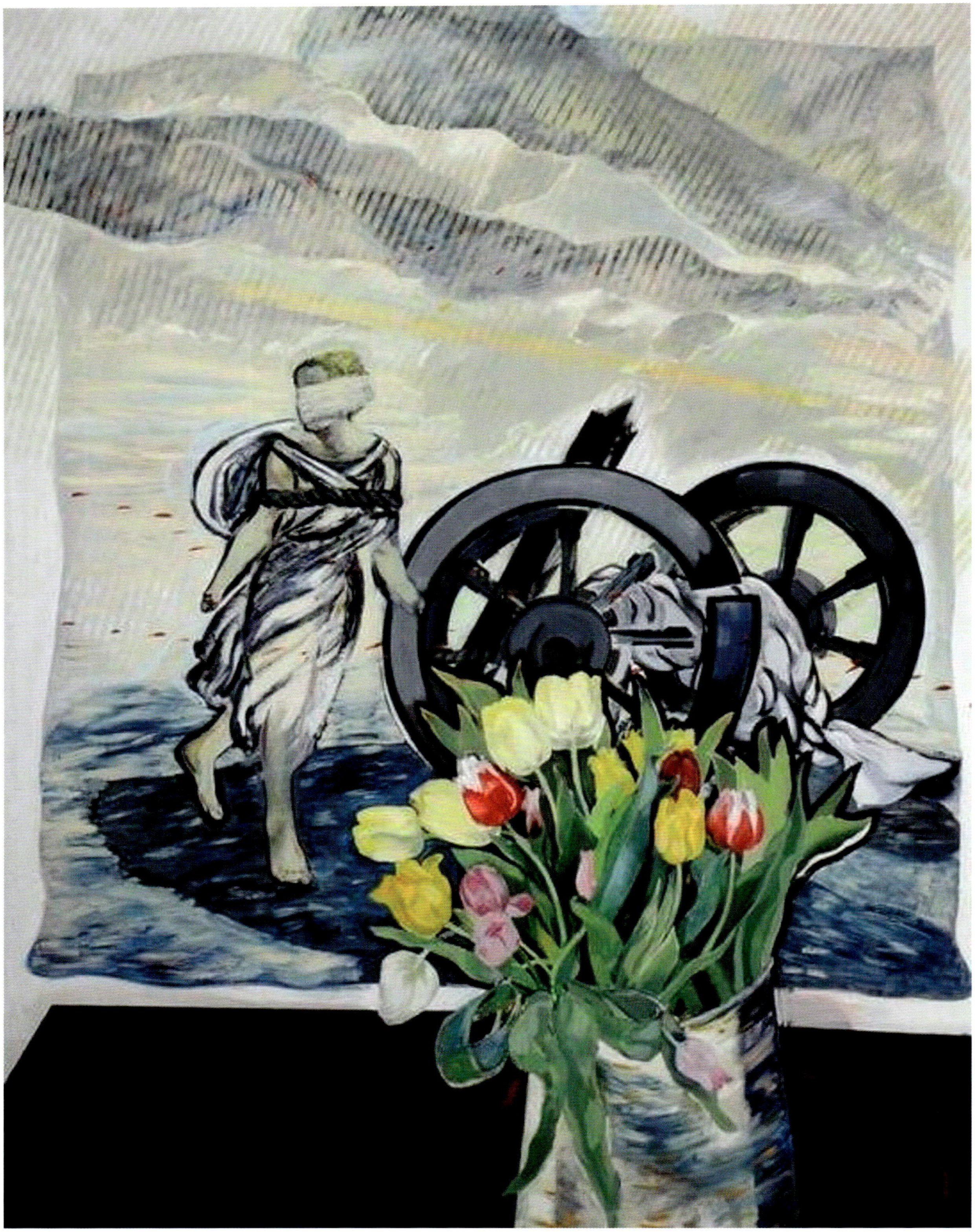

Frail Peace with Tulips c.1972, oil on canvas, 150 x 122 cm
Collection: Graves Art Gallery, Sheffield

Chapter 3

Cruelty has a human heart
And Jealousy a human face
Terror, the Human Form Divine
And Secrecy, the Human Dress

From *A Divine Image* by William Blake

Looked at with hindsight, the tendency towards a poetic, landscape-based abstraction which first emerged in Lawson's work as a student at the Royal College, rather than being only some kind of holding operation while she worked out her own particular artistic 'voice', can now clearly be seen instead as the first expression of that same significant abstract strand in her work to which she was finally to return much later in the 1990s. Abstract painting had, as she has subsequently reflected, provided her with a crucial form of liberation at the start of her career. By this I believe she means, above all, freedom from ties to any kind of older, and more limiting, narrative figurative tradition, even those practised by her artist parents to whom she always felt herself so indebted. But now, before she could arrive again at this freedom of abstraction, 'there were solid hard realities to deal with.' As a painter who has always felt herself to be an artist of conscience, this youthful realization 'of the inhumanity human kind deals out to all sentient forms,' seen now in the context of contemporary troubles, had to find expression first before she felt free enough to go on to explore any other, more personal, subject matter.

Her response was powerful and articulate – an extended series of paintings over the next decade or so (1966–77) encompassing themes of prisoners of conscience, the brutalising impact of war on men's and women's lives and the abuse of children – which, in their ferocious, engaged energy, visceral painting technique, astonishingly powerful and controlled use of colour and monumental formal structure – can be counted among the major (if still largely unrecognized) artistic achievements of the period. What is also quite remarkable about them, the first series on political prisoners and executions particularly, is that, rich and complex in their range and reference of allusion as they are, they nonetheless seem to emerge almost fully fledged, without any real sense of her gradually trying to find her way. And, in the context of Pop Art, Hard-Edged Abstraction, post-Bomberg realism (Auerbach and Kossoff) and Slade measured naturalism that dominated the late 60s, they also seemed set on a very separate artistic trajectory, one that owed nothing to any of them.

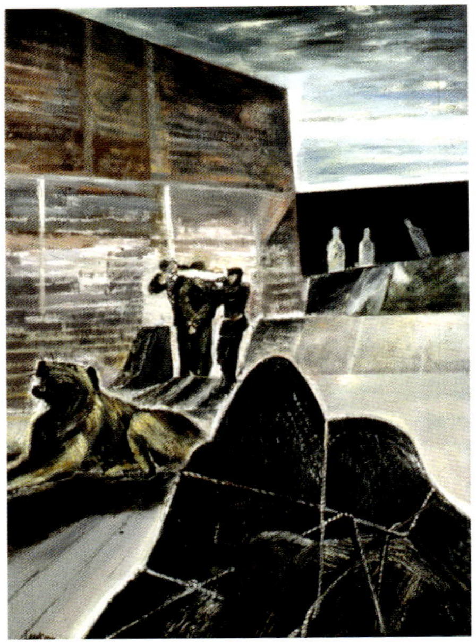

Execution at Daybreak

Over the years critics have wrestled with what stylistic label to put on such works which seem, at one point or another, to touch on Surrealism, Expressionism, Realism and English Romanticism and incorporate compositional methods that owe more than a little to the European films she had enjoyed watching since her student days at the RCA, Ingmar Bergman's *The Seventh Seal* in particular. In *Execution at Daybreak* (1967), for example, the man being blindfolded (a political prisoner, one imagines) prior to being shot, is viewed obliquely in the middle left ground, above and to one side of her painted version of Man Ray's *The Enigma of Isidore Ducasse*, itself a realization via a 'made' and then photographed object, of one of the classic Surrealist literary images – a sewing machine wrapped in a blanket and tied with string. With its fiercely oblique diagonals and arbitrary arrangement of objects, that also includes a sculpted lion, the setting she constructs for this drama has a distinctly laconic and highly ambiguous quality to it, clearly Chirico-esque in feeling. The atmosphere is then further complicated and made even more haunting by the unmistakable sense that one is, at the same time, somehow viewing a still from a film or even a documentary newsreel, the paint having a somewhat harsh, grainy quality that underlines this feeling. Given it is the kind of incident the media seems to bring into our homes now on an almost daily basis from Syria or Afghanistan or elsewhere in the world, it is a testament to the imaginative power of this work that the shock value of the image has become, if anything, even more intense over the half-century since it was painted.

The allusions to Man Ray have a further dimension in considering the other works in this first series, all painted around 1966/67, notably the bound figures in *Prisoner* (1967) and *Figure at Dawn* (1966–67). Man Ray had observed that form, when stripped of function becomes an enigma drawing the eye and mind through curiosity, and forms stripped of meaning become objects of focus and fascination and take on the resonating power of the unknown. In the process they bind the composition together hinting at something sinister or at the revelation of a mystery. In terms of these two compositions, each is weighted by the bound human figures which are the focus of the composition, drawing the eye ineluctably to the central drama being played out. Sonia herself elaborated very intriguingly on the ambiguous emotional resonances of the bound figure, in a film interview with the critic Mervyn Levy some 10 years later where she observed 'When people are emotionally in some sort of *extremis*, in some sort of predicament, they seem to hold themselves together rather well, sometimes in groups, in a ready-made composition. This painting *Figure at Dawn,* is only a single figure but the actual subject of a bound man is nicely held together so that, quite apart from the human predicament, it's got this nice sort of sculptural quality, this ready-made feeling, which I liked'. This is a reference again of course to Man Ray and to Dada and Surrealism in general but also looks back, on the one hand, to her own sculptural experiments earlier in the decade at the RCA and, on the other, forward to her renewed preoccupations with achieving a more sculptural quality in her painting from the 1990s onwards. The feeling for sculptural form is, in short, something that is always an important presence in her art, both in terms of the composition and the drawing that underlies her art, giving to it that sense of monumental presence that is such an inescapable and fundamental quality in all her major paintings from the 1960s to the present day.

In the same interview Sonia, talking about *Figure at Dawn,* also makes a revealing reference to the ecstatic dawn sky-scape behind the figure. 'In a sense the sky symbolizes (not that I want to talk about symbolism like that) a sort of freedom, and sometimes when I am painting these subjects I also need to go out into the fields where I do rather large paintings of skies, getting that nice form you find in heavy skies coming down the valleys, terrible and beautiful as an army with banners, as they come down the Yorkshire Dales where I live.' Immediately one's mind goes back to that 11-year-old girl at the end of the war, with her scrapbooks full of cuttings of human inhumanity to set alongside her earlier complex memories of an often idyllic childhood growing up among animals in a beautiful and untrammeled landscape but also with memories of those early family losses and emotional difficulties. In a conversation with the art-historian Norbert Lynton for her 1996 retrospective exhibition in Halifax she talks very clearly of the 'social comment about war, vulnerability and death' embodied in these works, and of family deaths etc, as part of a mental sketchbook that fed into their narrative content.' Thus, already, in this figure of a bound man awaiting execution or torture we can see at work that painterly process whereby Lawson seems to layer and interweave social comment, landscape and personal and public histories into a uniquely resonant form, one that, over the years, has found no parallel in British painting in its exhilarating emotional power. As Carel Weight thoughtfully observed in his introduction to Sonia's retrospective show at Milton Keynes in 1982, 'I don't believe Francis Bacon has done anything more disturbing.'

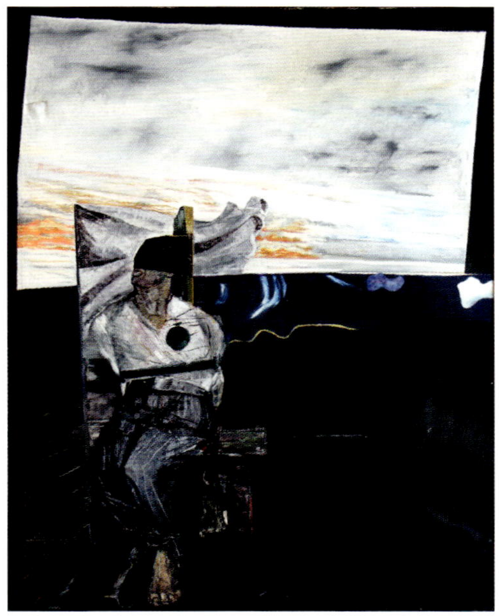

Figure at Dawn

The other major group of paintings on war- and violence-related themes from this period, represented here by *Untitled Anti War I* (1967) and *Untitled Anti War II* (1968) have an altogether different character, fields of war strewn with violently struggling figures, gun carriages, female corpses and dying horses set in landscapes of an unremitting bleakness. Goya immediately comes to mind though the way they are painted and composed are very much more twentieth century in character with Léger and Guttoso among the names that suggest themselves here. The landscape too echoes the harshness and relentlessness of its subject matter with its hard, often striated finish, a mechanical surface-making that was apparently achieved by painting certain areas through metal mesh.

Finally, though very different to these two pieces in the way it is painted, looking forward as it does to the *Mother and Child* paintings of c.1974–77, but, nonetheless with the same unremitting ferocity of mood, there is *Warlock* (1967). A grinning, wolf-headed-female figure, perched on the shoulder of an impassive bowler-hatted, bespectacled and suited man, is placed right up against the plane of the picture, both looking out from a darkened, ravaged landscape where buildings burn fiercely on the horizon, with firebrands and clouds of thick, dark smoke pouring into a stormy evening sky. It is a dark and terrifying image, redolent of an evil intent, of the dark magic that can lurk in even the most apparently respectable figure, of how war is so

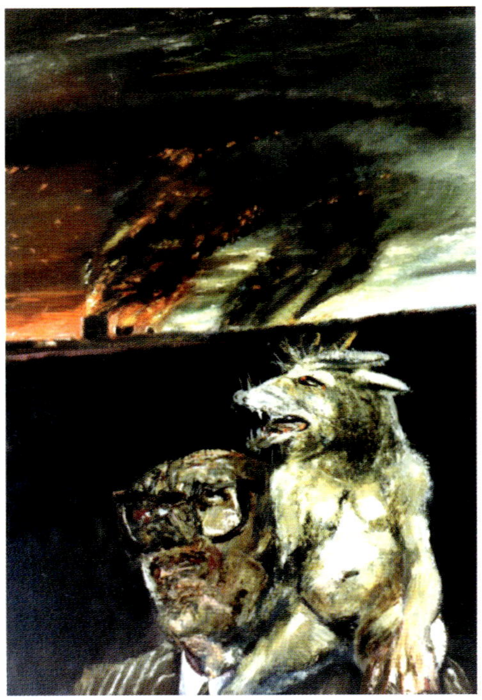

Warlock

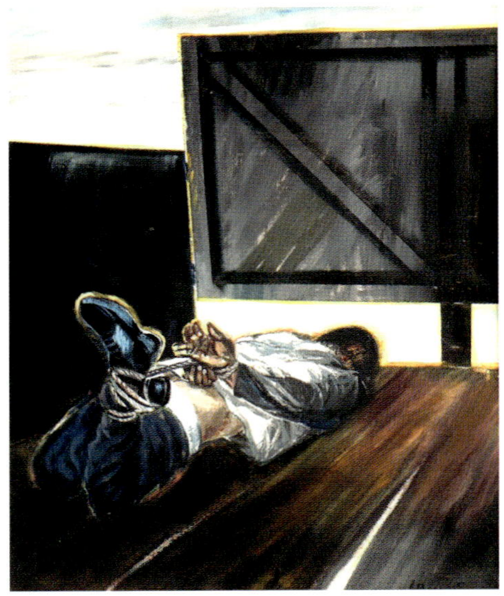

Prisoner

often orchestrated by men sitting behind desks. Where it comes from artistically is intriguing – it is so different in touch and feeling again from the *Prisoner* paintings of the same year. Bruegel's apocalyptic paintings of war would seem to be a significant background element while, in more contemporary terms, the German Expressionists Max Beckmann and Ludwig Meidner come to mind, together with the work of the Italian Modernist Mario Sironi, whose brooding Metaphysical urban landscapes of the 1920s have a similarly disturbing mood; they were all artists Sonia was already familiar with and greatly admired. Nearer to home also one shouldn't forget the example of her Royal College of Art tutor and good friend Carel Weight whose own art, strongly European in character with Munch an important influence on it, took on themes and subjects of a not entirely dissimilarly haunted atmosphere and black humour and were often painted with the same kind of febrile, broken brushstroke that lends this picture such an edgy quality.

That mood of anxiety that haunted her work in the lead up to this series of paintings – she had only recently broken up with a boyfriend also – was however about to change and change in ways that, while by no means affecting her determination and need to paint pictures that would continue to address those 'hard realities' she had recently identified within herself, nonetheless radically affected both her choice of subjects and the feeling she wanted to bring into them. The causes were a rapid sequence of highly significant events in her personal life, precipitated in the first instance by the death of her beloved father, Fred Lawson, after a long illness, in December 1968. This had meant the postponement of her marriage to her husband Charles (Charlie) Congo, whom she had met some time before, to early 1969, her only daughter, Zoe being born some 16 months later in 1970. Her marriage also meant leaving London – no great loss, one senses – and moving to Leighton Buzzard in Bedfordshire in 1969 (where Charlie had started a business making plastic industrial parts), to the same house she still lives in today. From a way of life which she looks back on as being somewhat lonely and isolated she now had a rather more settled existence, though she still travelled on a regular basis to Wensleydale to work and to keep an eye on her mother who continued to live and work in Castle Bolton for some two decades after her husband's death. For all the stresses and strains of motherhood as well and the fact that she was now seeing few artists and little of the art-world, it was a way of life that seems nonetheless to have suited her well temperamentally and artistically, her work now expanding and opening out still further over the next decade and beyond.

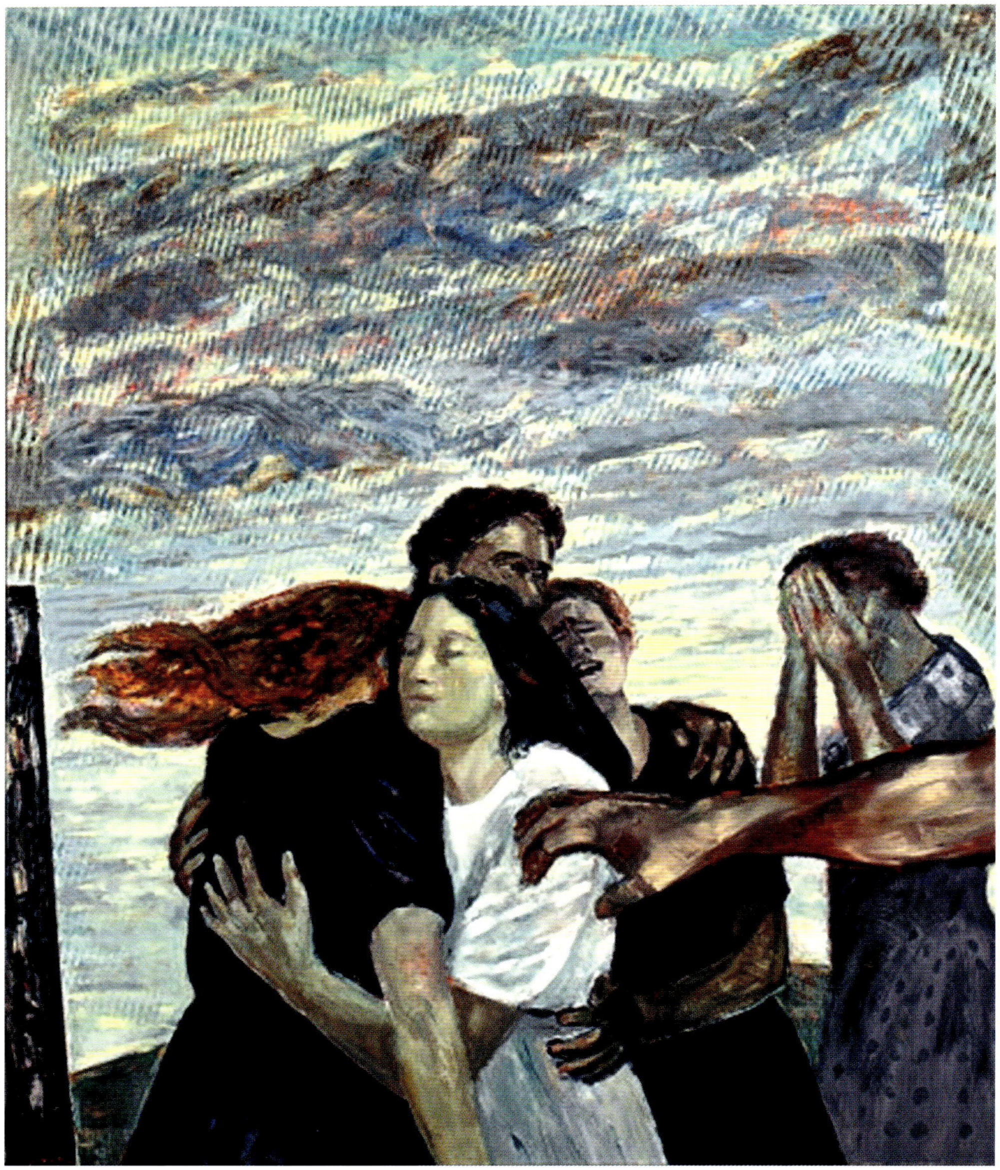

The Parting 1970, oil on canvas, 143 x 122 cm

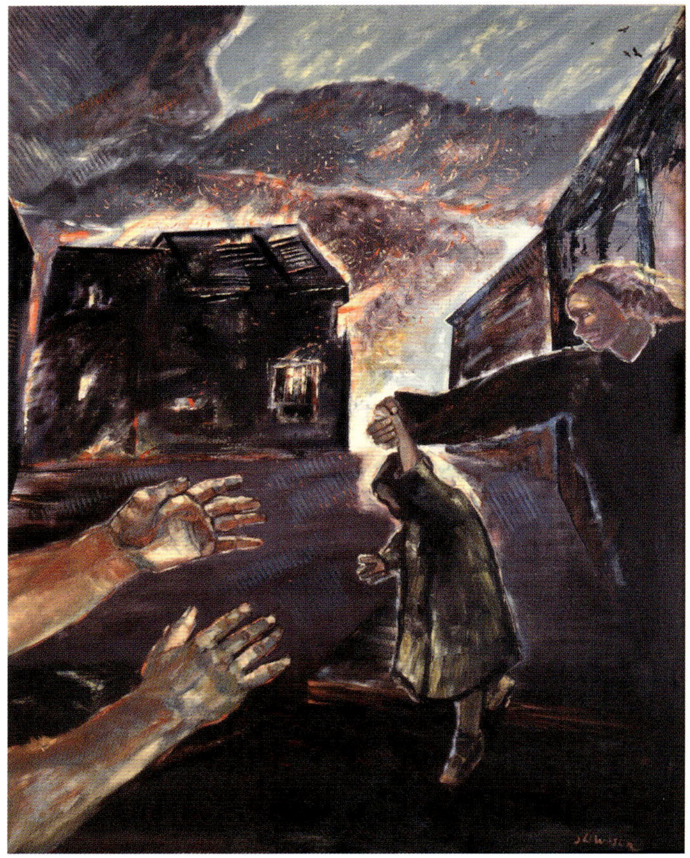

Incendiary 1979, oil on canvas, 153 x 122 cm
Private Collection

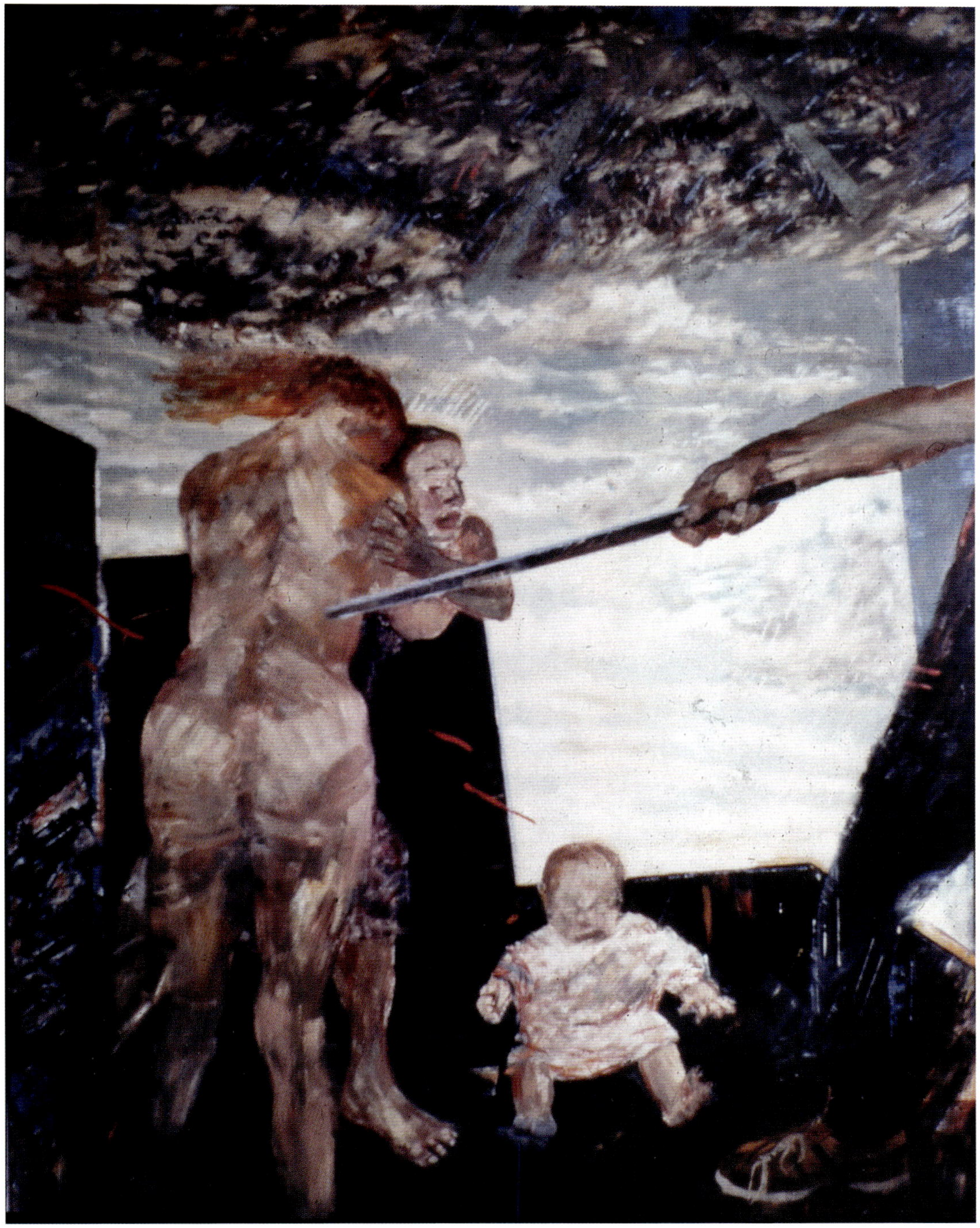

Separation 1970, oil on canvas, 153 × 122 cm
Private Collection

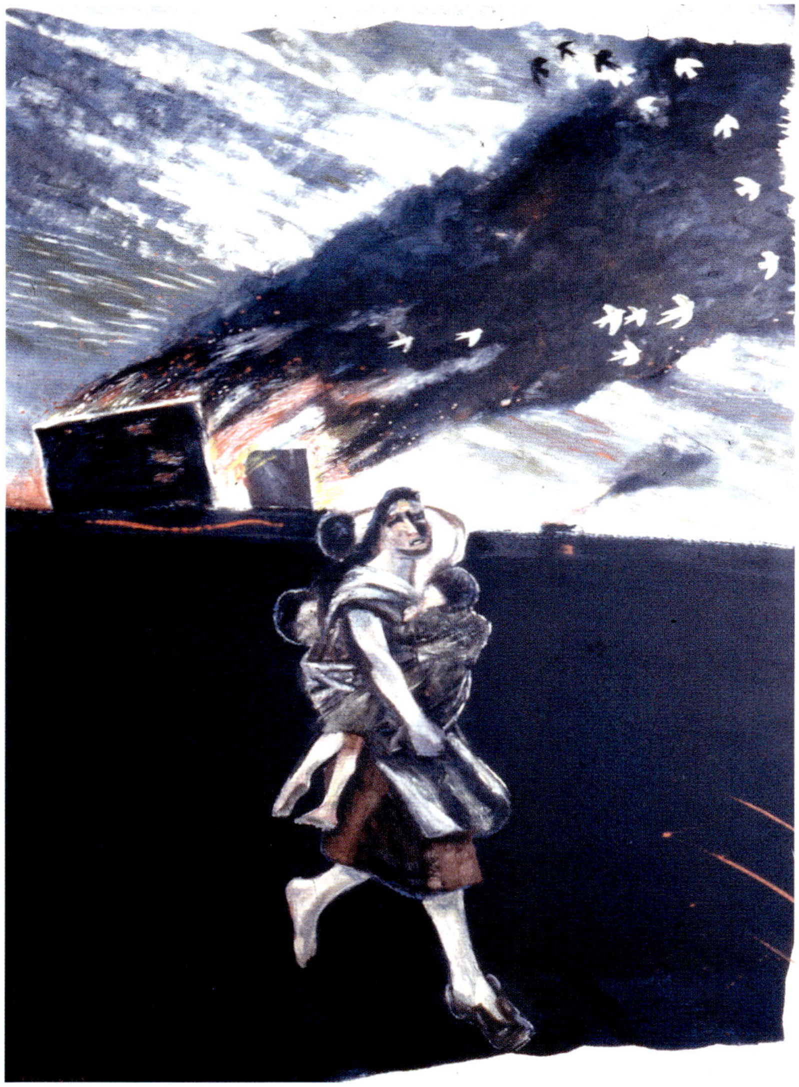

No Hiding Place 1974, oil on canvas, 153 × 122 cm

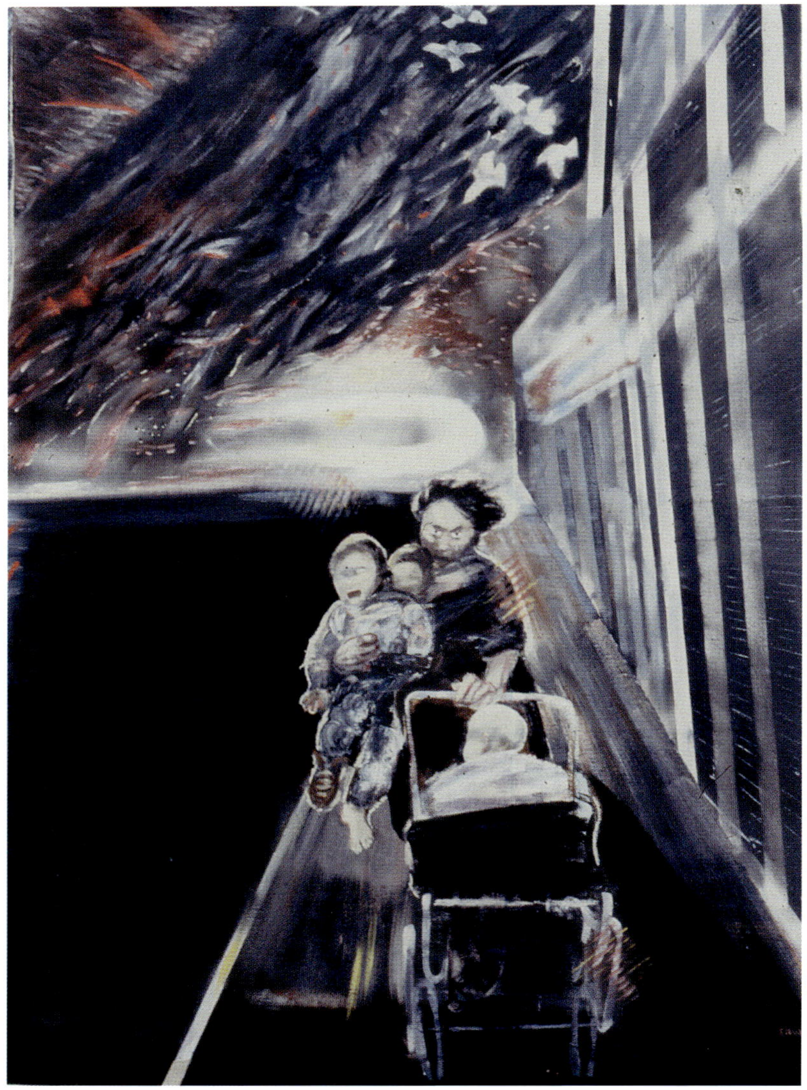

Fire at Noon 1977, oil on canvas, 153 × 122 cm

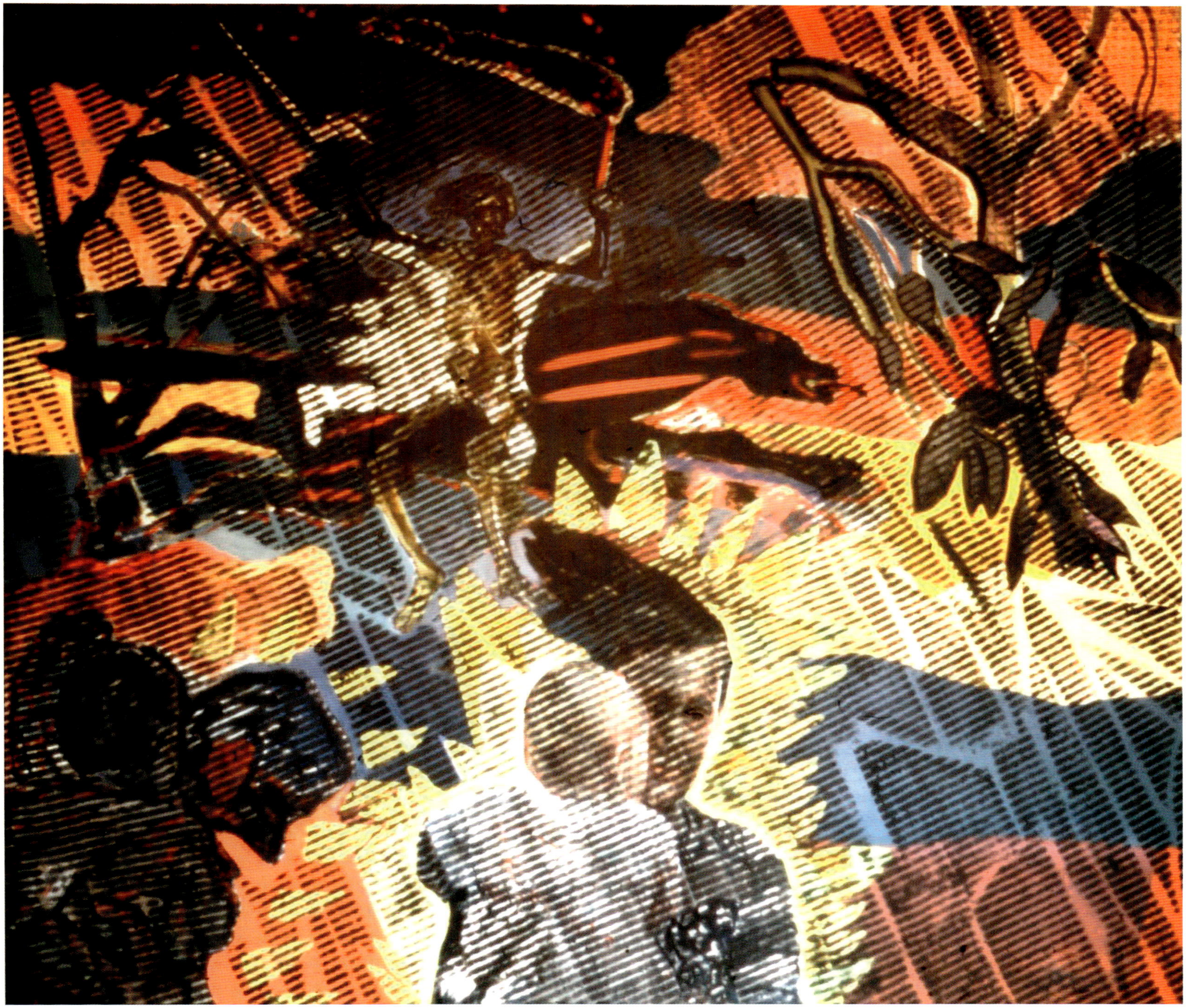

Blaze 1981, oil on canvas, 153 x 244 cm

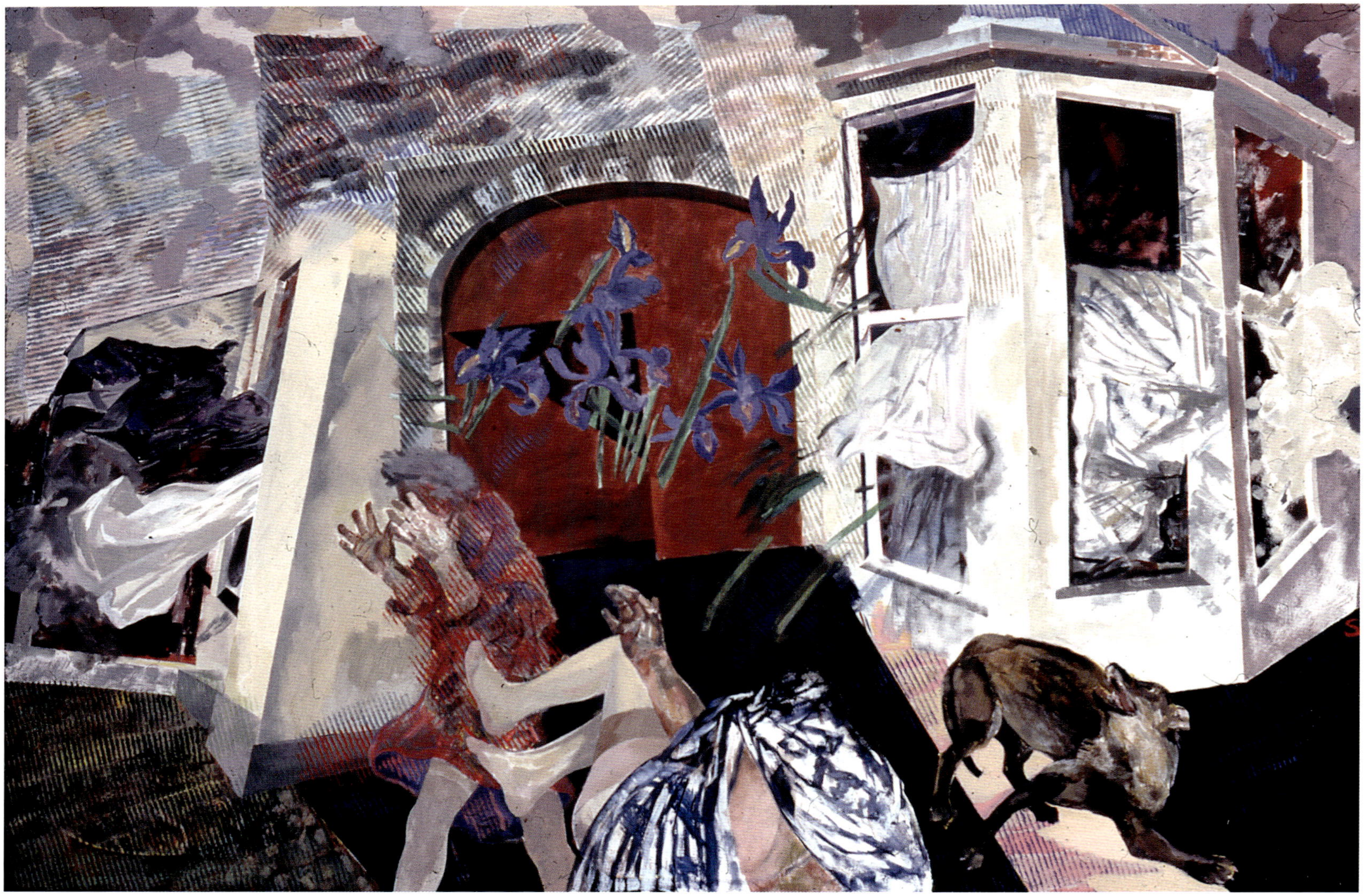

Sudden Event 1981, oil on canvas, 153 x 244 cm

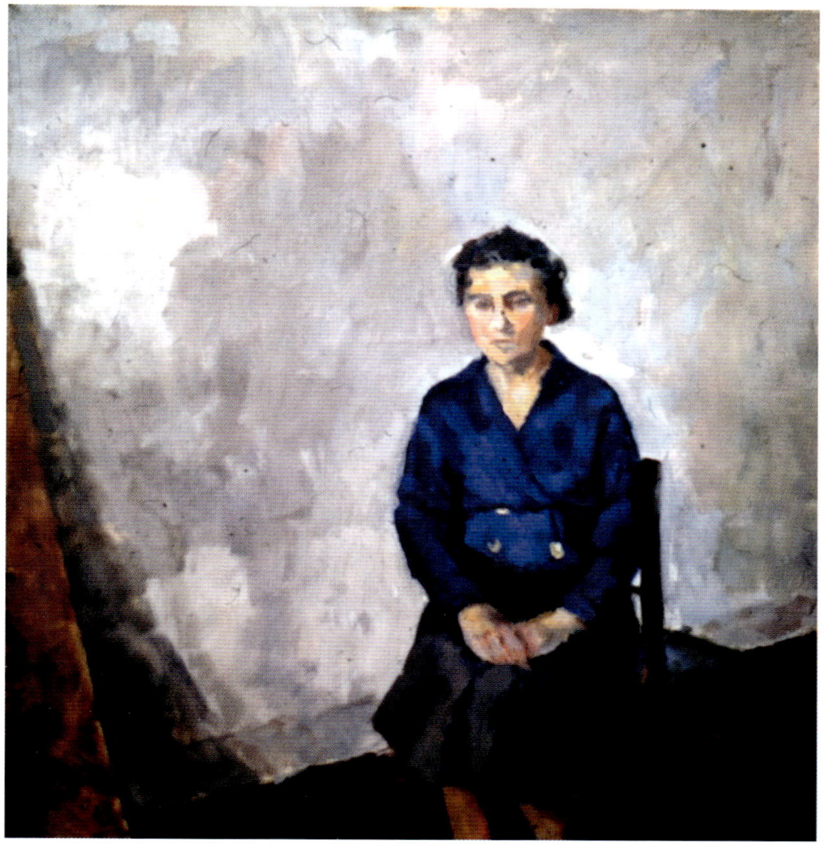

Woman in Blue 1959, oil on canvas, 64 x 57 cm

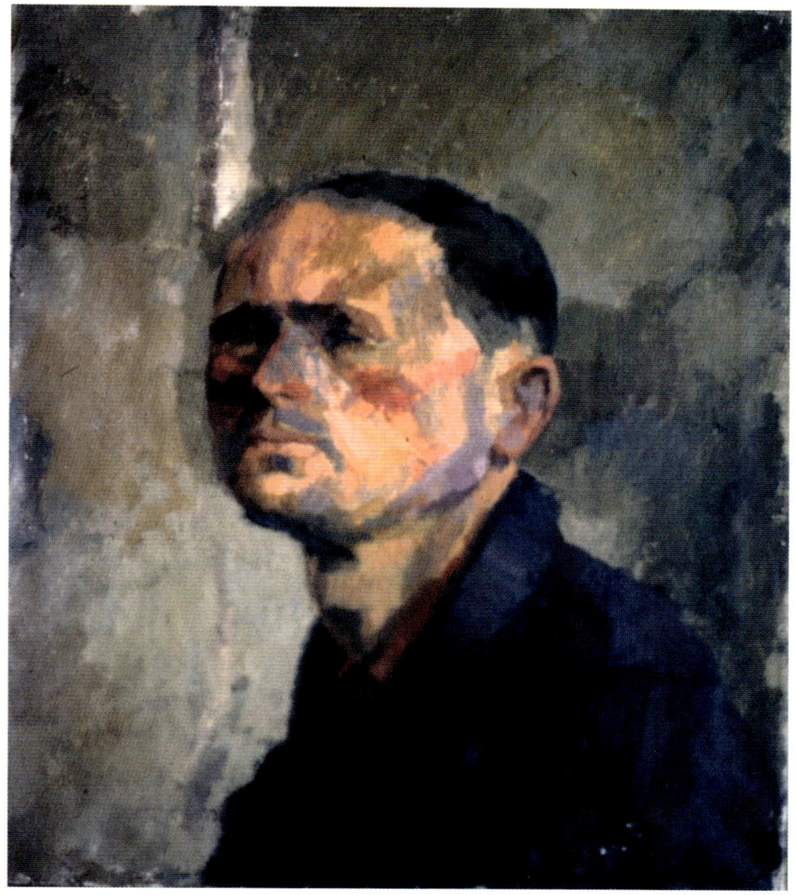

Man recovered from T.B. 1958, oil on canvas, 64 x 57 cm

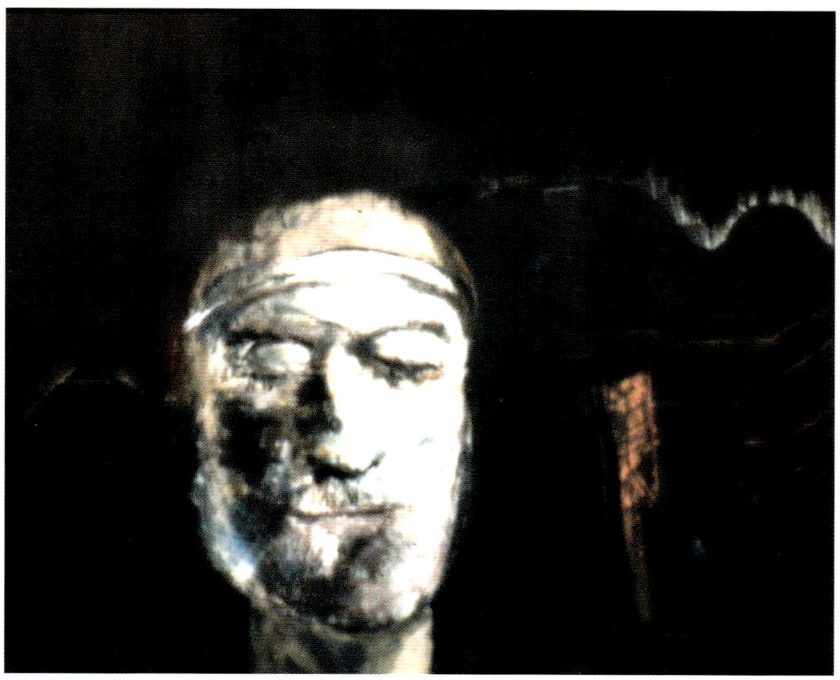

Lazarus Head 1979, oil on canvas, 57 x 64 cm

Chapter 4

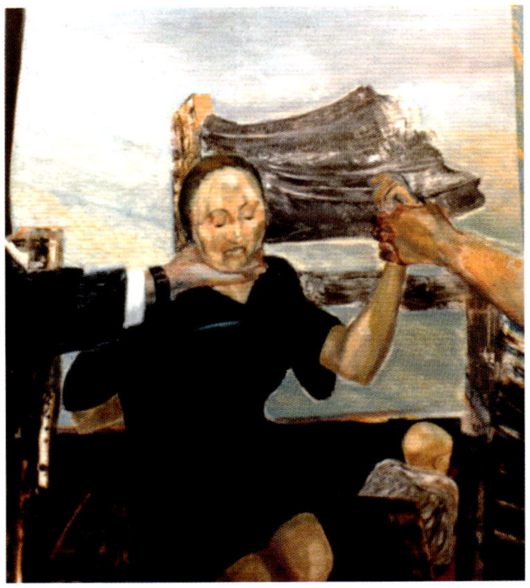

Separation at Dawn

After the birth of her daughter Zoe in spring 1970, the character of Sonia Lawson's still very committed approach to painting starts to change quite distinctly: the themes of war and its brutal fall-out continue – the suffering of the innocent as she has termed it – but now, over the next decade, it was with an increasing emphasis on the sufferings of women and children in particular. Two events particularly, in the wider world, now made a deep impression on her imaginative sympathies, the emergence of the Baader-Meinhof terrorist group (and the position of Ulrike Meinhof with her two small children in particular) in West Germany and the tragic death of 6-year-old Maria Colwell in 1973. There had been premonitions of such a shift of emphasis in the sprawling and fallen bodies of dead and wounded women depicted in the two *Untitled Anti War* paintings of 1967 and 1968 but now, in trying to come to terms with the implications of these two stories against her own now more profoundly engaged maternal feelings, the position of women and children caught up in the terrors of the modern world gains an increasing and immediate emphasis. It is apparent initially in two major paintings of c.1972–3 – *Separation* and *Separation at Dawn* and then, in a much more lyrical work also from 1972, *Frail Peace with Tulips*, and finally, very differently again, in a series of paintings from c.1974–79, *No Hiding Place, Fire at Noon* and *Incendiary.*

With their enclosed, almost claustrophobic, settings and lyrical backdrops of radiant skies, the first pair of paintings bears a broad compositional similarity to the *Figure at Dawn* group but, with women and children rather than single men now the focus of the composition, the atmosphere of these paintings is very different again, concerning as they do, her reaction to the arrest of Ulrike Meinhof by a policeman and plain-clothes detective. Rather than the physical and mental brutality simply being implied we see instead the authority figures as active participants in the drama, albeit still anonymous and intruding dramatically from the wings as it were. In *Separation* this takes the form of a man's leg and an arm holding a long stick, with which he forcibly separates the mother and her two children while, in *Separation at Dawn,* two male arms project from either side of the canvas's edge, one of them neatly pin-suited and with a wrist watch (a haunting touch, this, in its feeling of a bureaucratic correctness of dress – the man from *Warlock* again perhaps?) and forcibly manhandle a young, seated woman as her child, squatting in the background turns away. Some critics have claimed to see a degree of optimism in this second group of 'political' paintings, the sense that the women will ultimately be alright, and while that might be true of those subjects from later in the 70s there really is no sense of that yet in either of these intensely disturbing works. It is also important perhaps to point out the complexity of Sonia's moral attitude to the whole Baader-Meinhof; that there is no sense here that she agreed with the brutality of their murderous actions – she was well aware of how and why they had done what they had done and thus felt able to make a judgement about it. It is rather an identification with the underdog trapped in a situation and, at another level below that, and perhaps most significantly of all for her, the implications for the two tiny children that are such vital emotional elements of the composition. As Leslie Fillingham thoughtfully observed in an article of 1992, with her own closeness both to her mother and her own daughter 'Lawson was quite as puzzled by this mother's abandonment of her own children as by her terrorist crimes. This, to her, is just as great a crime against humanity …'

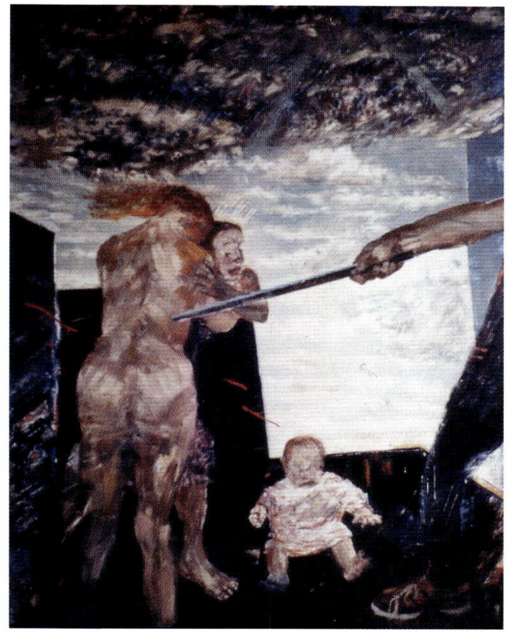

Separation

Originally entitled 'The silk and rough love that breaks all rocks', *Frail peace with tulips* (1972), with its broken gun-carriage, blindfolded and partly-bound female figure like a classical statue, looks back, meanwhile, to the two *Untitled Anti War* paintings of 1967 and 1968. With the woman seemingly fleeing towards us from an unknown threat under a cloud-filled sky, all painted in the same mechanical, striated technique that she had used for those earlier works, it carries a bleak message though one, in this case, that Sonia chooses to counter with the lyrical painting of a large and exquisitely painted vase of multi-coloured tulips in the foreground. The fact of it being positioned there, right up to the picture plane, between the scene of war and us, not only makes it clear that this is a painting within a painting but also provides a very touching and potent assertion of the beauty and life of the world. She herself, in a commentary written when this painting entered the Graves Art Gallery, Sheffield in 1985, observed 'I believe [it] holds a lot of optimism. That, although the figure of woman, of truth, of peace, of whatever breakable has been broken, nonetheless the gun-carriage is also broken and the flowers, delicate and gentle as they are, have the resilience and cheerfulness to bloom. They have kept faith.'

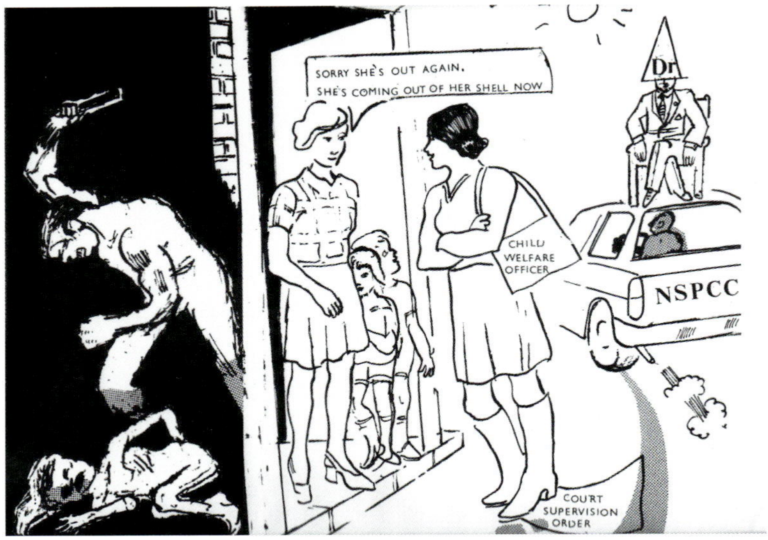

Coming out of her Shell 1974, ink and mixed media
Drawn to assist the group: Justice for Maria Colwell

At this point in Sonia's career another horrific current event erupts into her world, the Maria Colwell scandal of 1973, in which the girl was starved and beaten to death by her step-father. A widely-publicised event at the time, one that involved a lack of proper oversight by social services, it was among the first cases in post-war British history to bring such issues into the public eye. It also became apparent that this was not just an isolated case and it was this aspect, above all, that led Sonia, with her now three-year-old daughter, to get involved in a wider campaign for child protection, setting up a Child at Risk vigilante group in her town. She proved a determined publicist for it both at a grass-roots level, producing several forceful political cartoons on the subject (see ills) and also, more indirectly, through her art, producing, in 1973/4 a substantial 5' × 4' canvas entitled *Evermore Statement* (present whereabouts unknown) in which a distressed child forms a central part in a complex figure composition. It was not only accepted for the Royal Academy Summer exhibition in 1974 but used by her to help publicise her campaign, with a photograph and substantial accompanying text in the local paper in which she talked of how it represented 'the world's wound and society's gut-rot.'

The theme of human vulnerability in particular had now become the key theme in her work and over the next three years she produced a number of astonishing canvases

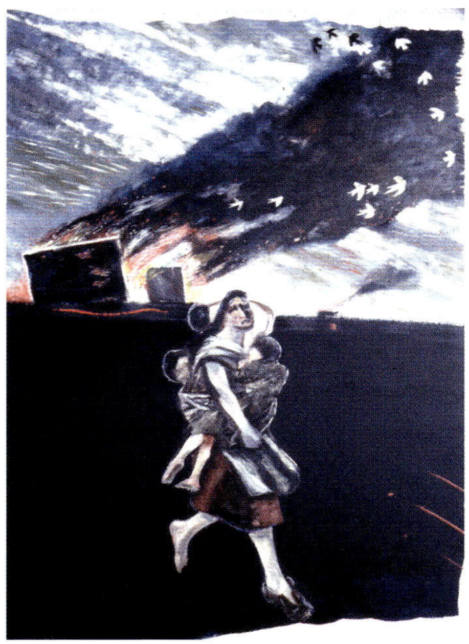

No Hiding Place

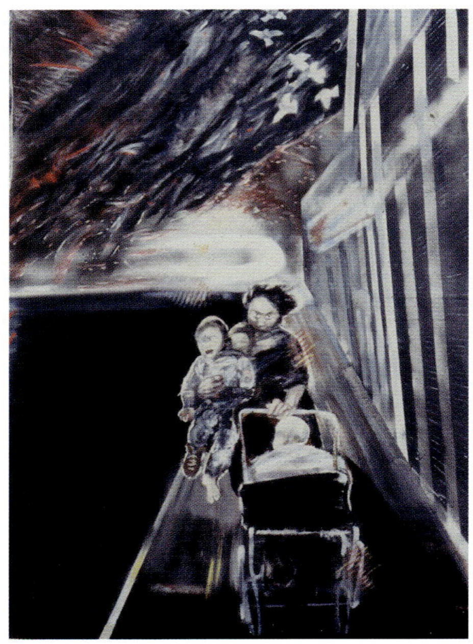

Fire at Noon

depicting mothers and children in conditions of extreme distress, in particular *Fire at Noon* (1977), *No Hiding Place* (1974) and *Incendiary* (1978–9). The first of these depicts a woman, burdened with three small children, fleeing bombs in a state of terror. Everything about the painting's composition – the buildings leaning in on the group from one side and the streamers of cloud and smoke that sweep diagonally above her head carrying birds (she was to write in 1985 how 'with the Bomb not only people but all creatures would perish, even the birds would fall burning from the sky') driven helplessly along in the fire-storm – create a sense of enveloping claustrophobia while the flickering scarlet, black, white and blue-black paint-strokes of the clouds seem to embody the very essence of the human distress and anguish apparent on the family's faces. It is in short painting as an act of profound imaginative empathy, even down to the tiny detail of the child's missing shoe.

The missing shoe is in fact a recurrent image of helplessness in the paintings of the 1960s and 70s – it first appears in the bound man in *Figure at Dawn* – and it appears again in the running woman in *Fire at Noon* (1977), Sonia later apparently being astonished and moved to find this same image echoed in Kieślowski's 1988 film *A Short Film about Killing.* With its conflicting diagonals of windswept blue sky and streaks of scarlet flames and blue-black clouds of smoke issuing from the burning buildings in mid- and far distance as the woman flees almost anywhere just to get away, *Fire at Noon* is, at first sight, another image of despair but, as Norbert Lynton, in his 1996 essay for her Dean Clough retrospective, points out very perceptively, none of these paintings 'shock for shock's sake: they are not ghoulish. It is life that matters: it is for the sake of life and love that one protests against violence, destruction, cruelties, legal as well as illegal deaths.' There is, too, in these latter paintings a rather different, a rather more hopeful mood, one in which there is the just possible sense that the women and children may perhaps survive. They are, in some way, images of 'Mother Courage', imbued with the profoundest sense of compassion, an intensely personal female compassion that derives ultimately from a gradual coming to terms with all those complex feelings of childhood, her wartime scrapbooks, family deaths and illnesses as well as her own often idyllic childhood among the animals on her uncle's farm. They are works fuelled, too, with her own intensely buoyant, spirited personality and curiosity about the world and the way it works.

They are though, the last major examples of this strand of subject matter and by 1977 her life and her art were changing once again and there was the feeling that she had now said what she had felt so strongly had needed to be said about the world at large – she had exorcised her demons as she has put it. Added to which she had, over the last decade, been spending an increasing amount of time travelling up to a rented house in

Wensleydale both to paint and also keep an eye on her mother who had suffered three heart-attacks in the course of the 70s (her mother also spent every winter with Sonia and her family in Leighton Buzzard to avoid getting snowed in in her Castle Bolton cottage). That pattern changed again in 1977 with the purchase she and Charlie made of a house, in the village of West Witton just across the valley from Castle Bolton. They still own it and she gets there as often as she can. It was to help effect a profound alteration in her work as it took an altogether more personal and celebratory direction.

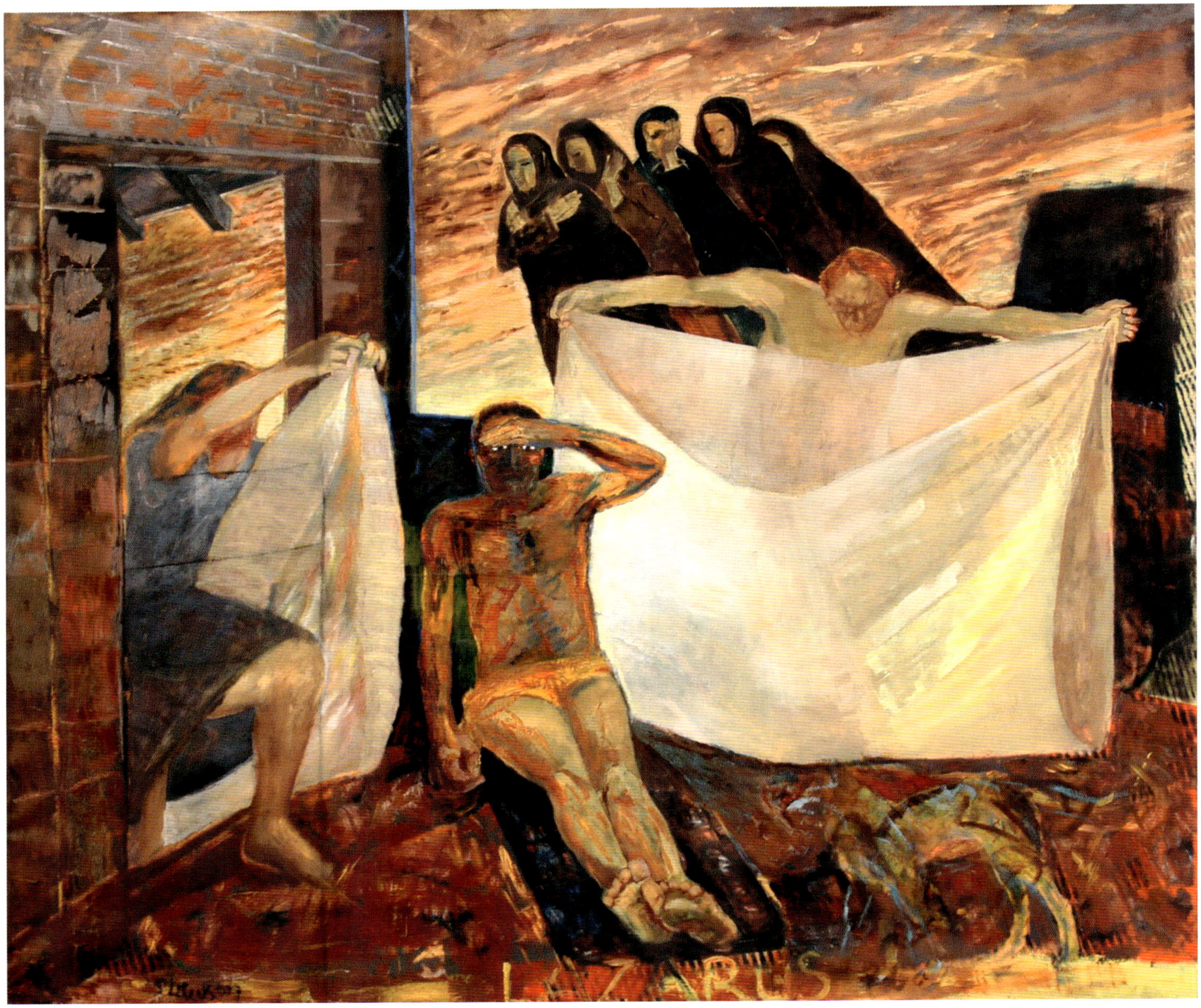

Lazarus 1980, oil on canvas, 152 x 184 cm

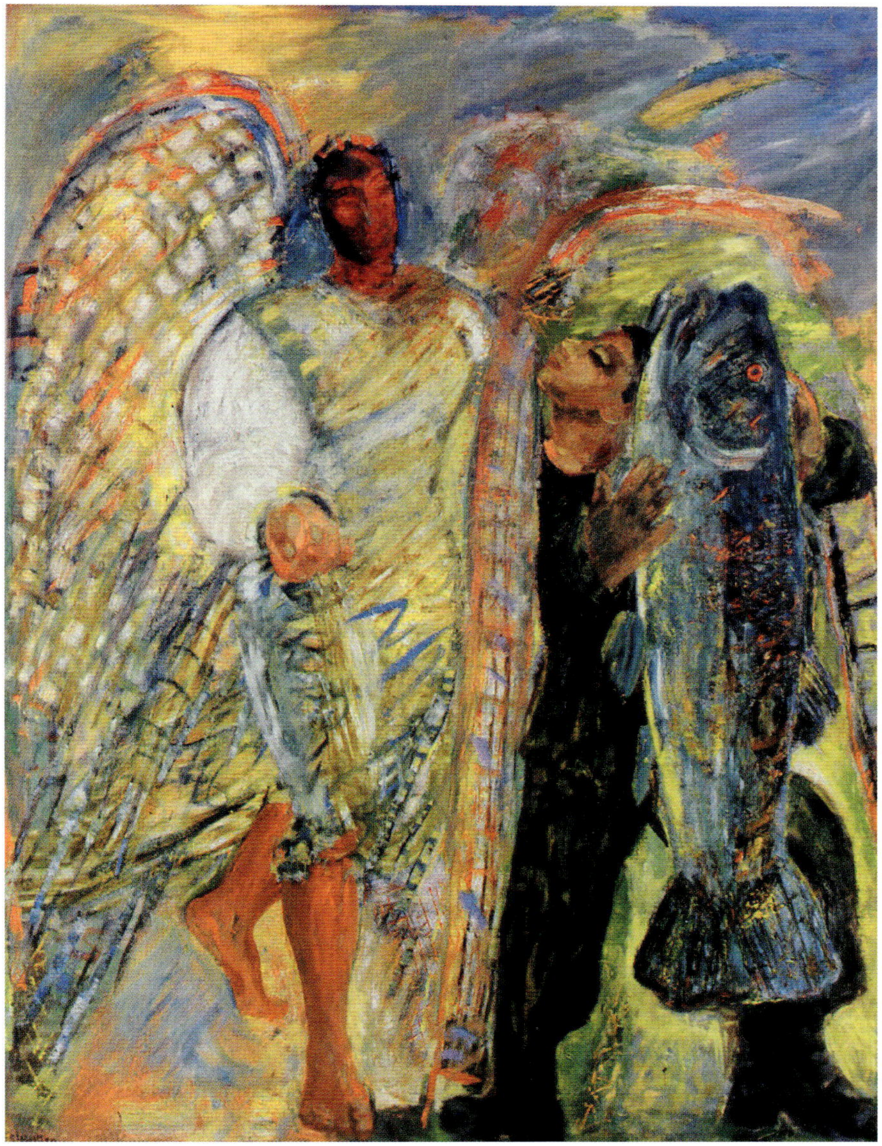

Tobias and the Angel 1982, oil on canvas, 156 x 126 cm
Collection: Royal Academy of Arts, London

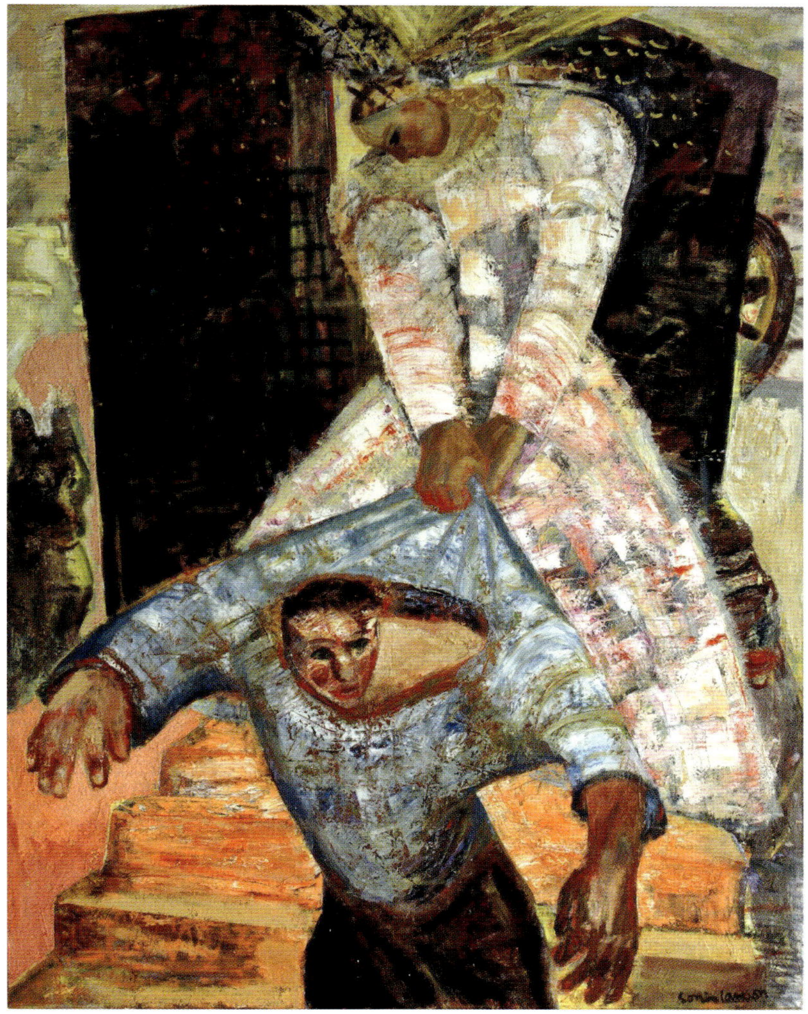

Fallen Angels 1987, oil on canvas, 152 x 121 cm
Collection: Royal West of England Academy, Bristol

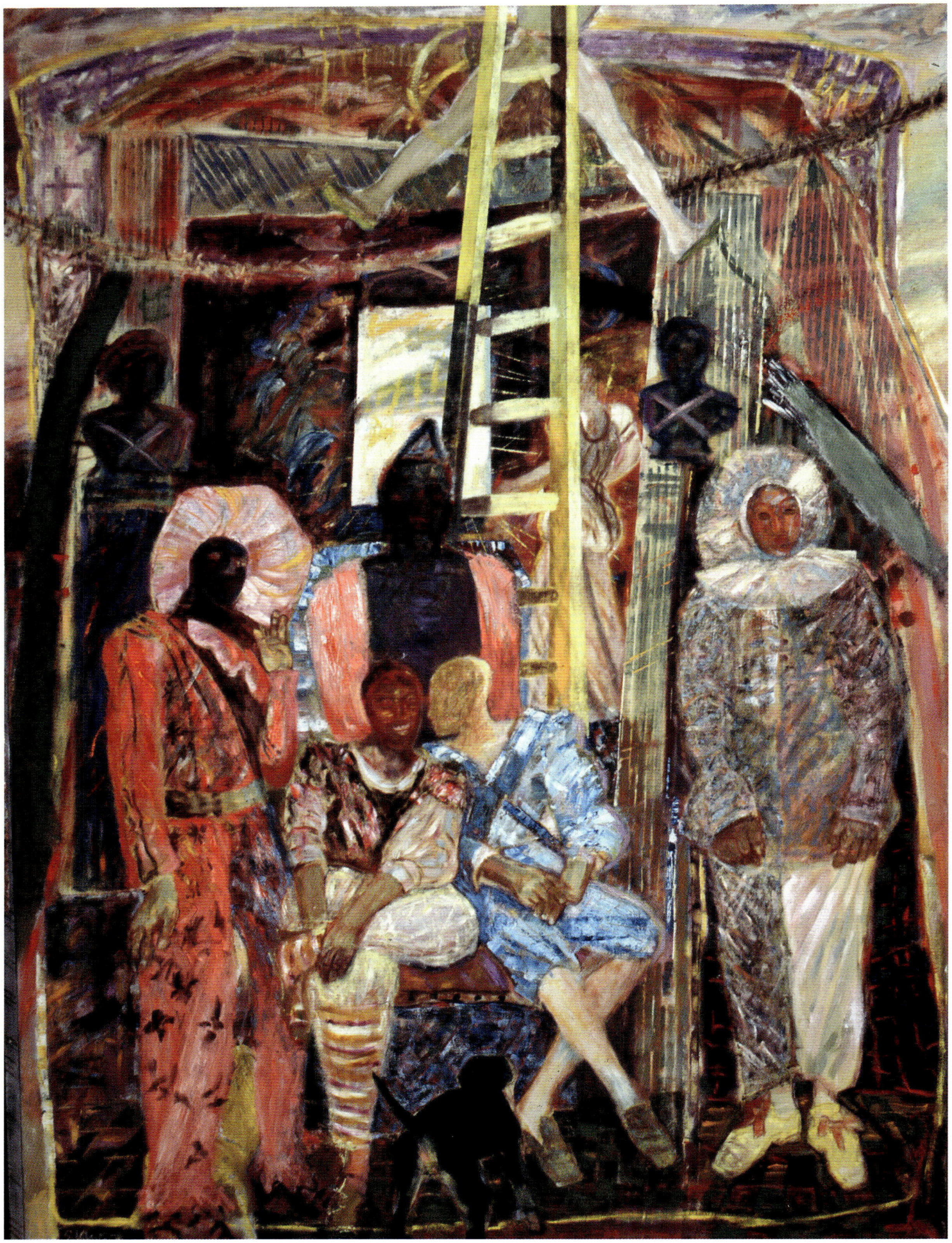

Homage to Molière and Watteau 1981, oil on canvas, 198 × 153 cm

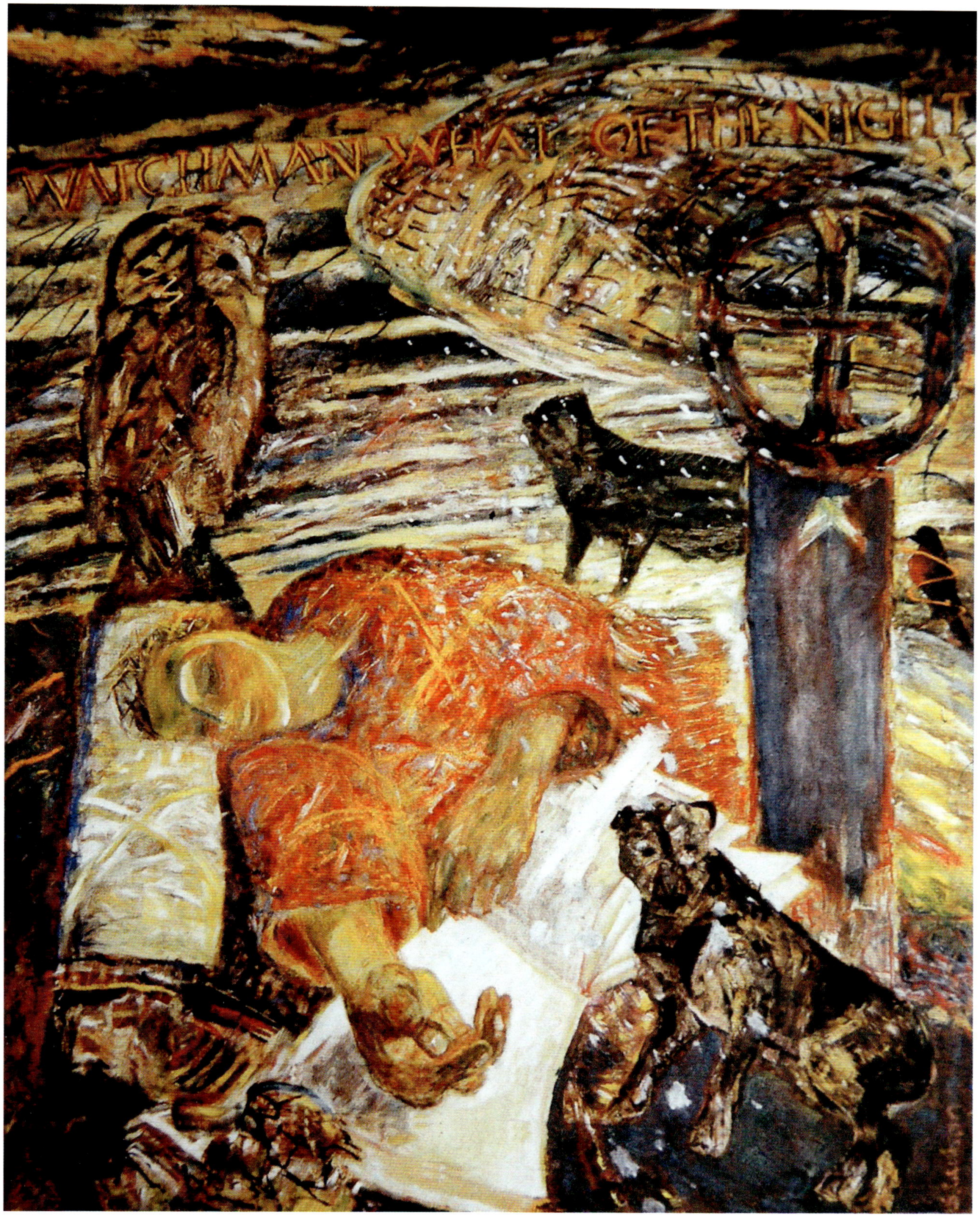

Watchman, What of the Night? 1982, oil on canvas, 198 × 165 cm

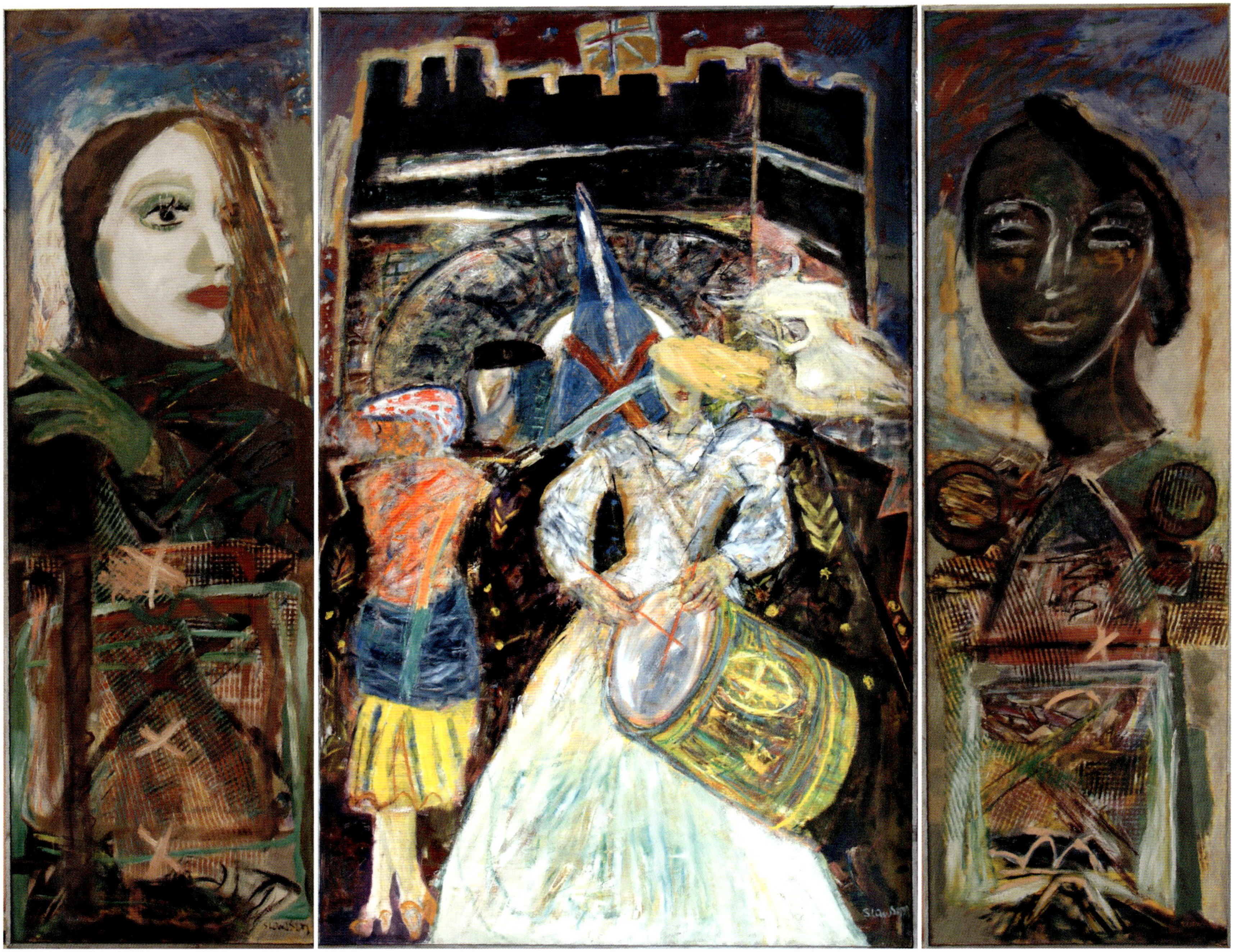

Garrison Town 1981, triptych, oil on canvas, 246.5 x 304 cm

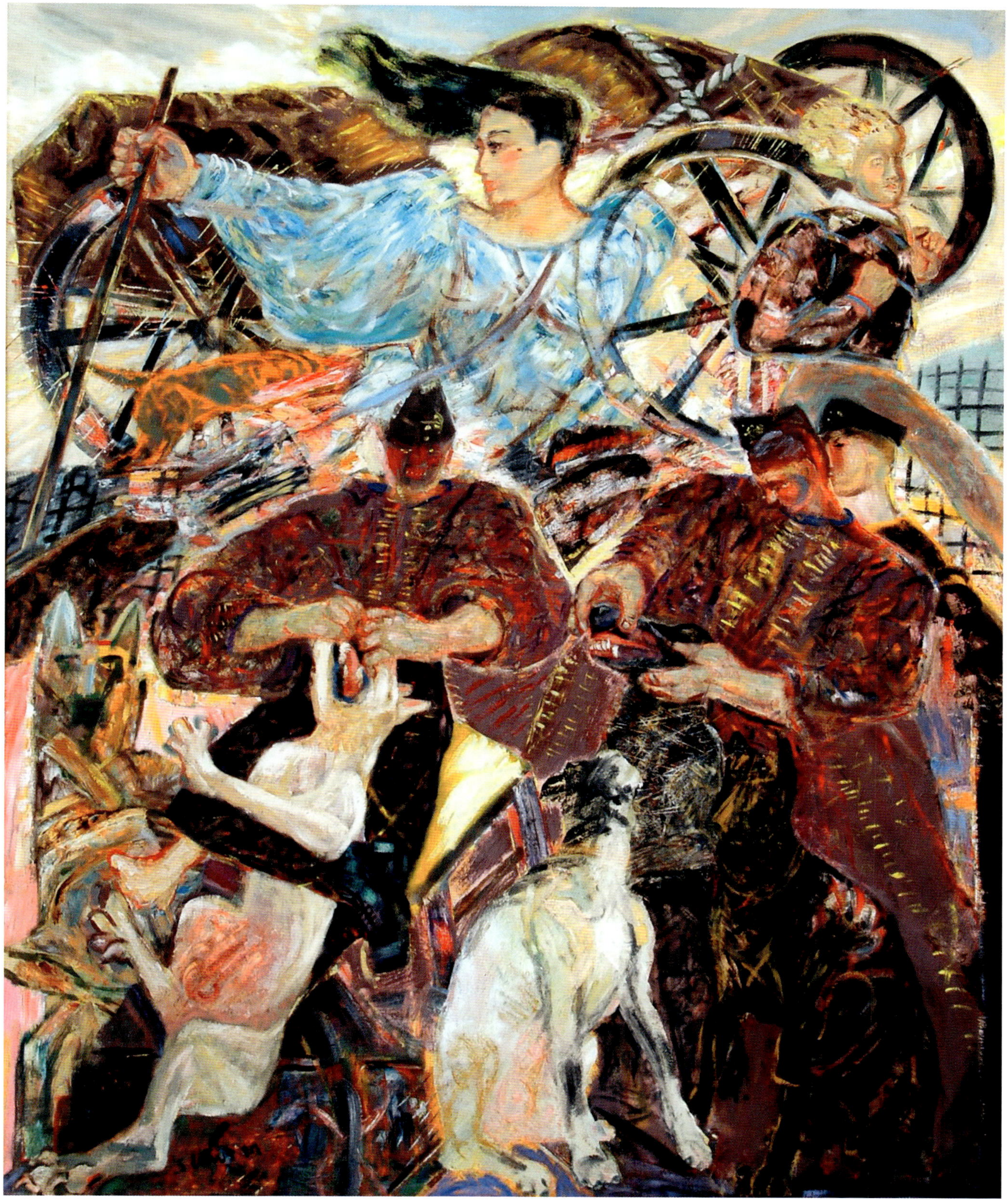

Northern Garrison 1986, oil on canvas, 186 x 155 cm

Chapter 5

> Who, if I cried out, would hear me among the angels'
> hierarchies? and even if one of them pressed me
> suddenly against his heart: I would be consumed
> in that overwhelming existence. For beauty is nothing
> but the beginning of terror, which we are still just able to endure,
> and we are so awed because it serenely disdains
> to annihilate us. Every angel is terrifying.
>
> From 'The First Elegy: The Duino Elegies' (trans Stephen Mitchell)

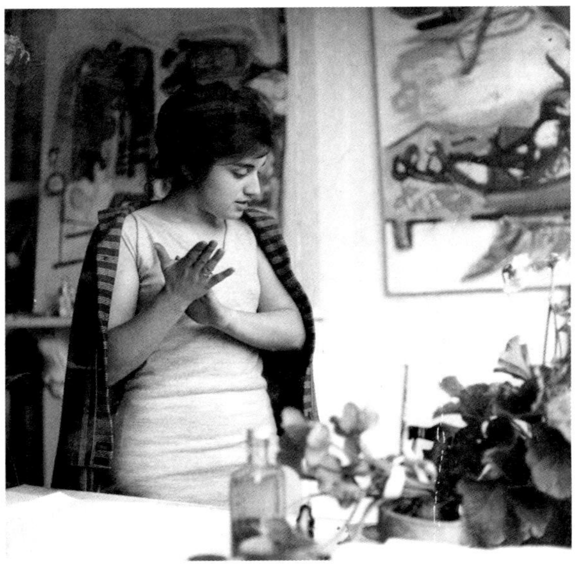

Sonia Lawson in her studio, 1960

For Rilke the angel in his 'Duino Elegies' stood for 'that being who guarantees the recognition of a higher level of reality in the invisible. Therefore "terrifying" for us, because we, its lovers and transformers, still cling to the visible.' In the move that now took place in Sonia's work from the late 70s onwards there was a clear and dramatic move towards an altogether more inwardly directed kind of painting, one that aimed to encompass a much greater complexity of feelings that related not only to her autobiography and family history but also started to give expression to those layered and hidden histories of the landscape she had grown up in and felt for instinctually. In short her concerns came to be with precisely that same 'invisible' reality Rilke had intuited – now she was having to come to terms with her 'angel'.

Although it can often be difficult for artists to make such a necessary break with the kind of work for which they had become known to critics, dealers and collectors over a period of time, Sonia was, simply in career terms, remarkably free of any ties and constrictions of this kind. On the one hand, while she had not been linked closely with any commercial galleries in the 18 years or so since she had left the RCA, she had, nonetheless, begun to gain a quiet reputation among curators, fellow artists and certain influential critics. Showing steadily in Royal Academy Summer exhibitions from the early 1960s onwards – she only missed one year, in 1975 – she was not only selected for the big Queen's Jubilee exhibition '25 years of British Art' at the Academy in 1977,

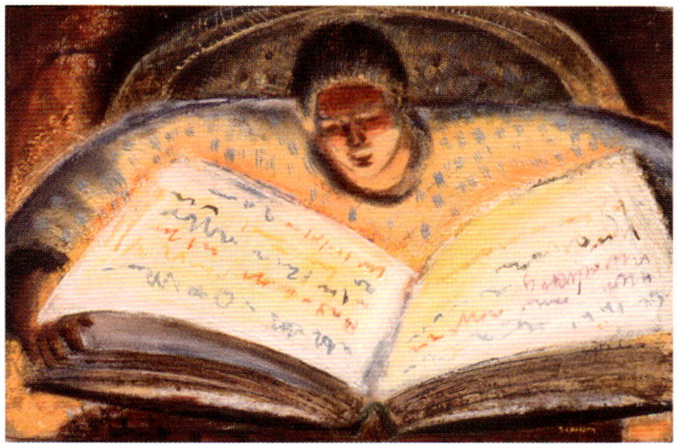

Night Reader

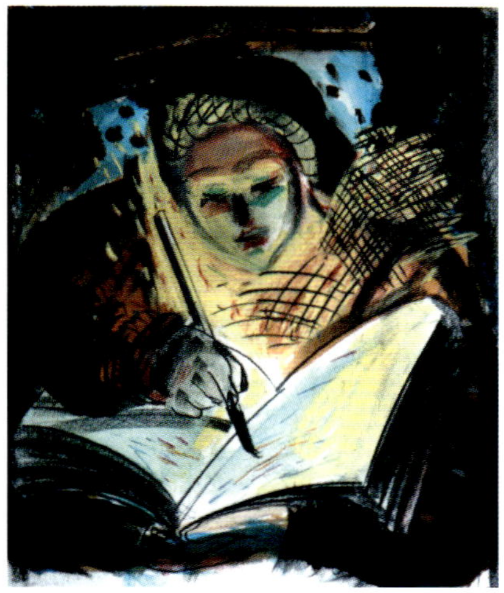

Night Writing Series, **Diarist**

a mark of some respect in itself, but was chosen by the critic Mervyn Levy as one of the half dozen artists he interviewed as part of a substantial BBC TV documentary about the show, along with John Hoyland and Carel Weight.

This had all been achieved, even more remarkably, over a period when not only had she been very preoccupied first with her father's illness and death and her mother's ongoing health problems but, from 1970 onwards, with the care of a small child. With typical resourcefulness she had got round this, in part at least, by working at night, a habit that she also shared with her mother and which remained with her for much of the rest of her life, itself becoming the subject of the extended series of paintings and large watercolours from 1980 onwards that she entitled 'Night Reading'. Also, in order to avoid letting people down, she had decided to limit very carefully the number of exhibiting commitments she took on during the 1970s; apart from the Royal Academy (where her entry for several years in the mid-70s was often limited to one or two pieces) she had only one solo show between 1970 and 1977, the 'Homage to my Friends' exhibition at Billingham in 1973, and only one mixed exhibition, at the Trafford Gallery, London, 1970.

It had remained work of such distinctive quality, power and originality of approach however that it had been more than enough to keep her name in people's minds and, by the end of the decade, there is the distinct sense that, with her daughter now of school age, the tempo and volume of her painting steadily starts to pick up again with two solo shows, at Bradford Central Library in 1977 and an Open University exhibition at Milton Keynes (and touring to Darlington, Harrogate, Hull Ferens, and Leicester polytechnic) in 1979. These were to prove only the precursors to what became, from 1980 on, a stream of exhibitions, public commissions and scholarships that rapidly projected her into wider public consciousness. Meanwhile election to the Royal Academy in 1982 gave her a platform of an ideal kind for work that still, puzzlingly, didn't seem to attract solo shows in commercial galleries – that would have to wait for another decade.

What she had also done throughout the 70s, alongside the big subject pieces, was to keep up a steady flow of slightly smaller landscape, or rather sky-scape paintings, the subjects for which originally derived from her regular visits to see her mother in Wensleydale. These luminous skyscapes had, as we have already seen of course,

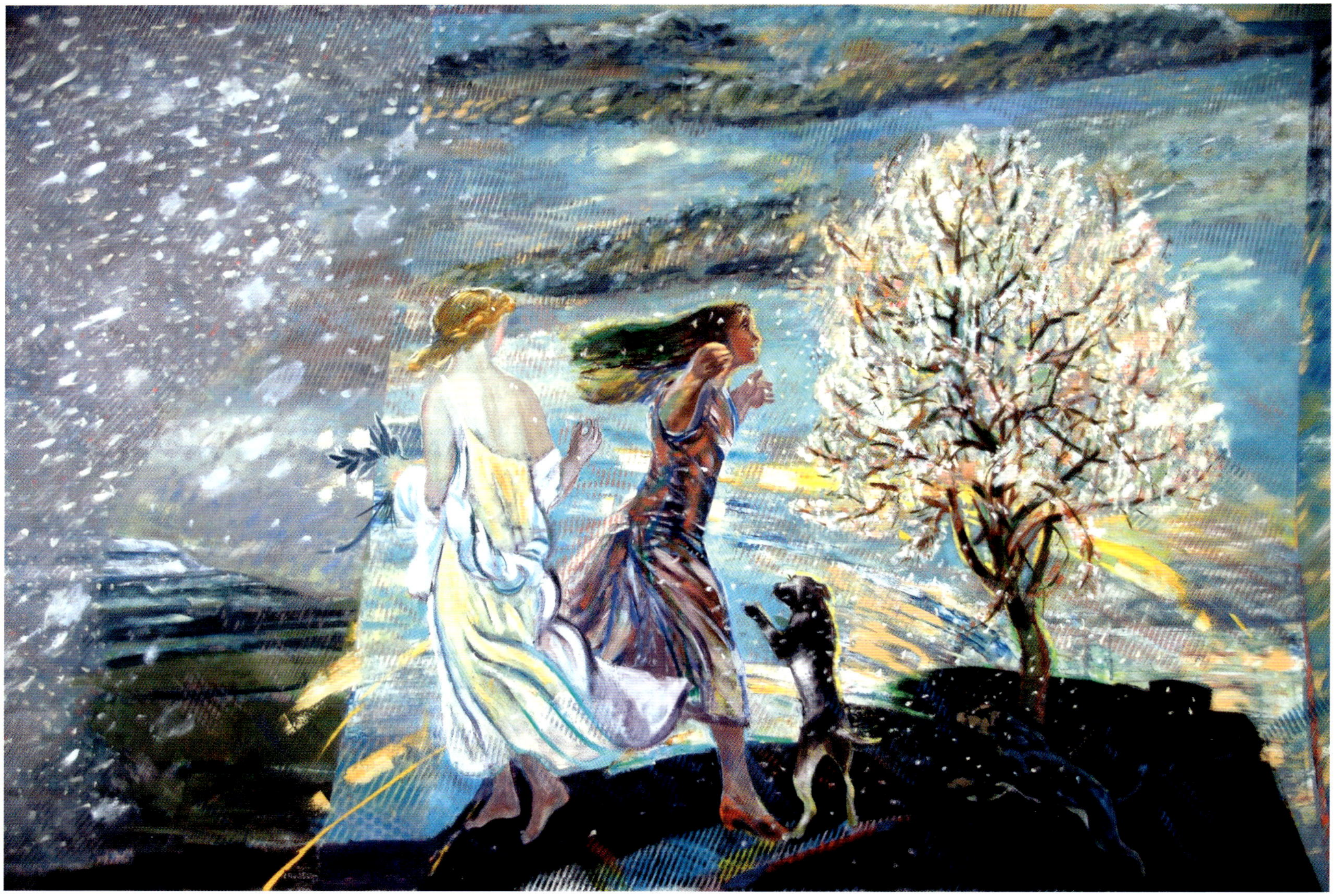

From Blizzard To Blossom 1978, oil on canvas, 153 x 244 cm. Collection: Cranfield University

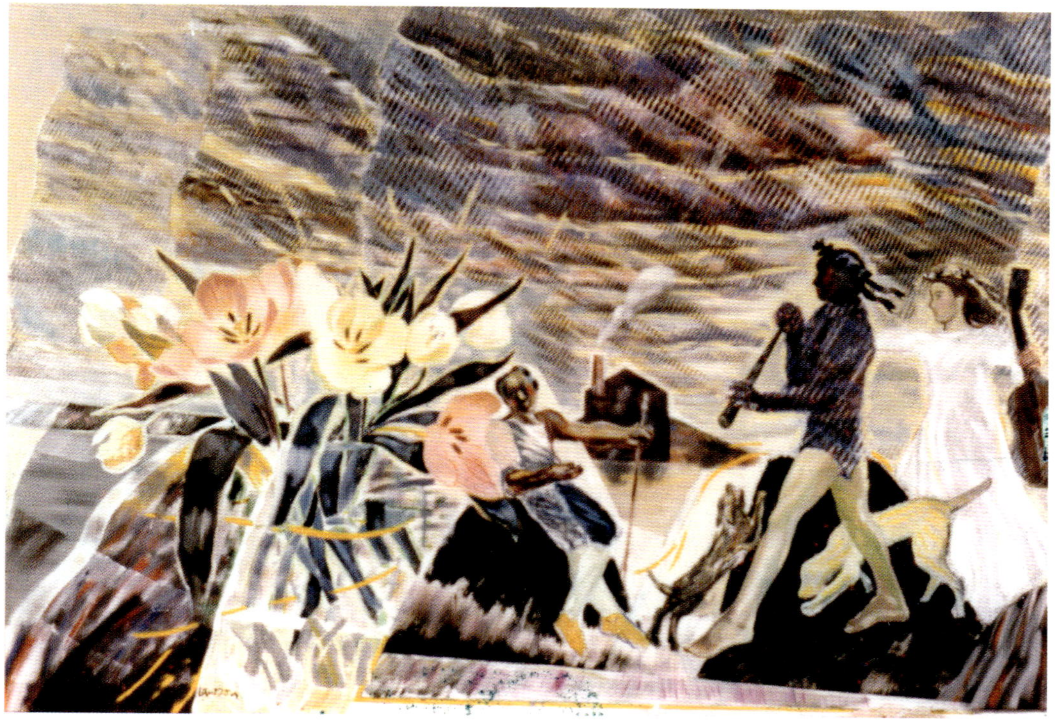

Spring Rendezvous 1978, oil on canvas, 153 × 244 cm. Collection: Sir William Gladstone

provided an often poignant counterpoint to the scenes of human inhumanity enacted beneath them but they also made wonderfully exhilarating paintings on their own account, full of dramatic weather effects and gleaming light. *From Blizzard to Blossom* (1978) and *Spring Rendezvous* (1978) are superb examples, expressing her deep-seated feelings of identification and affection for the landscape of her childhood and with a romantic intensity and detailed, joyful observation that brings to mind not only her beloved Wordsworth – 'Rolled round in earth's diurnal course,/With rocks, and stones, and trees' – but, more particularly, John Clare, whose poem 'The Thrush's Nest' she had first encountered at the age of 11. Now, at the end of the 70s, with her 'demons exorcised' as she put it, a permanent base in Wensleydale and a growing daughter of her own, her artistic thinking turned increasingly to reconsiderations of her relationship to her own mother and, more particularly, her mother's artistic and intellectual inheritance. Out of that, in turn, came a flooding back of autobiographical memory, of childhood, landscape, stories and histories. It was to prove the most astonishingly fruitful source of inspiration with, over the next four years or so, an impressive sequence of major paintings on a wide range of narrative themes. In their richness of poetic reference, intense painterliness and huge ambition there is nothing quite like them in English figurative painting of the late twentieth century.

The sequence opens with a group of religious or spiritually themed paintings – *Lazarus* (1979), *Moorland Benediction* (1981) and *Watchman, What of the Night?* (1981) and *Tobias and the Angel* (1982). Her mother, Muriel Metcalfe had undertaken a number of religious paintings and watercolour and wash studies on religious themes in the 1930s, including a large mural of The Crucifixion at St Margaret's, Preston-under-Scar, close to her Castle Bolton home, so the impulse to explore this narrative strand for herself represented an important and necessary first step in re-examining her relationship to her mother's art and life. It was a brave thing to do. When she had first gone to the Royal College in 1955, she had turned to abstract and then semi-abstract still-life and landscape painting, almost deliberately, as a means almost of distancing herself from the kind of art practised by her parents. Now that she had the confidence of having established her own, very different, artistic voice, she was ready to go back and explore her and her family's experience and legacy.

Compared with what was about to follow though, *Lazarus* still seems closer, in the almost anguished intensity of its mood and agitated brushstrokes, to the more political, figurative compositions of the late early 70s. And while the sunset sky behind the figures is depicted in marvellous, striated streamers of red and gold, overall that quite ecstatic explosion of layered colour with its febrile, broken brushstrokes which was about to transform the character of her painting is not yet apparent. At the same time, too, the miracle is played out in the same kind of distinctly enclosed and quite narrow, almost stage-like compositional space that characterises the *Judgement and Separation* series from c.1972/3. Interestingly her old tutor from the Royal College, Carel Weight, writing in the introduction to the major retrospective show she was to have two years or so later, in 1982, at the Milton Keynes Gallery, in commenting very specifically on this painting – 'one of the few people today who can paint a moving religious picture' – ties it in direct lineage to 'the horrific *Figure at Dawn*' and other similar paintings from the 60s. As far as he was concerned these were all quite as much religious as political pictures and, looking back from this point, it becomes apparent that the extraordinary emotional power of those 'political' paintings derives quite as much from the spiritual compassion she shows for her victims as her outrage that human beings could even think of doing such things to one another.

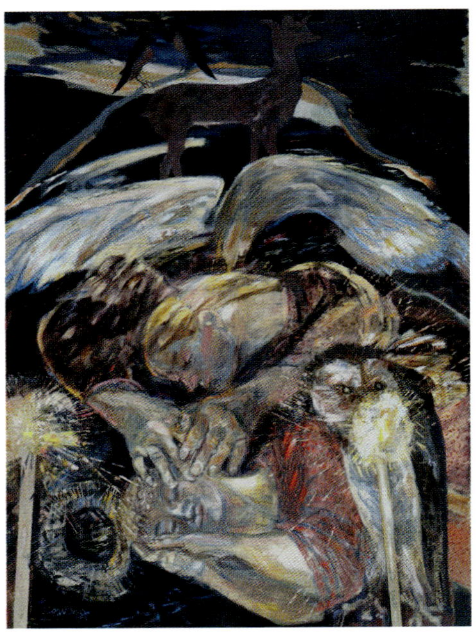

Moorland Benediction

The remarkable changes in painting technique that so strikingly take place as we move from this to the later paintings in this group are largely down to one, very practical matter – the building of the separate and very spacious top-lit studio space to one side of the family home she still works from today. Having always painted in one of the rooms of their late Victorian house before, suddenly 'There was light!'

Thus, in *Moorland Benediction* (1980), a painting from only a year later than *Lazarus,* everything has effectively changed – the sleeping woman's pinky-red dress, illumined by the candles to either side of her, is shot through with bluey shadows, the owl's whitish front is similarly flecked with blue and goldish tones while the presiding angel's face and arms are painted in a remarkable range of pinks, blues, rusty-reds and golds, the wings in a blur of white, blue and gold. The dramatic tenderness of this brilliantly illuminated group is then further enhanced by being set against a dark and mysterious moorland landscape at dusk with its quietly presiding deer and two birds on a bare branch of a tree.

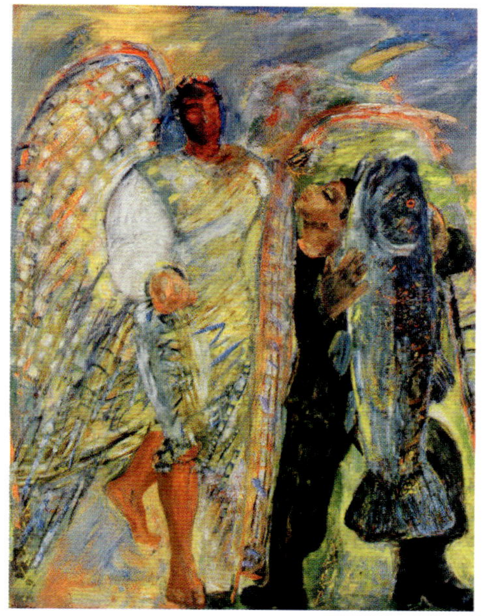

Tobias and the Angel

It is a painting technique that she was to develop to great effect, not just in the next painting in this series, *Watchman, What of the Night?*, but also in other works of this same period inspired by more literary and historical themes – the 'Garrison' and 'Homage' series of which the Brontë subjects can perhaps be considered an integral part – each feeding into the other increasing layers of autobiographical and poetic cross-reference. Meanwhile, *Watchman, What of the Night?*, a subject derived from the Book of Isaiah in which the watchman's enigmatic response is 'The morning cometh and also the night, if ye will enquire', takes a similar compositional idea, of a brilliantly illuminated foreground sleeping figure encircled by an enigmatic, possibly rather ferocious, cast of animals – an owl, a dog, a wolf and a bird as well as a totem figure – and bathes the whole scene in an intense sunset light of reds, golds and blacky-browns. It is an unmistakably consoling statement that whatever evil forces we fear in the night, reading and sleep will strengthen and protect us. As in many of Lawson's paintings, there is the idea again here that good and bad co-exist in this world – for her it is the simile of a dark shadow being ever present when the sun shines brightest – which, like Wordsworth's use of the word 'deep' to imply darkness, is the necessary emotional counterpoint to all sensations of the ecstatic. Meanwhile, in the final painting in this series, *Tobias and the Angel* (1981–2), a comparatively straightforward rendering of the Biblical narrative, Sonia allows the colour absolutely to take off, the figure of the angel, his wings and robe particularly, set against a luminous sky, a dazzling radiance of pinky-reds, golds, blues and creamy whites. The almost aerial lightness of the figure is then rather wittily and touchingly emphasized by the darkly clad, plodding figure of Tobias with his hobnail boots, staggering along beside him under the burden of a giant, darkly luminescent fish almost as big as he is!

A similar pictorial and colouristic evolution can be seen to take place in the two other key groups of major paintings that Sonia developed over this same period 1979–82: the mytho-historical paintings of garrisons and ancient roadways – *Exercising Dogs on Watling Street* (1979–80), *Northern Garrison* (1980–81) and *Garrison Town* (1982–3) –

and the Homage paintings, *Homage to Molière and Watteau* (1981), *Homage to Muriel Metcalfe, my Mother* (1981), *Pilgrimage to the Ridings, Homage to my Family* and the loose-knit triptych of Brontë/Haworth-inspired paintings *Homage to Emily Brontë, Night Writing I & II* (1981) and *Tea-Time at Haworth with the Brontës* (1981).

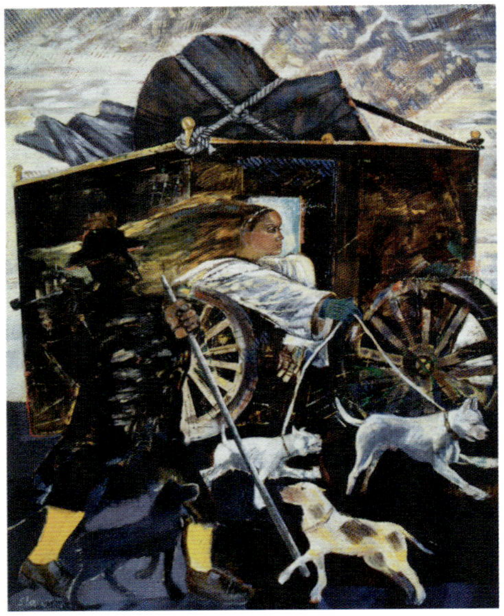
Exercising Dogs on Watling Street

Looking at the earliest of the Garrison/Ancient Roadway paintings first, *Exercising Dogs on Watling Street* is, in the sheer dark mystery and sense of adventure the composition engenders in the onlooker, a *tour de force* and quite unlike anything Sonia had painted before. In terms of the subject matter, there is no specific incident contemporary or historical to which it refers in any way, other than that Watling Street, the old Roman Road to the Midlands and a major road artery right up until the building of the M1 some 50 years ago – down which Dick Whittington travelled in search of a fortune and Samuel Johnson looking for literary fame, (and now dully rechristened the A5) – runs only a few miles from her Leighton Buzzard home. In a 1981 conversation with the curator Julian Spalding, who had recently bought the painting for the Arts Council of Great Britain, Sonia observes that the picture was not an illustration of anything specific – it is more general than that – but rather that she hopes to capture an atmosphere, to gather together some of the richness of her experiences of life. This painting apparently began with the dogs – a memory of handling the cows and dogs on her uncle's farm and by this means learning their anatomy. Their lithe activity then fed into a painting concerned, above all, with movement (which, in itself, she saw as being a reaction to the stillness of so much modern art) and the dominating form of the hurtling stagecoach out of which leans a determined young woman with streaming blond hair, fluttering white sleeves and two ferocious-looking dogs on a lead – there is too a distinct suggestion of Boadicea about her and her defeat at the Battle of Watling Street. This sensation is then further reinforced by the figure of an archaically dressed man in breeches, with a staff and deep yellow socks striding energetically forward with two dogs of his own, the suggestion here being of someone like Dr Johnson, the period referred to feeling broadly late eighteen century in spirit. A dark trussed-up parcel is on top of the coach, same as 'Execution at Daybreak' has a trussed parcel in the foreground, giving all a touch of mystery and enigma. As the critic Edward Lucie-Smith pointed out at the time though, 'it is not a commonplace activity but an epic event … deliberately public and oratorical … and paradoxically domestic', also noting the 'huge fervency with which she paints … pushing both experience itself, and the artist's response to it as far as it will go.'

Looked at in terms of Sonia's own development however, *Exercising Dogs on Watling Street* still bears certain points of similarity to *Lazarus* (of more or less the same date) with its tightly enclosed, quite claustrophobic 'stage' on which the action takes place right up at the front of the picture plane. It also retains the same comparatively restrained colour scheme of the earlier/mid-70s, while the sky has similarly striated brushmarks as, for example, *Spring Rendezvous* (1978). Through 1980 however, as things start to change radically in Sonia's painting, *Northern Garrison* (1980–81) can be seen as representing a further radical step forward in her work, an astonishingly confident statement of intent. Indeed when it was shown alongside *Moorland Benediction* (with which it bears many points of similarity in technique) at the Summer Exhibition in 1981, more than one critic pointed out the huge irony that these paintings were hanging in the same main room at the RA that De Kooning, Balthus and Baselitz had occupied just a couple of months before in the major, and hugely publicised, international exhibition of contemporary painters 'A New Spirit in Painting?' Her work, so very much in the 'new spirit' of early 1980s international painting had, in short, found its way past the apparently traditional RA selectors but been ignored by the supposedly avant-garde curators of that show, yet by every criteria – above all its full-blooded espousal of what paint was capable of doing in taking on a large-scale, contemporary and largely figurative agenda – Sonia should have been in included in it. Not least for the huge range of reference points in Twentieth Century and Contemporary art that these works of hers contain, which range from Mexican Muralists like Orozco to elements drawn from some of the Italian Transavantguardia painters like Chia, Paladino and Clemente whose work she had also been aware of from a comparatively early date. At the same time, almost in Post-Modernist fashion, the dynamic presiding figure of the woman in blue can be seen to have much in common with an iconic nineteeth-century image – Rude's sculpture of the *Marseillaise* on the Arc de Triomphe. It is in short an astonishing synthesis of artistic ideas and personal emotions and histories – the sensation of those childhood memories of a small town close to large wartime garrisons of soldiers is part of this painting too – fierce, passionate and exhilarating and, in the end, utterly her own.

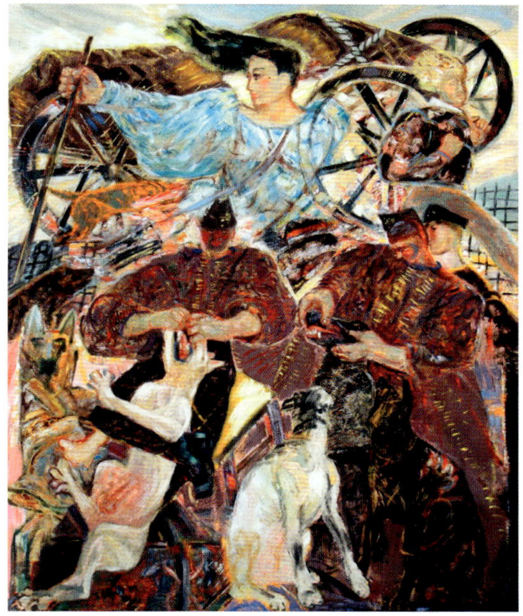

Northern Garrison

Meanwhile the final, and largest painting in this 'Garrison' series, the triptych entitled *Garrison Town,* started in 1981 but possibly was not completed until 1984 following a fire at Sonia's house, strikes a rather different note again. With its much brighter colour and fluid flurries of brushstrokes, the central scene, of soldiers meeting girls by the town gate has, as Norbert Lynton once described it, the sense of an entertainment – the striking blonde girl in the centre vigorously beating a side drum, the gaily dressed girl with the headscarf chatting to a soldier with her back turned to us, the sense of exciting forward impulsion towards the viewer all part of it. Look closer though and a rather more disturbing note is sounded – the soldier to whom the girl appears to be in conversation with, has a dog's skull face, for example, while the predominant

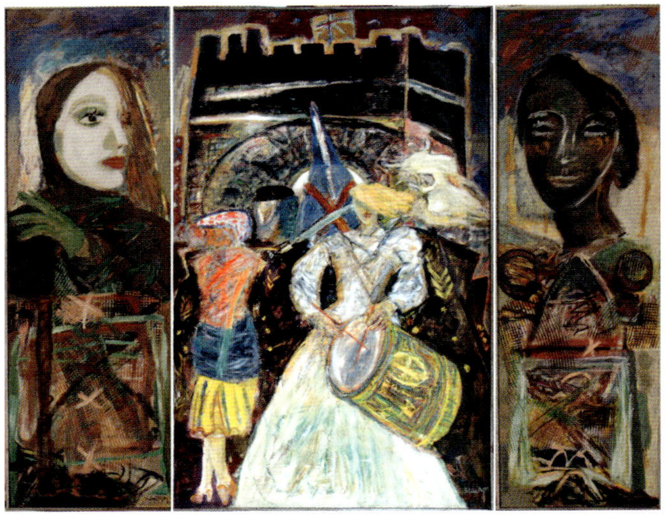

Garrison Town

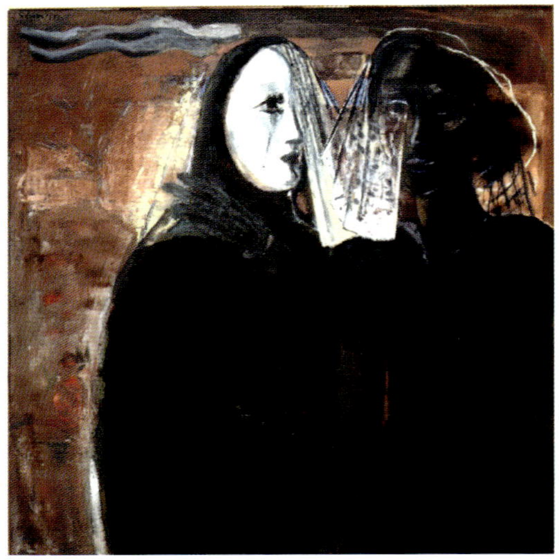

Grieving Women

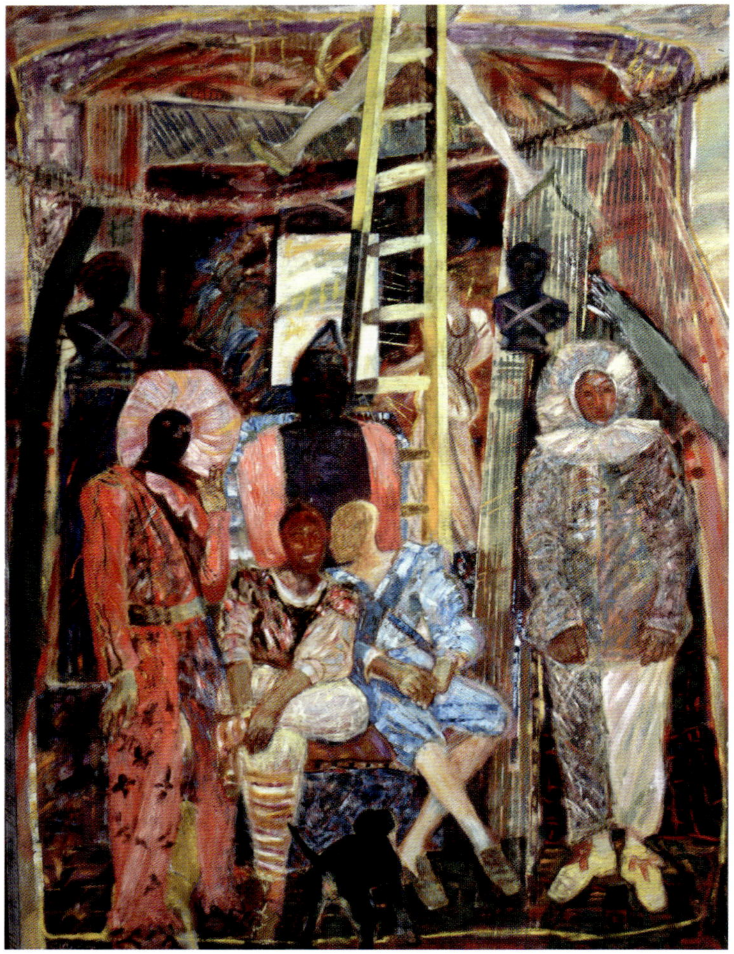

Homage to Molière and Watteau

colour tonalities of yellow, red, white and blue have a certain stridency of mood – the white and red-spotted scarf of the second girl conveys a sense of blood and latent violence that the black uniforms, escutcheons and fortification behind seem to reinforce. War and oppression echo even here. It is an ambiguity of mood further reinforced by the two monumental faces of women that brood reflectively over the scene, figures that look forward presciently to the archetypal large-scale single female pictures Sonia starts to paint at the end of the decade. In artistic and compositional terms too, the painting shows signs of having been influenced by seeing once again the Beckmann triptychs that went on show at the Whitechapel Art Gallery over the winter of 1981/2 – Sonia had, of course, admired Beckmann since her student days. This was not simply a matter of the triptych format however but also the accentuated layering and massing of the figures on a tight, frontally flattened, plane – which helps to underline the painting's sense of almost overwhelming physical urgency. Like *Exercising Dogs on Watling Street* this is a painting you can hear almost as much as see, smell almost as much as you can feel vibrating around you.

Beckmann's example was very important to another major painting of this same period also, *Homage to Molière and Watteau* (1981), the first in a series of paintings in which Sonia explored her feelings about the creative figures she admired and had been of greatest significance to her as a painter. She had always been very open in expressing these allegiances – her show at Billingham in 1973 had been entitled 'Homage to my Friends: From Giotto to Janis Joplin' and apart from numerous painters had also cited Mary Wollstonecraft, Billie Holiday, Germaine Greer, Emily Brontë among some 20 others – but she had never attempted to express these feelings quite so directly in her painting before. In an article she wrote before her 1996 Dean Clough retrospective she set down her intentions in this painting very clearly and straightforwardly: 'though Molière and Watteau were a generation apart, one can be very dismissive of the gap or age gap between them, and between them and us. One is supported in this by the weight of tradition, nothing to do with nostalgia but of people doing their own creative thing. Watteau's *Gilles* [standing on the right] has about him an innocence, an air of invulnerability. His quiet, decorous stance contrasts compositionally with the implied busy hubbub of *la troupe de Molière*.'

Meanwhile the Beckmann influence can be felt very distinctly not only in the carnival/circus-like subject matter itself but also in the crowded, densely layered complexities and bluntnesses of the composition, the eye being led in at the base of the painting by the small black dog, seen from the rear, to the pair of seated foreground actors and then being taken vertiginously up a steep ladder to the spread-eagled legs of an acrobat (her face cut off by the top edge of the canvas in what feels like a notably Beckmannesque touch!) which then return us, equally forcibly, back down to the standing figures of an actor and Gilles standing to the far right and left of the canvas edge. Compared with the 'Garrison' subjects, the colour tonality of the whole painting is prismatic, largely brilliant and benign, reinforcing the strong sense that this painting's subject is essentially that of intense creative harmony and exhilaration. It was an important painting, too, for her career because when it was first shown at the Royal Academy in 1982, it had been, along with *Pilgrimage to the Ridings* (1981–2) and *Fallen Angels* (1981/2), the key work of the group which had seen her finally elected to the RA that same year. Apart from the honour, this was an important moment for an artist who had yet to have the support of a major commercial gallery in which to show, in that it now allowed her to exhibit 6 works *hors de concours*, rather than a maximum of three if selected.

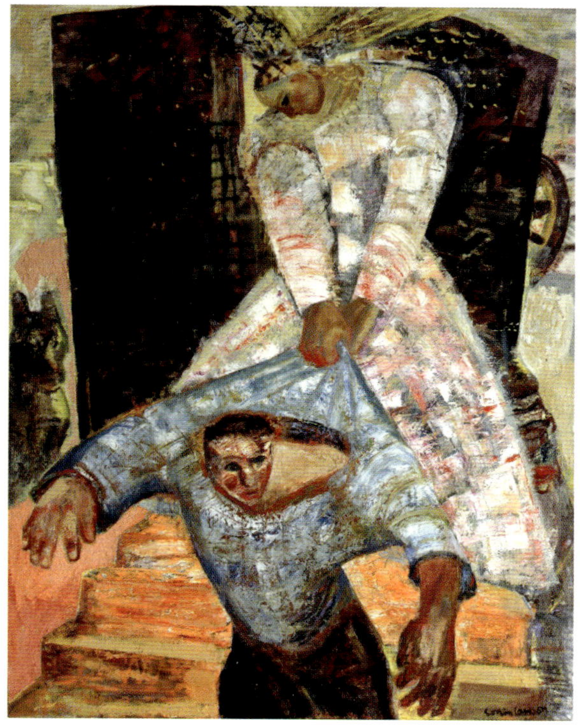

Fallen Angels

The final group of major paintings from this incredibly prolific period up to spring 1982 also can be seen as belonging within this same 'Homage' series – the three *Brontë Revisited* paintings and *Portrait of my Mother, Muriel Metcalfe* (1981) – alternatively entitled *Homage to Muriel Metcalfe, my Mother* – and *Pilgrimage to the Ridings, Homage to my Family* (1981–2). Sonia had, of course been to see the Brontë Museum/Parsonage at Haworth several times as a child; now, in 1981, she returned with her mother and her daughter, Zoe, aged 11. This visit had the profoundest of repercussions for her art, not just for that immediate moment but also for the long term as the extended (and extensive) series of 'Night Reading/Writing' paintings and watercolours that came out of it have recurred at intervals right up to the present day. At that moment though, in the early 80s, accompanied by her mother and daughter, the autobiographical narrative is central, as her reading of the Brontës and their biographies and remembrances of those childhood visits become entwined with all those earlier memories that her mother's growing ill-health had now released – that 'huge sketchbook' of her own history as she once put it. The Brontës now became the means for an imaginative transformation of material which had a huge resonance for her though, as ever in Sonia's work, the tone is never allowed to become one of Romantic doom and gloom, 'ice and winds and baleful passion' as she once put it. In *Teatime at Haworth with the Brontës* (1981) the scene is painted with an intense high-pitched colour, the sense she wanted to get across from her readings was of the story behind the fiction being one of 'tea-time and the warmth and the daily round of living and sunshine' an atmosphere of laughter, food warmth, a communal creative activity. In this it had, of course, a great deal also to do with recollections of those childhood gatherings of artists, poets and academics at her parents' Castle Bolton cottage. More than that again though, with the table laid out with food and the three archetypal figures at the head of the table, there is the powerful suggestion also of the Last Supper at Emmaus theme, Sonia thereby adding a powerful sense of the sacred to the scene as well.

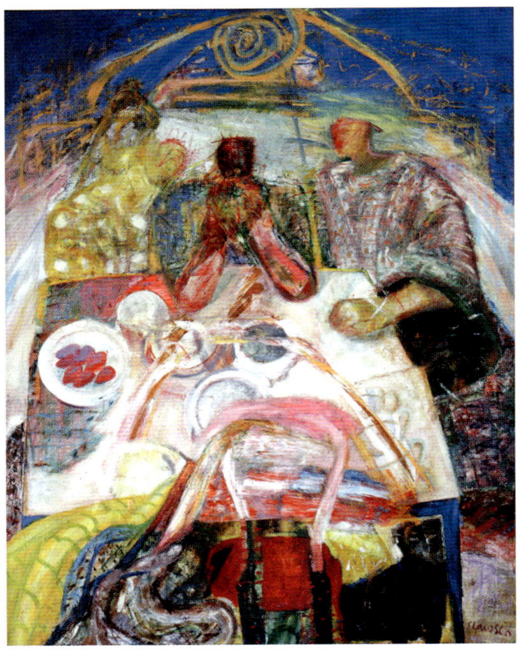

Teatime at Haworth with the Brontës

The two other Brontë themes illustrated here, originally exhibited together with *Teatime at Haworth with the Brontës* at the Royal Academy as a loose-knit series entitled *Brontës Revisited: Triptych* (1981), *Night Writing, Homage to Emily Brontë* (1981) and *Night Writing: The Brontës* (1981) meanwhile take up and develop ideas implicit in *Watchman, What of the Night?* and *Moorland Benediction*, namely of night-vigils, dreaming and reverie, the metaphors implicit in darkness and light, while also linking the camararderie of the three Brontë sisters at their night-writing with her mother's lifetime habit of reading and writing into the small hours of the morning. As this was an activity, as we have seen, that she had come to adopt for herself as a means of sustaining her art – the elusive muse as she termed it – while also bringing up a young child, she also saw herself as becoming part of a complex sisterhood of creative activity that links backwards and forwards in time. Again these ideas are given a pictorial coherence by the adoption of an enclosing, pointed, almost tent-like, compositional structure containing the brilliant, candle-lit figures (and Emily Brontë's dog, Keeper) engaged in reading and writing, and then surrounding them by suggestions of a swirling landscape darkness outside. Meanwhile the much more gestural painting technique she adopts for these works also seems to parallel the creative fervour that is really the central subject of these absorbing paintings.

In many ways – composition, colour and feeling – *Homage to Muriel Metcalfe, my mother* (1981) can almost be read as a fourth member of this Brontë group. Her mother, shown as a young woman, is depicted working at a drawing at night-time while, above her, rises a similarly brilliantly lit, triangular architectural 'tent' form filled with cushions and fabrics and, closing in on this, the sense of a general darkness beyond. Meanwhile, at the base of the painting is a tablet inscribed with the words drawn from Wordsworth's 'Intimations of Immortality' – 'And you, you valleys/streams and groves/forbode not any severing of our loves' – the painting a sharing, in effect, of a deep affection between mother and daughter for the valley landscape and its people in which they had both been brought up in and come to love and from which they both drew mutual inspiration.

Finally among this group of Homage paintings, and in a rather more exuberant and light-hearted spirit, there is *Pilgrimage to the Ridings, Homage to my Family* (1981–2), a splendid compilation of motifs very much in the spirit of *Exercising Dogs on Watling Street*, in which a male figure laden with folding stool, drawing board and paint satchel, is seen striding out past a backdrop of smoking chimneys towards the Dales landscape, surrounded by dogs and passing a dreaming figure of a woman working at her notebooks. With a curved, encircling composition similar to *Moorland Benediction,* it raises myriad feelings and interpretations, the essential one being of benign and joyous encounter with a familiar, loved landscape, its homage, in one sense, being both to her father and mother (the figures in this painting) and, now, to her own engagement with it.

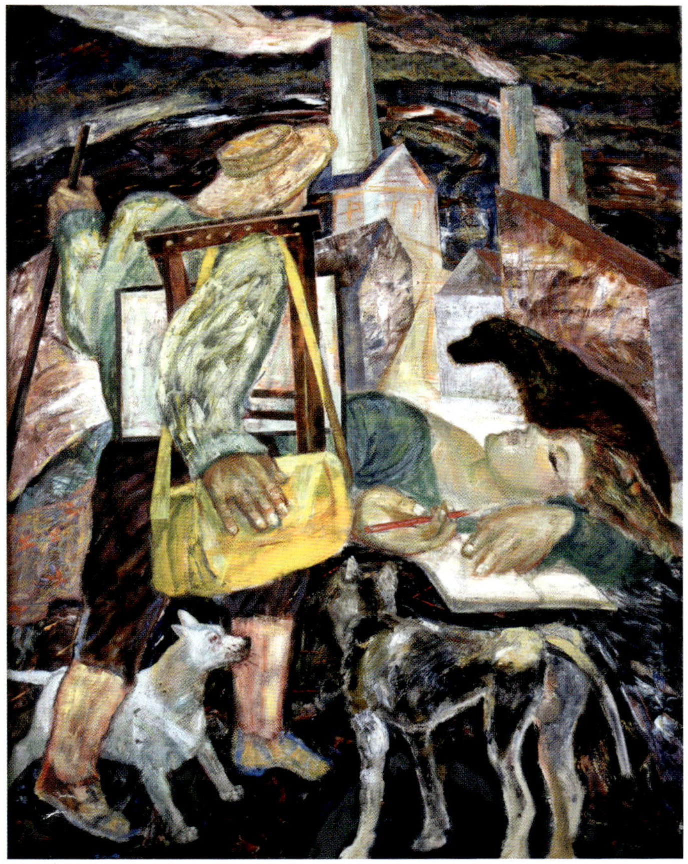

Pilgrimage to the Ridings, Homage to my Family

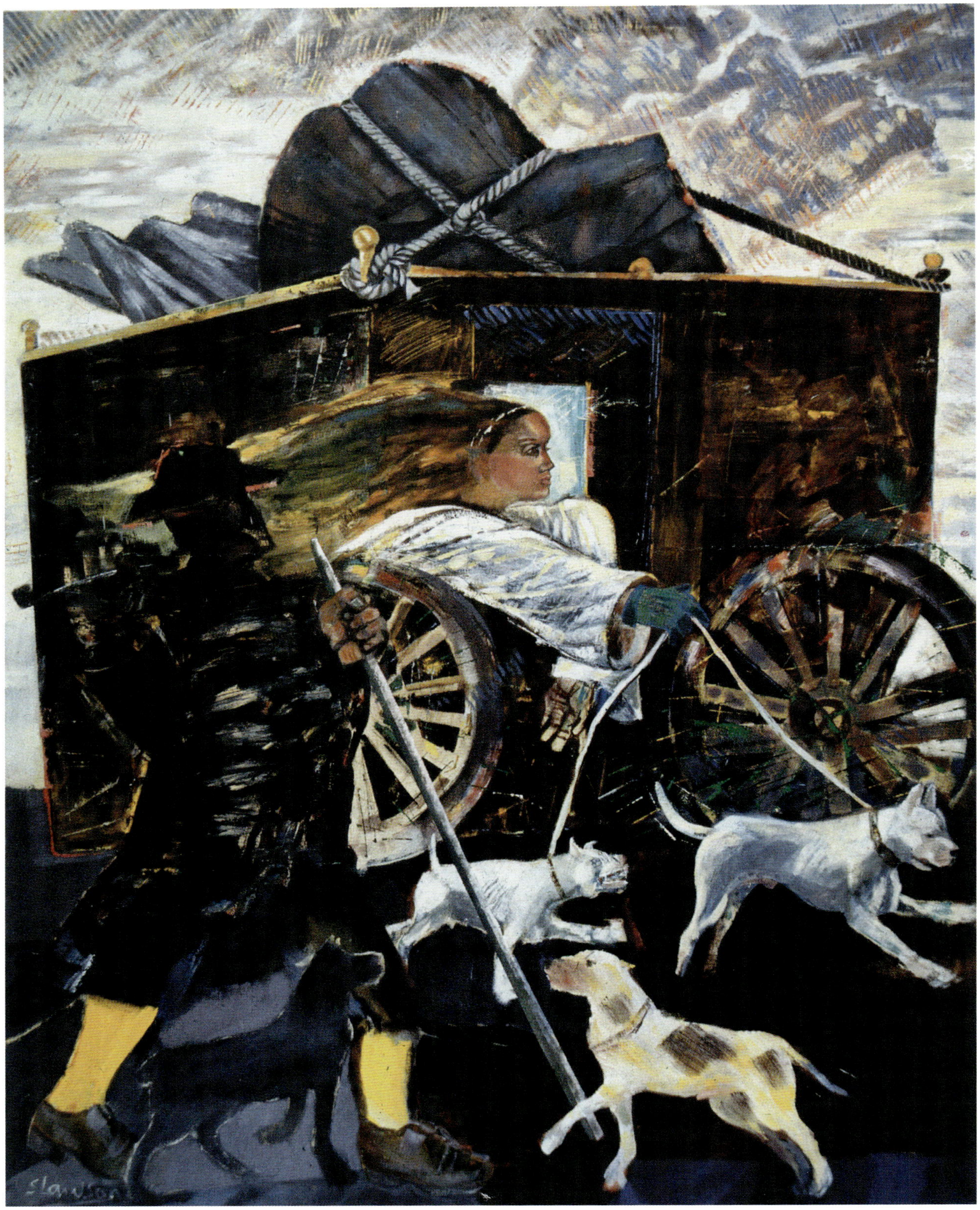

Exercising Dogs on Watling Street 1980, oil on canvas, 153 × 122 cm
Collection: Arts Council of England

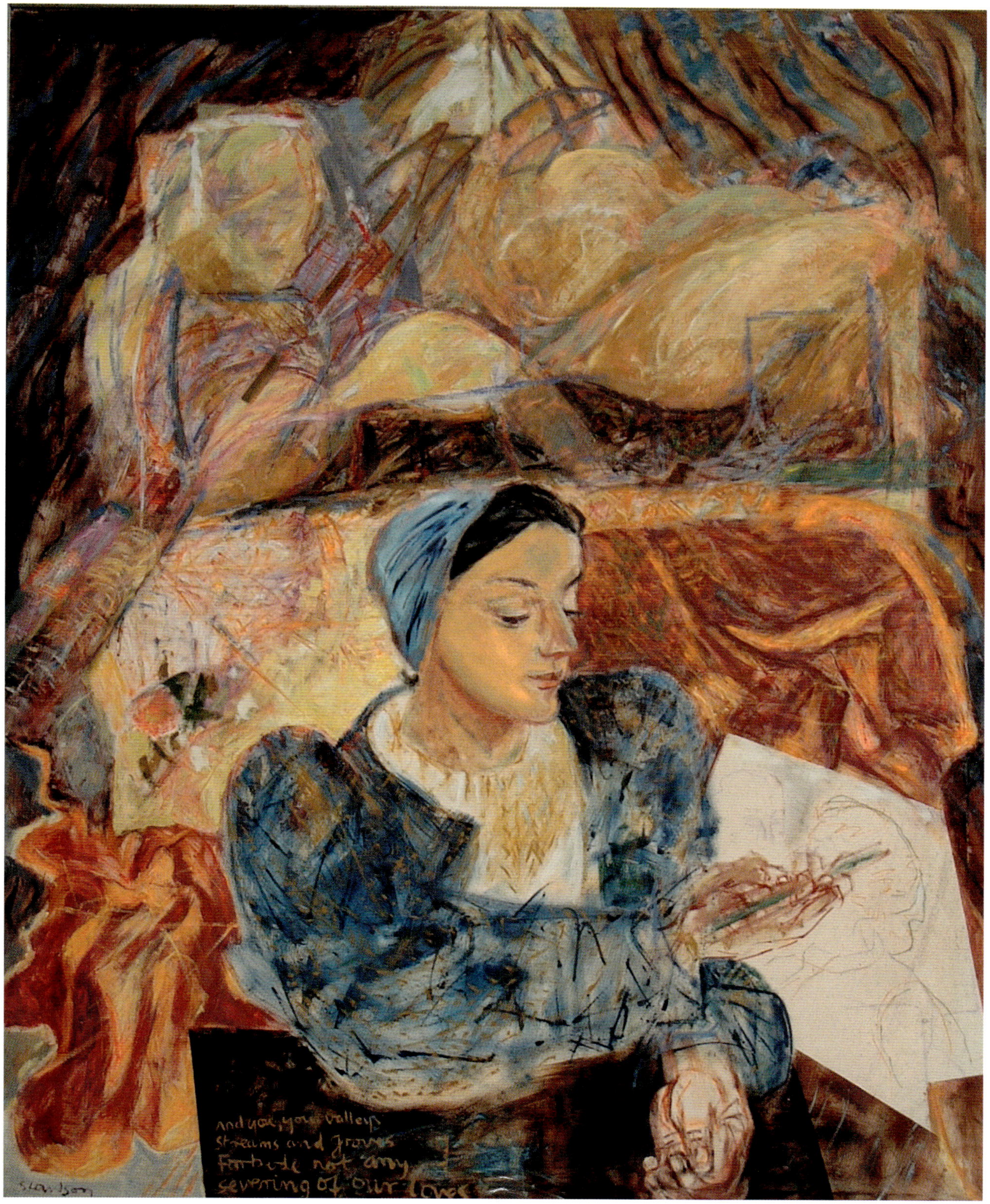

Portrait of my Mother, Muriel Metcalfe 1981, oil on canvas, 289 x 191 cm

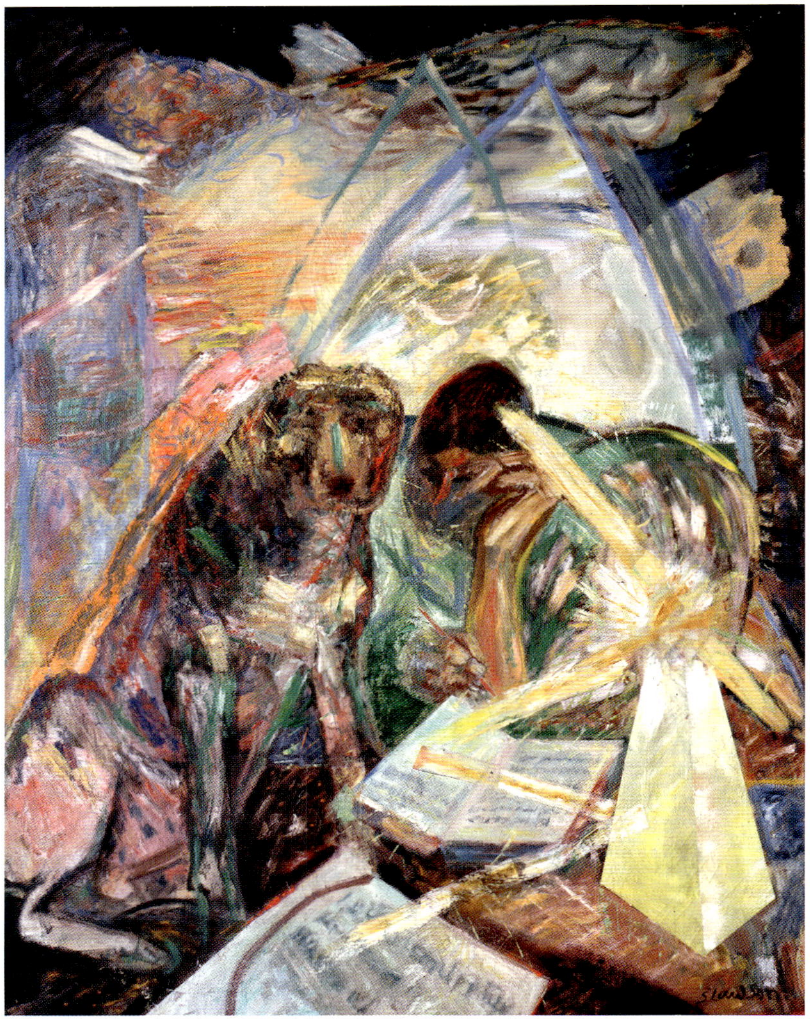

Homage to Emily Brontë, Night Writing 1981, oil on canvas, 153 x 122 cm

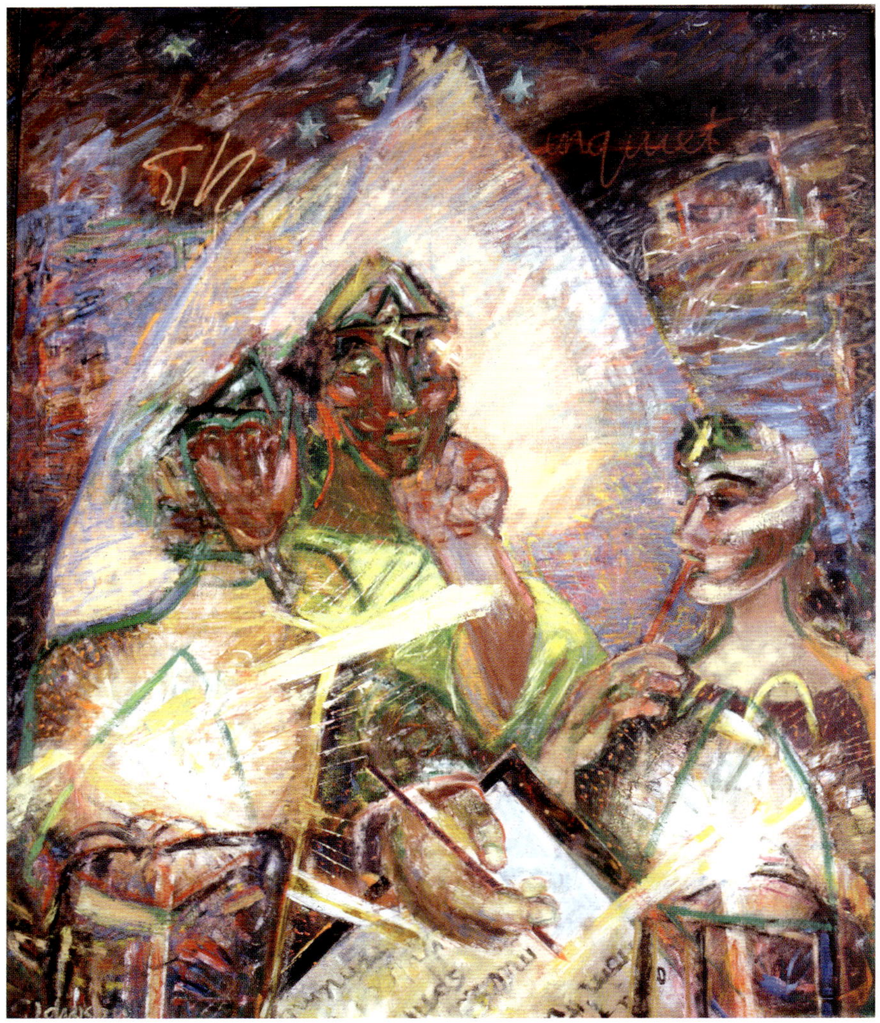

Night Writing, The Brontës 1981, oil on canvas, 153 x 122 cm

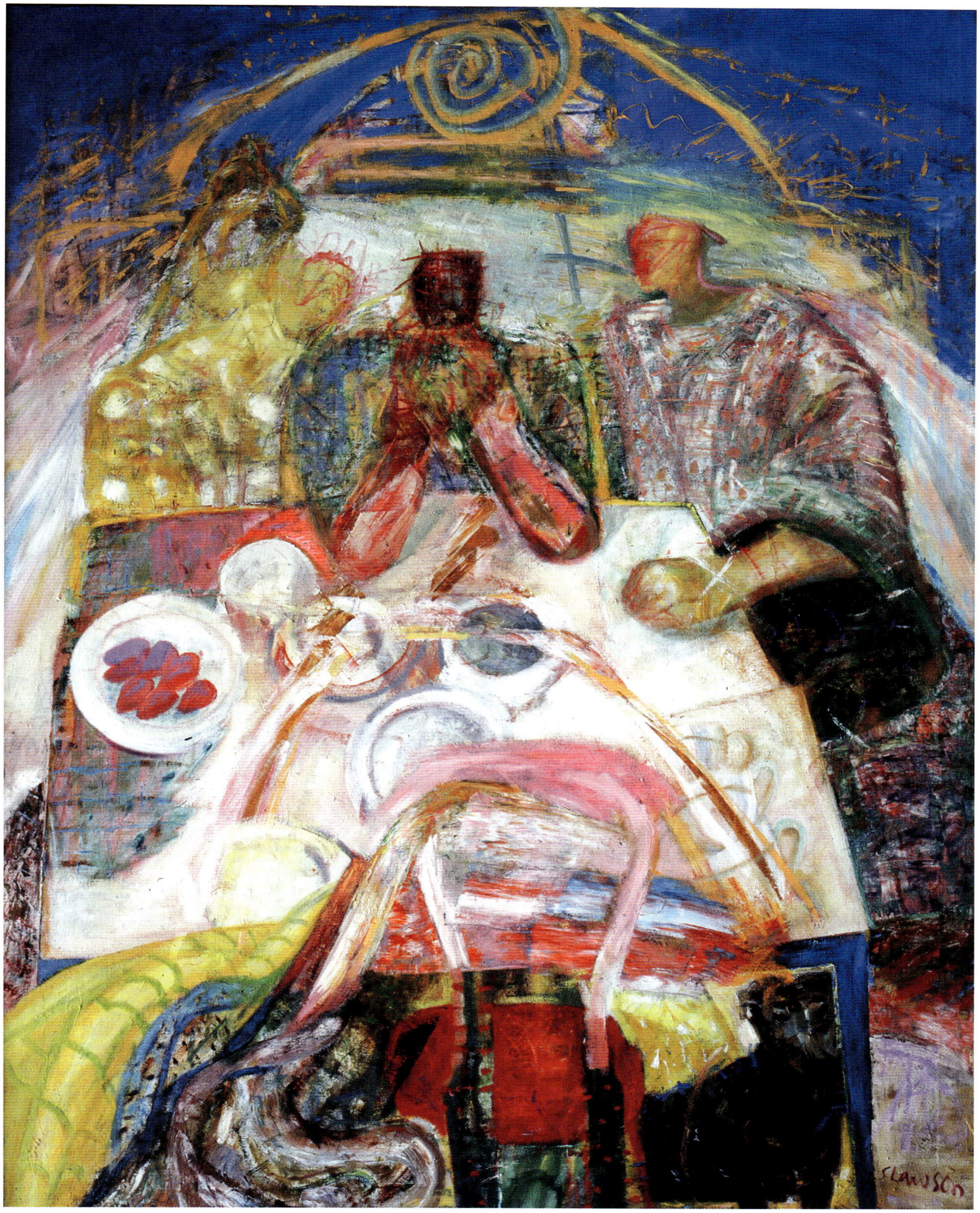

Teatime at Haworth with the Brontës 1981–82, oil on canvas, 153 x 122 cm

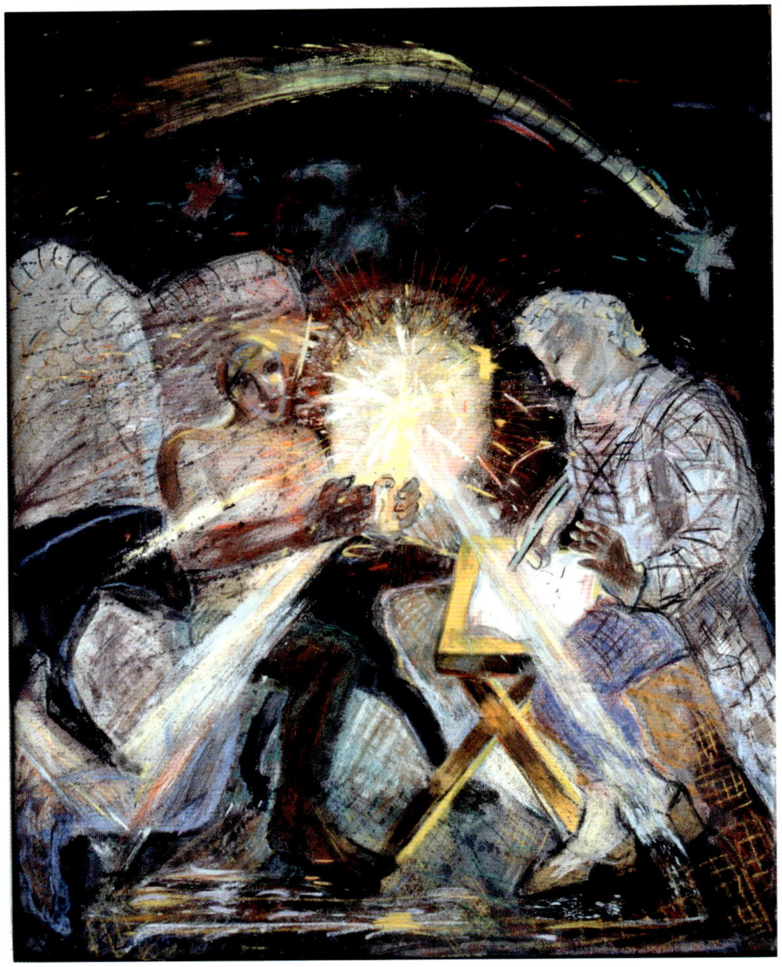

Night Writing Series, watercolour and chalk on paper

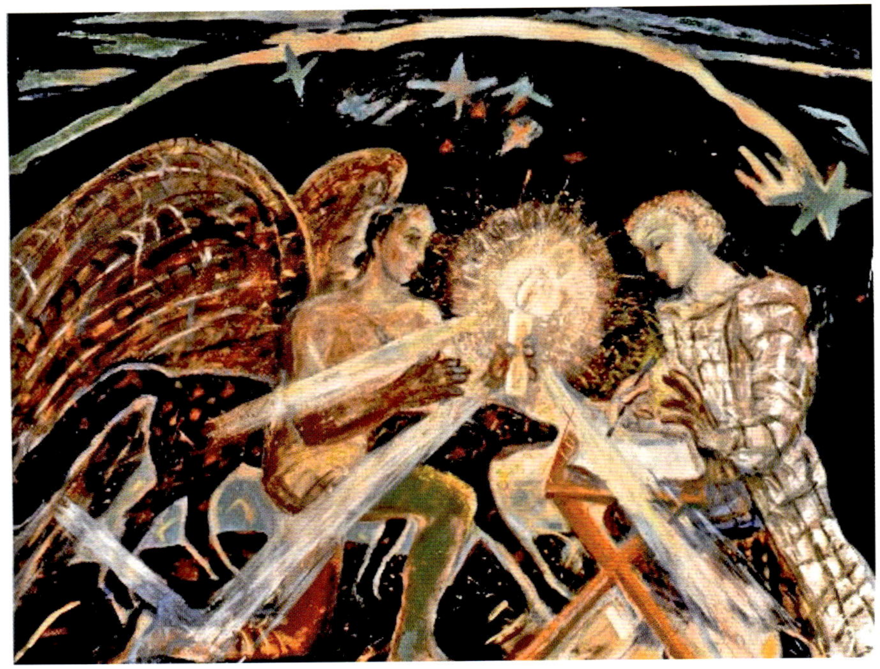

Night Writing II, mixed media

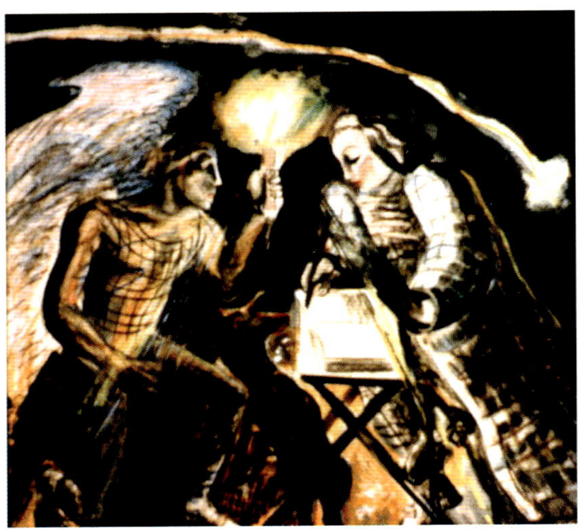

Guiding Light, ink and watercolour on paper

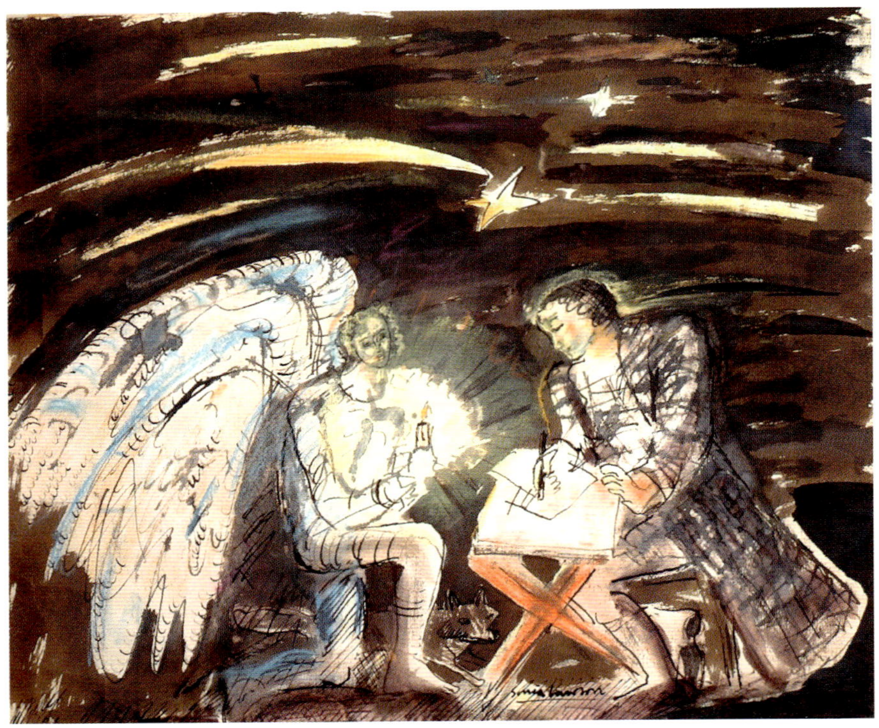

Angel Reader, ink and watercolour on paper

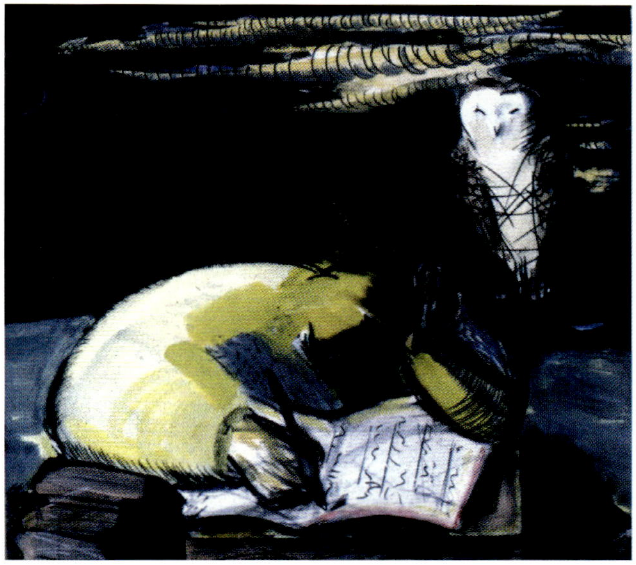

Night Writing Series 1990s

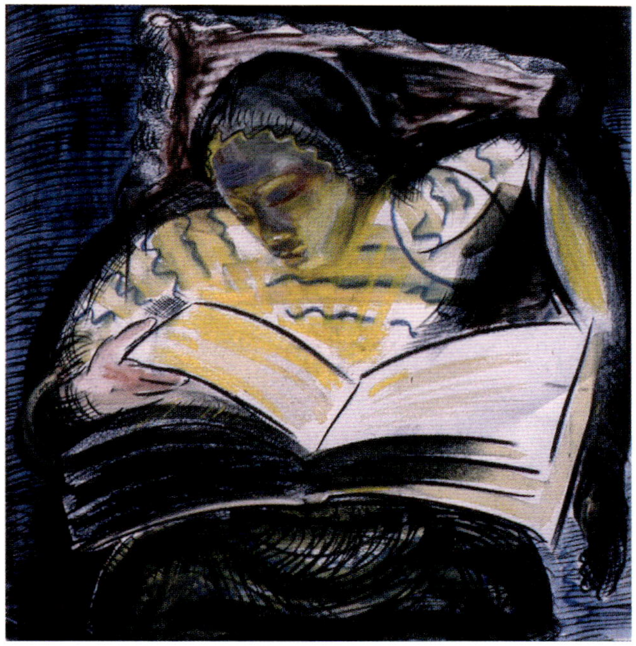

Reader, watercolour and chalk on paper, 40 x 30 cm

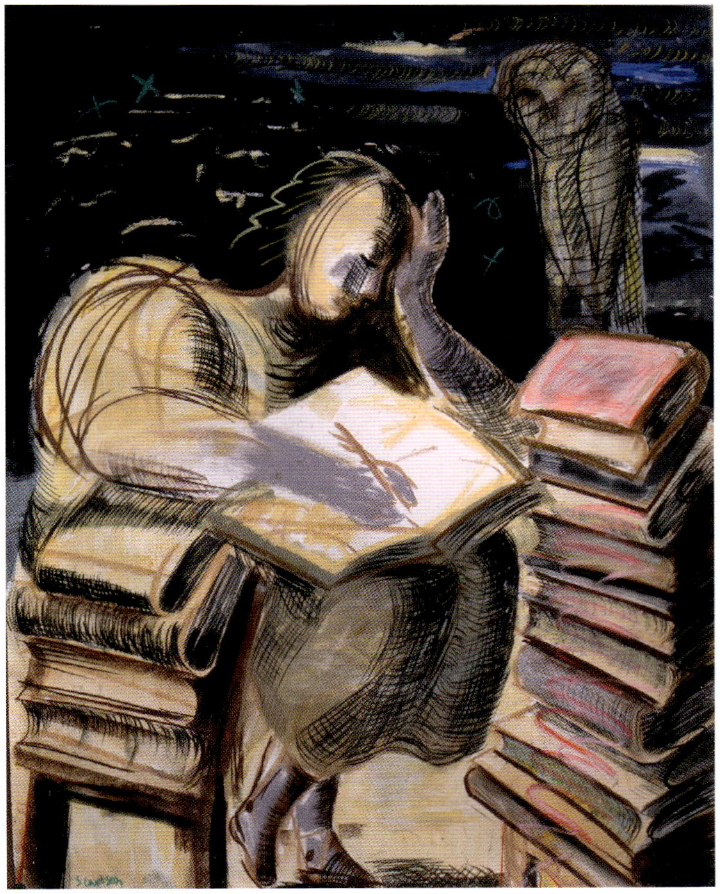

Night Writing 1991, watercolour and chalk on paper, 95 x 77.5 cm

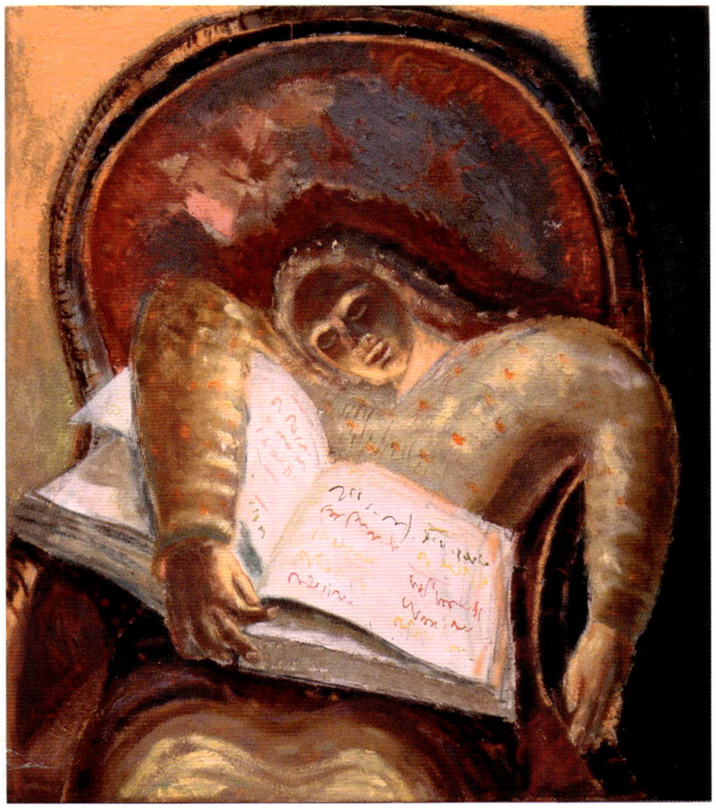

Book of Delights II, oil on canvas, 67 x 50 cm

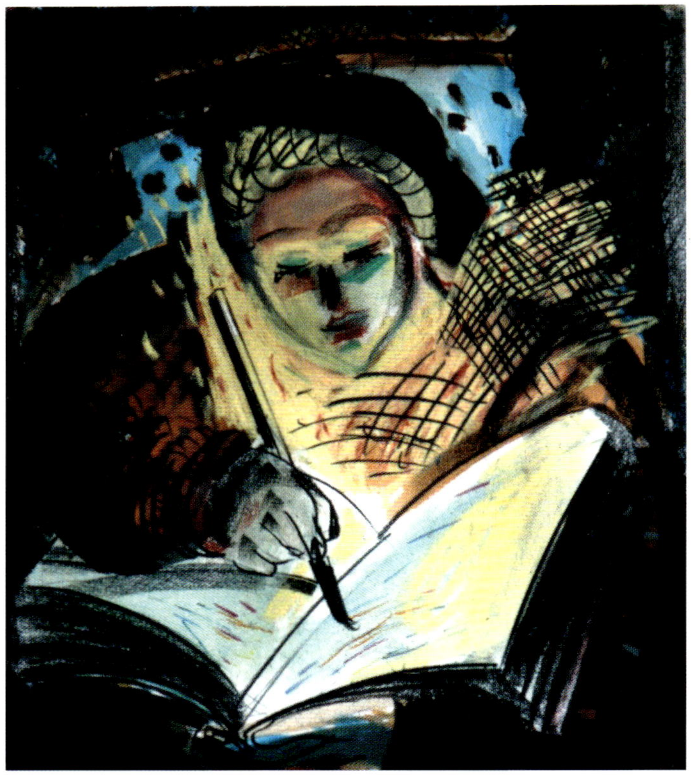

Night Writing Series, **Diarist** 1992, watercolour on paper, 46 x 40 cm

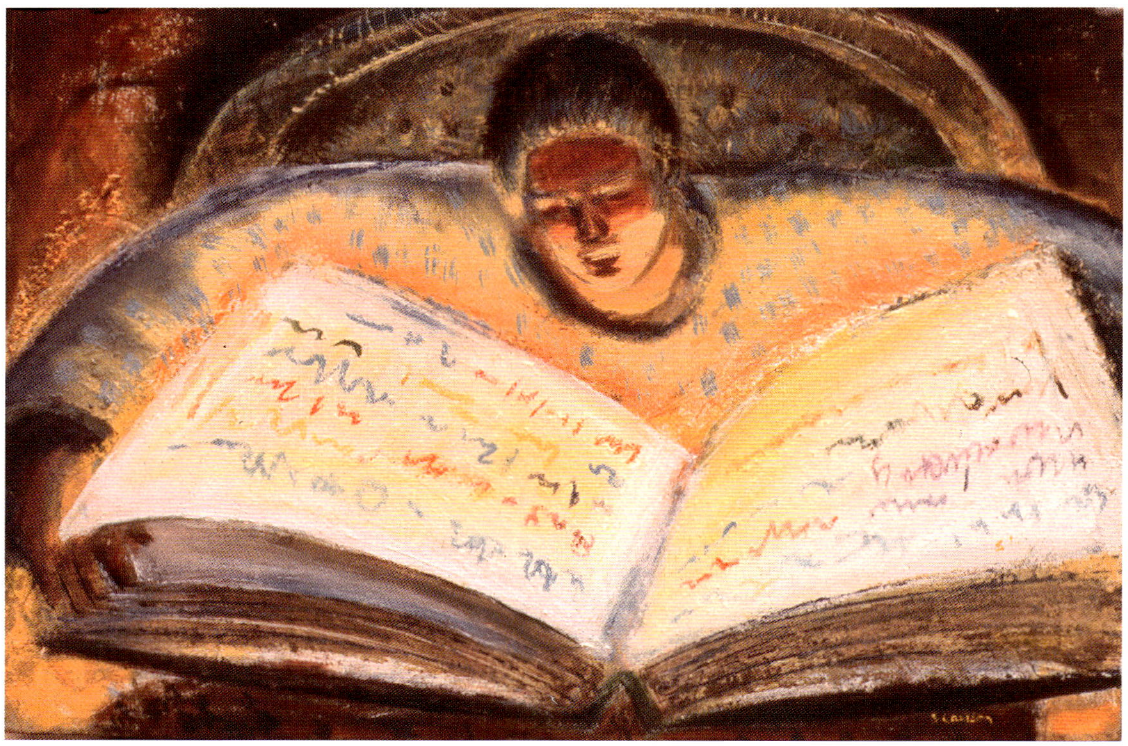

Night Reader 1992, oil on canvas, 30 x 46 cm

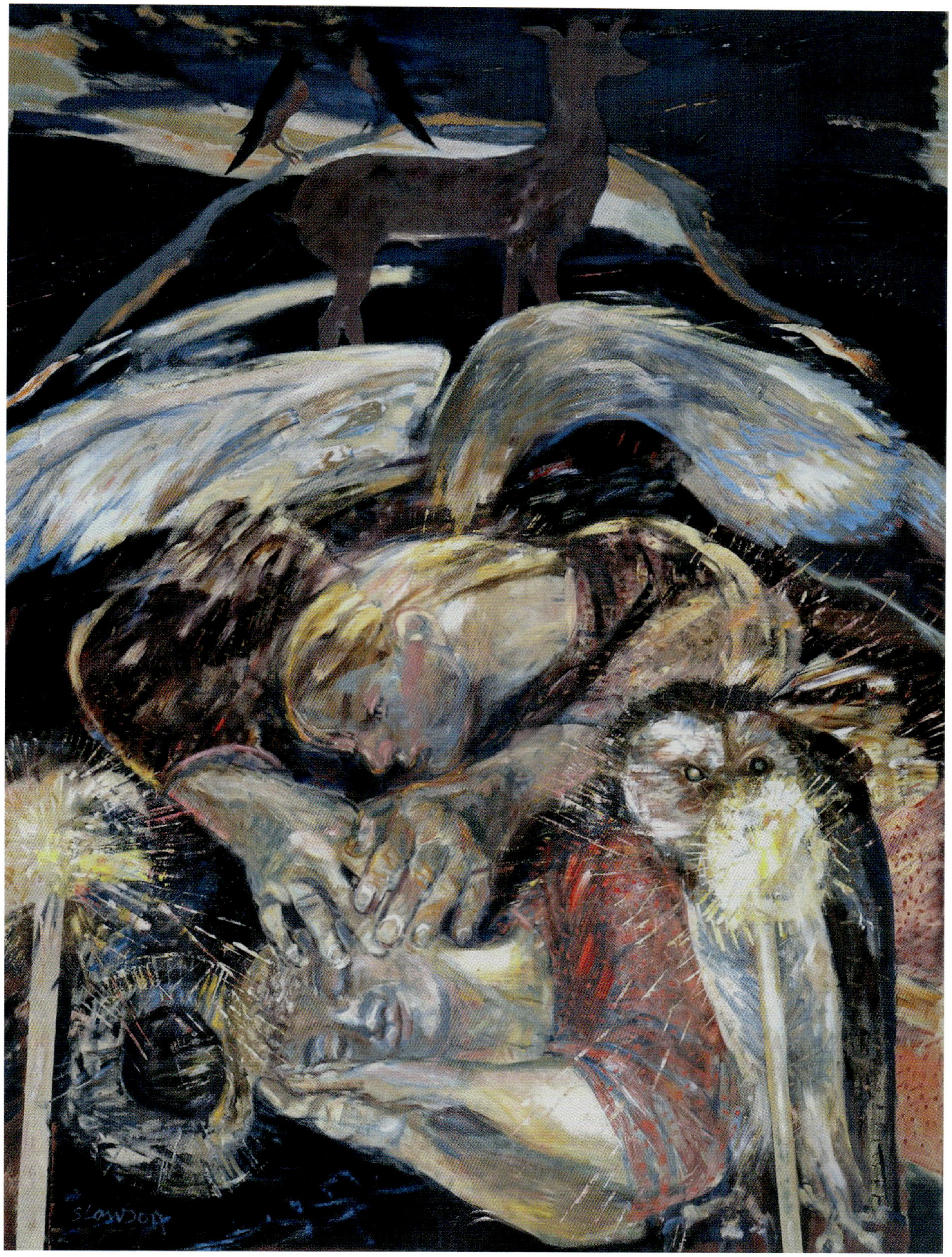

Moorland Benediction 1980, oil on canvas, 202 × 152.5 cm. Collection: Kirklees Museums and Galleries

Chapter 6

> Even this late it happens:
> the coming of love, the coming of light.
> You wake and the candles are lit as if by themselves,
> Stars gather, dreams pour into your pillows,
> Sending up warm bouquets of air.
> Even this late the bones of the body shine
> And tomorrow's dust flares into breath.
>
> From 'The Coming of Light' by Mark Strand

This spell of intense productivity came to an abrupt halt on April 2nd 1982 ('the same day as the launch of the Falklands invasion' Sonia wryly notes) when a serious fire, caused by a faulty gas appliance, swept through their house. Both Sonia and her husband Charlie were lucky to escape with their lives, suffering second-degree burns that caused them both prolonged hospitalization at Stoke Mandeville Special Burns Unit. The house itself was severely damaged though, as she asked of the first visitor to her bedside in hospital, the studio, miraculously, was intact. Even so she had lost half a dozen or so paintings and two folders of drawings and, with the house taking a year or more to clean and repair and Sonia living meanwhile with her mother-in-law in nearby Bletchley, no painting or drawing of any kind was remotely possible – to begin with she had had to go around with her arms bandaged and raised shoulder high for some considerable time. It was the kind of setback from which Sonia seemed to suffer at periodic intervals throughout her life; quite apart from parental illnesses and care, there was another domestic disaster a few years later when a large inflatable swimming-pool on their upper lawn gave way, releasing a torrent of water into the house. As her friend, the painter Carel Weight, affectionately observed at the time 'My dear Sonia, you've had the fire and the flood, one wonders when the pestilence is coming!'

This new domestic disaster happened at a moment, though, when her professional career and critical recognition had really just begun to gather momentum and she seems to have surmounted the frustration and difficulties it imposed with an astonishing energy and determination. She had just had a major touring retrospective show – 'Shrines of Life' – open at the respected Milton Keynes Gallery in February 1982 and, later that same year she had (as has already been noted) been elected an Associate of the Royal Academy. In 1984 she served on the Selection and Hanging Committees of the Summer Exhibition where the large room of large-scale figurative and contemporary painting she had selected had caused a good deal of favourable comment. A noted 'modernist' critic, Waldemar Januszczek, for example, opened his *Guardian* review of the show with the observation that 'Sonia Lawson is clearly a growing force at the Royal Academy Summer Show, a fact which I welcome. On several recent occasions her own paintings have rescued the exhibition, almost single-handedly, from a complete lack of awareness of the art of the Eighties. Dark, moody, aggressive, packed with elusive symbols, they push you into a confrontation with someone else's private mythology.' He then went on to comment on her 'room' which 'she has chosen and hung with powerful examples of modern expressionism … the casual visitor might imagine he had wandered into a celebration of progressive painting rather than the 216th Royal Academy Summer Show.'

That September of 1984 she had also been selected for the first of what would soon turn out to be a series of prestigious public commissions over the next decade or so, in this case the Imperial War Museum commissioning her to be the 'official' artist covering the major BAOR (British Army of the Rhine) military exercise Exercise Lionheart in West Germany. Looking at her official itinerary it seems to have been a highly intensive week's visit in the course of which she observed mobility movements involving Chinook and other helicopters and night-time troop deployments and also sketched tanks being serviced and visiting their exercise areas. It also resulted in a very substantial body of work – three large (5' × 4') canvases and one smaller one as well as over 30 works on paper – watercolours, chalk and conté and mixed media studies.

Her approach to this complex range of intense experiences is, looked at overall, very typical of her approach to her art in general up to this date, the bigger oil paintings, for example, with their strong sense of drama, movement, imminent action, being very much in the vein of her larger canvases from the early 80s, the 'Garrison' series and *Exercising Dogs on Watling Street* in particular. Above all, they share with those paintings very similar compositional schemes so that in a painting like *Two Minds with but a Single Thought* (1984) the leading tank of what would appear to be some four others ranged behind it, is placed right up to the front of the picture plane and seen very much

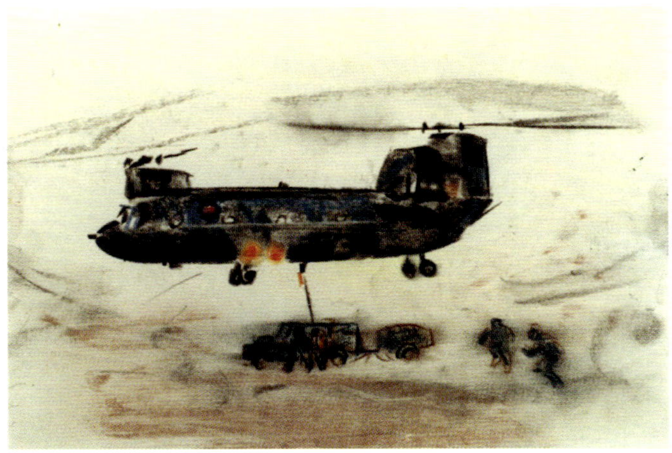

B.A.O.R. Exercise Lionheart, September 1984, Westphalia, **Chinook moving troops and vehicles**

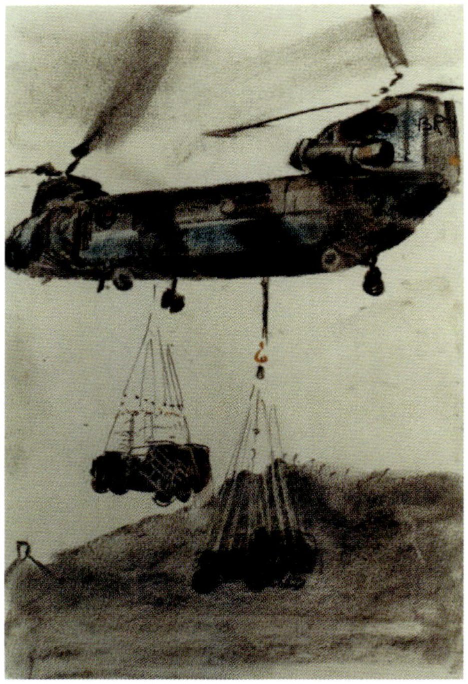
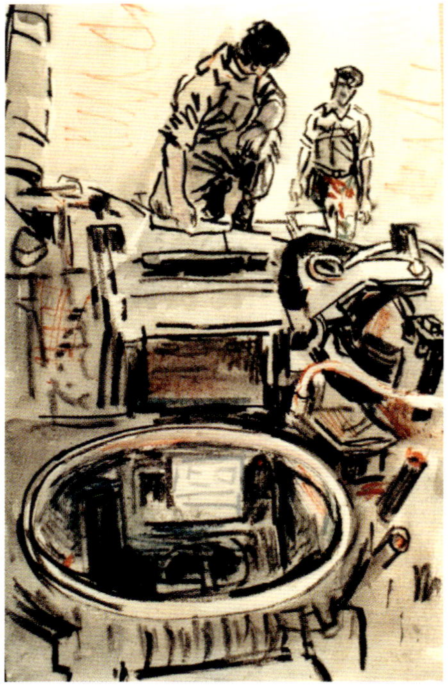
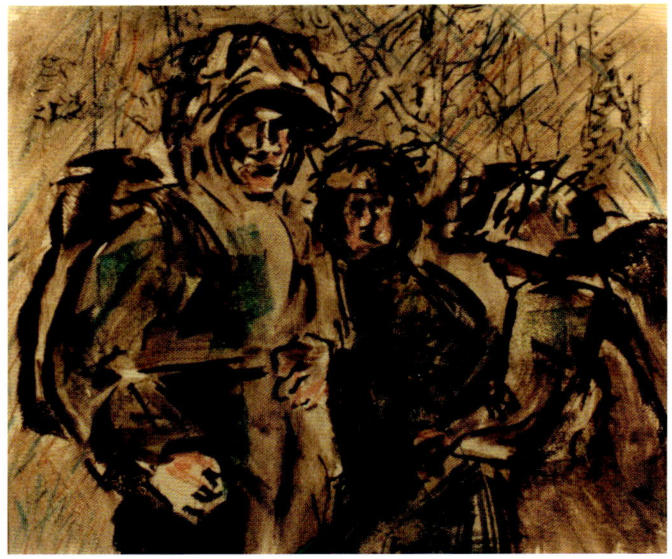
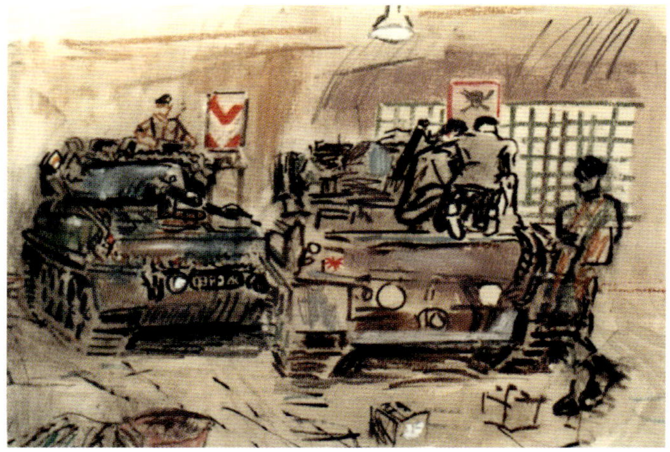
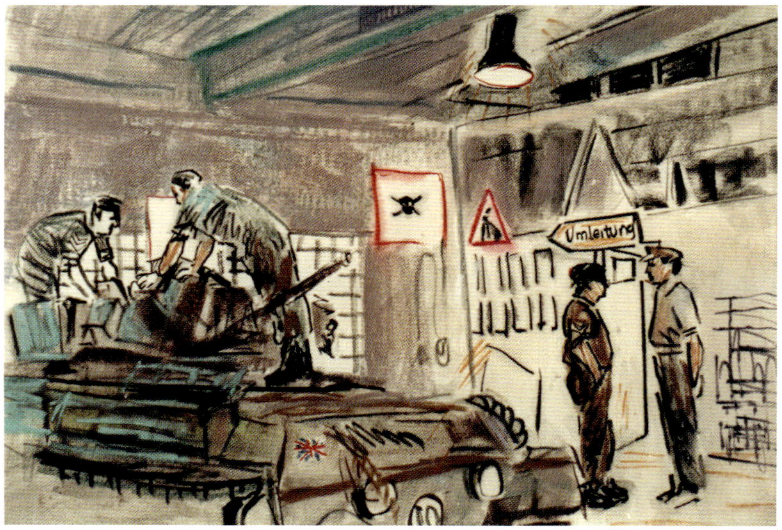

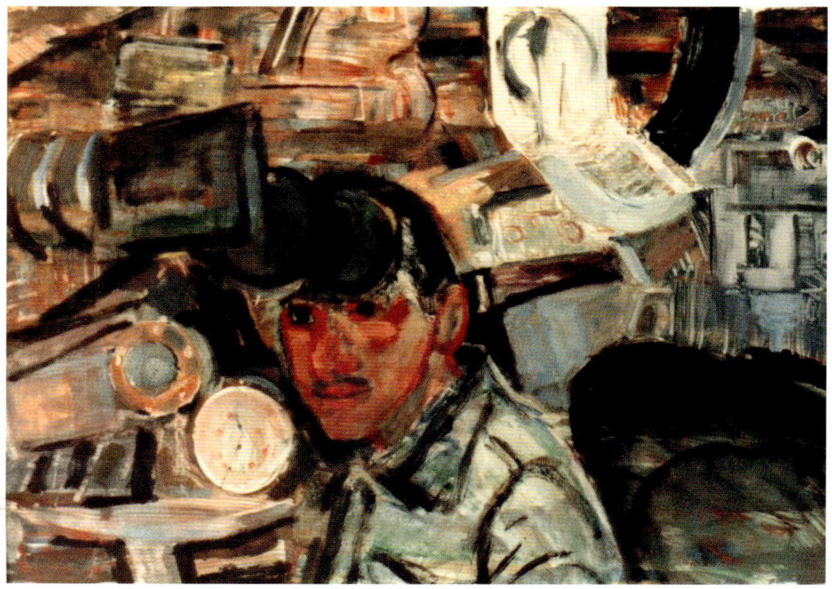

Selection of images from sketches and drawings Lawson completed during her commission to record Exercise Lionheart, Westphalia, B.A.O.R., 1984

from the point of view of a spectator at street level. With the massive tracks of the leading tank seemingly moving forward to within feet of us, the aggressively thrusting gun-barrels of all five are draped with curious writhing forms that at first sight almost seem to be garlands of flowers but are, looked at more carefully, swags of camouflage. The immediate impression the painting conveys is of a visceral sense of overwhelming noise and dramatic movement but it is also something rather more than just a depiction of the fearsome nature of military force; a blue flag adorned with its white dove of peace flutters among the gun-barrels, making it clear, as the title itself

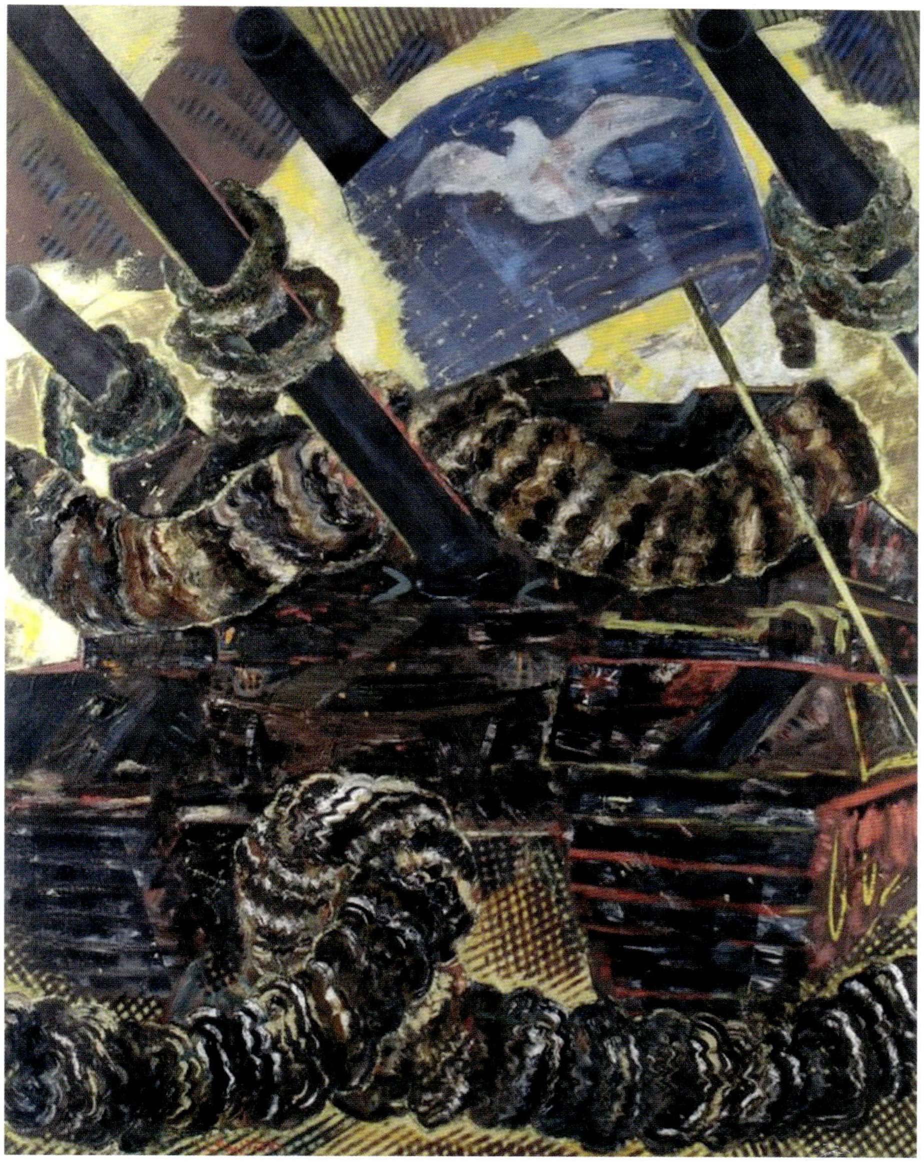

Two Minds with but a Single Thought (Peace Demonstration and Tanks)
1984, oil on canvas, 153 x 122 cm. Collection: Imperial War Museum

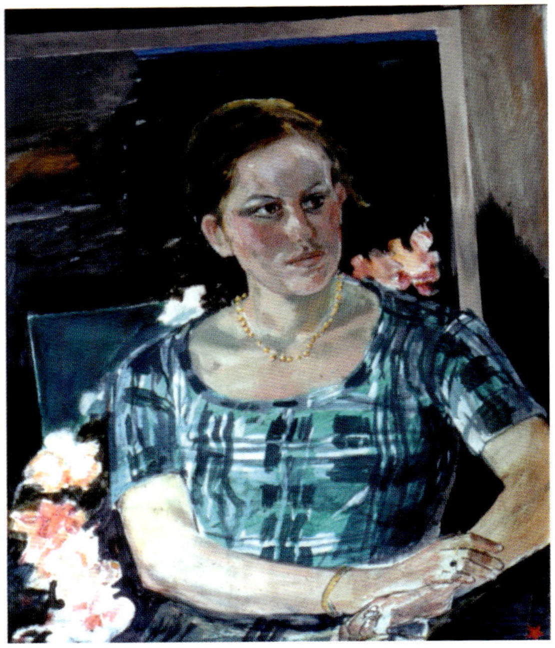

Dominique 1972, oil on canvas, 64 × 57 cm

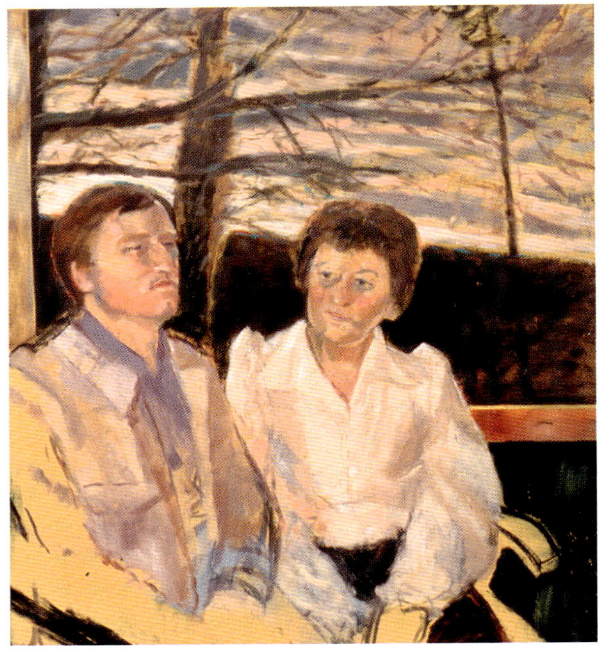

Ann and Dick Hammond 1982, oil on canvas, 64 × 57 cm

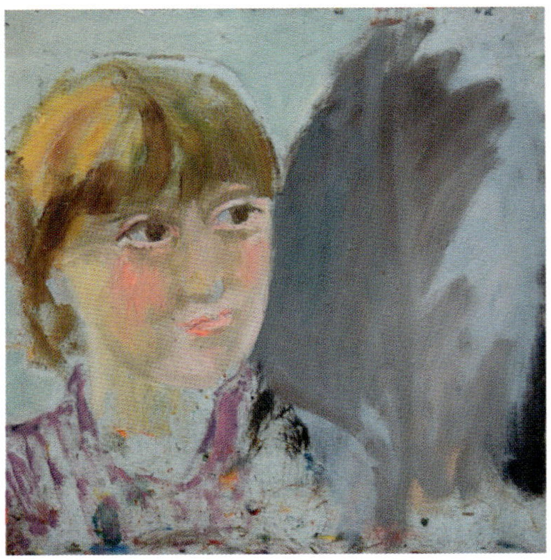

Joanne 1981, oil on canvas, 43 × 30 cm

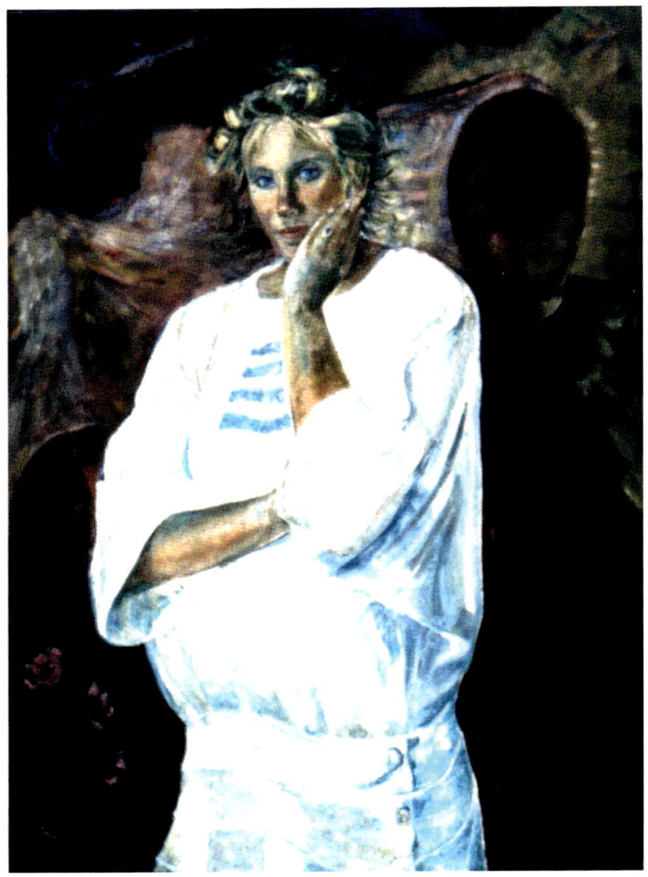

Mrs Gilks 8 Months Pregnant 1989, oil on canvas, 250 × 120 cm

suggests, that this is also a representation of a peace demonstration, an event also recorded in some of the sketch drawings she made on this same visit. It was, on reflection, a rather bold choice of subject for an artist commissioned by the military though one which, in the light of her work from the late 60s and 70s with its underlying sense of the human impacts of war, should not have been entirely surprising in its unmistakable sympathies. The work, along with the rest of the drawings and sketches, is now in the collection of the Imperial War Museum though, with the Museum's official incorrect description of there being 'tinsel' and 'bunting' on the tanks rather than camouflage, one cannot really be too sure what quite they, or the BAOR generals, made of it.

Meanwhile for the works on paper – mostly oil sketches, watercolour studies, conté crayon and pencil drawings – Sonia made full use of those skills in observational drawing that she had first developed at Doncaster School of Art back in the 1950s – those studies of workers in factories, markets and streets discussed in Chapter One. The outcome is some wonderfully vivid and sympathetic studies of the soldiers, not just in the excitements of helicopter-borne exercises but also wet and sodden as they participate in exercises in German forests or wait, bored, for an overdue helicopter to arrive. In all of them it is her shrewd and often humorous appreciation that these are still men at their work quite as much as soldiers full of brisk efficiency and bold action that makes them so vividly human and revealing of the nature of military life. In short she shows her love of people and the particularities of their everyday activities while, somewhere in the background, there are her childhood memories of those soldiers she had seen and observed in wartime Yorkshire and, behind that again, her deep-seated historical sense of the soldiering life right back in time.

The mid- to late 80s were not marked by any radical new developments stylistically in Sonia's painting and, judging by her submissions to the RA Summer Exhibition at this time, there is, understandably enough in view of the fire and its aftermath plus the work the substantial Imperial War Museum commission c.1984/5 had involved, a slight lessening in the volume of work compared to the previous four or five years of intense activity c.1978–1982. There is a distinct sense, too, of a consolidating of forces, of trying different things out before the next radical move forward that was to come over the next decade. There are, for example, a number of portrait studies painted just for the sheer enjoyment of painting people that she had been doing since the start of the decade such as *Joanne* (1981), a school friend of Zoe's and *Dominique* (1972), a French *au pair* who looked after Zoe, and *Ann and Dick Hammond* (1982), local friends of Sonia's. Meanwhile, later in the decade, there was a larger commissioned piece, *Mrs Gilks – 8 Months Pregnant* (1989), a dramatic and substantial work in which the striking three-quarter length figure of Mrs Gilks in a dazzling white dress is flanked by two more shadowy female figures and, stylistically, that is very much in the manner of her more imaginative paintings of this period.

The other, perhaps more significant, theme for the future however are the two related 'Night Reading/ Night Writing' series which she had now began to develop out of her Brontë paintings of 1981/1982 and works like *Moorland Benediction* (1980). Consisting of both oils and watercolour and chalk drawings, this was to become a substantial theme for her throughout the 1980s particularly, as the dozen or so examples from that period illustrated here make clear, but it was also one she has returned to at intervals right up to the present day. It is a subject matter of intense private significance – comparatively few of them have been exhibited publicly over the years – in which those past memories of her mother's reading and writing late into the night coalesce with her own present experience when both child-care and care for her increasingly invalid mother made night-time into a vital moment for creative reflection and inspiration. The critic Norbert Lynton saw them as 'dramatic modern successors to the author images and the Evangelists of the Romans and Early Christians' to which, with their intense meditative qualities, one could also add perhaps those depictions of the Early Christian Saints beloved of Early Renaissance artists, St Jerome above all. They represent most significantly though a slow turning away from the narrative mode towards the lyric that was to become the core characteristic of her painting from the 1990s onwards.

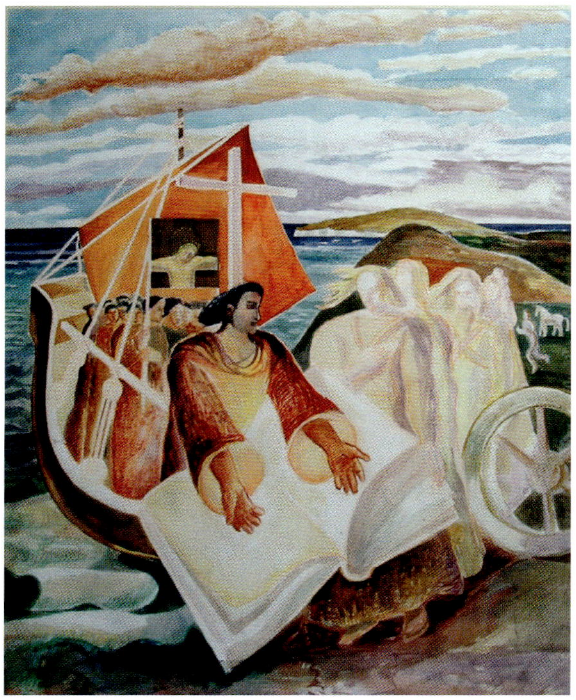

St Augustine Landing in England 1989, watercolour, 102 x 91 cm
Lambeth Palace Commission. Presented to the Pope
Collection: Vatican

Filled as they are with an intense sense of the sacred Sonia still always saw them as being, like the rest of her work, quite as much about real life as the rest of her work, in this instance a visualizing of the realities of the imaginative process. Writing about this period of work in the catalogue for a small show of this group of paintings at Manchester City Art Gallery in 1987, 'The Midnight Muse', she observed 'always there is comfort, a sort of benediction. There's time for celebration somewhere along the line and benign sentinels who do not acknowledge time so that everything is perpetual and new … I am not interested in mythology. I see everything as fact (not to be interpreted as realism) and paint it as fact and very much of the present.' Thus, in the paintings of single reading or writing female figures, mother and daughter are fused in a creative unity of both reverie and intense thought and activity that draws its poetic power from the very truth and reality of its feeling while in the double figures of artist and angel, Rilke's angels of the unseen are envisioned here as the vital forces of imaginative empathy – reverie, as it is in any form of intellectual activity, as a means to revelation. As Bach once remarked when someone asked him how he wrote so divinely answered 'I play the notes, in order as they are written. It is God who makes the music.'

The 1980s end for Sonia with several significant but unrelated events – an exhibition at Wakefield Art Gallery in late 1988 entitled 'A Family of Artists', in which her mother's and father's work was shown together with Sonia's in another, and separate, space close by (and which then went on to Ilkley/Carwright Hall in early 1989), her first commercial gallery show in London since the late 60s at the Boundary Gallery in 1989 and, in the same year, a major commission from the Archbishop of Canterbury for a work to present to the Pope in celebration of ecumenical accord. The Boundary was to prove an extremely useful connection – there were to be two further shows at the gallery over the next decade or so, both with good catalogues and useful sales, while the gallery was also heavily involved in the organizing, compiling and production of her major retrospective show and catalogue at the Dean Clough in Halifax in 1996.

For the Lambeth Palace commission meanwhile, Sonia made an interesting choice of medium, deciding that, rather than an oil on canvas, she would make a large-scale watercolour. At some 3'6" × 3' and on the subject of *St Augustine landing in England,* it proved a luminous and serene work, with its predominant tones of blue, gold and white. With its comparatively complex compositional scheme it remains closer in feeling to the kind of paintings she had been making at the start of the decade though, and it is more in the 'Night Reading/ Writing' series as well as a number of large-scale double-figure drawings also from the late 80s, for example, *Actors I* (1987) and *Actors II* (1989), that you get the overriding sense of a significant shift starting to take place in her practice. In this context the Papal commission seems to represent perhaps the last of its kind in this more strictly narrative tradition.

This shift was soon to be further accelerated by another of those sudden and dramatic personal events that seem to punctuate Sonia's career. Only a few months after the Ilkley show had closed, her mother, Muriel Metcalfe, suffered a major stoke which left her without speech and unable to walk or look after herself any longer. As a consequence she now came to live with Sonia who, somehow, had to find ways of continuing to work – she had also started to teach at the Royal Academy Schools in 1987 – while taking on the full-time care of her mother. As so often in the past though, Sonia found, in her dramatically changed circumstances, answers that were ultimately to deepen the emotional intensity of her work still further, taking it in quite radical new directions.

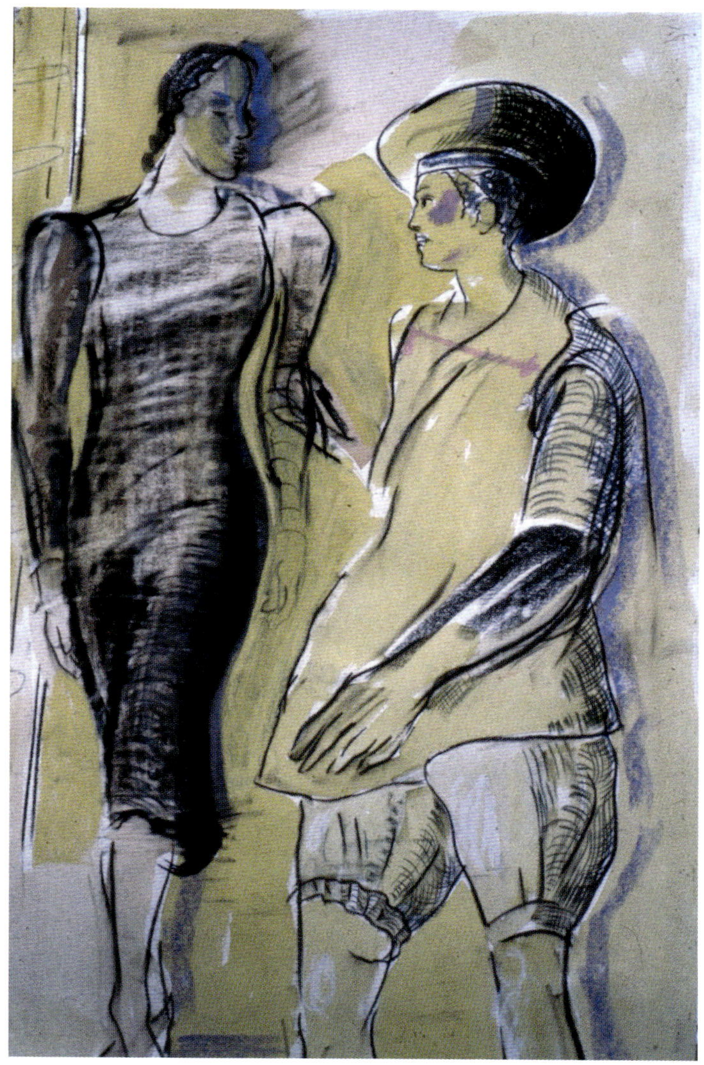

Actors II 1989, watercolour, 98 × 60 cm

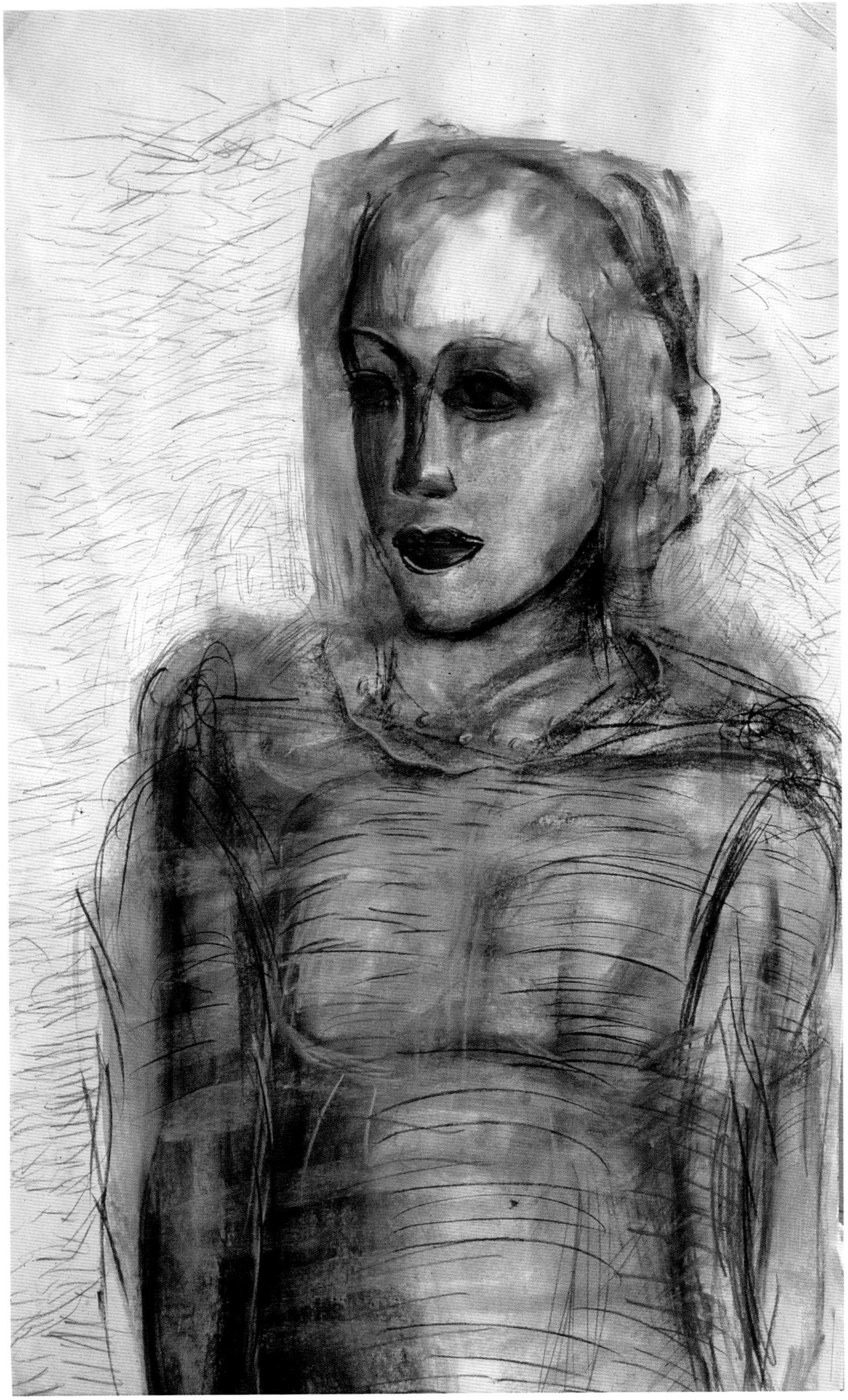

Standing Girl 1997, charcoal and watercolour on paper, 100 x 63 cm

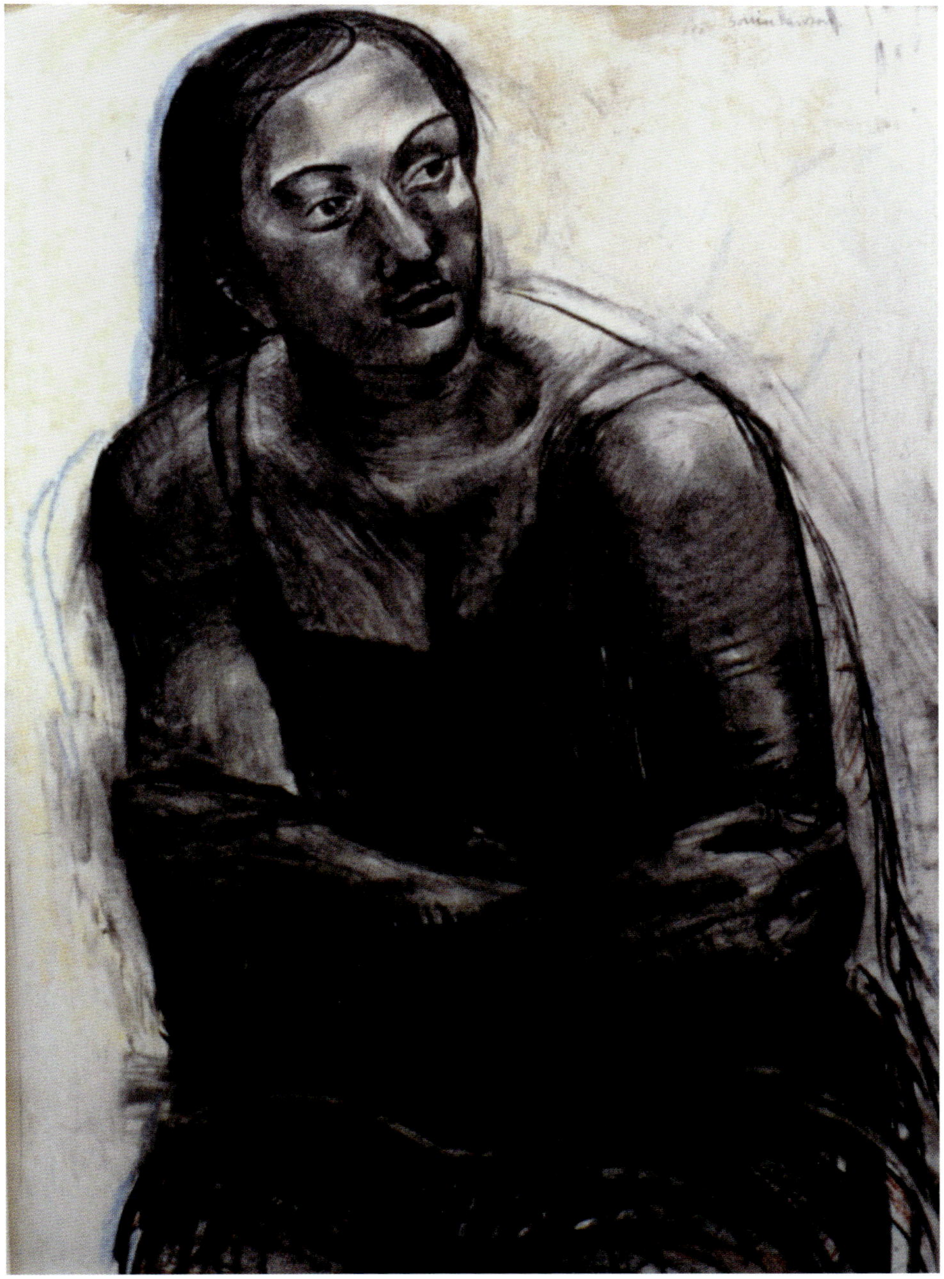

Seated Woman 1997, conté and charcoal on paper, 80 x 60 cm

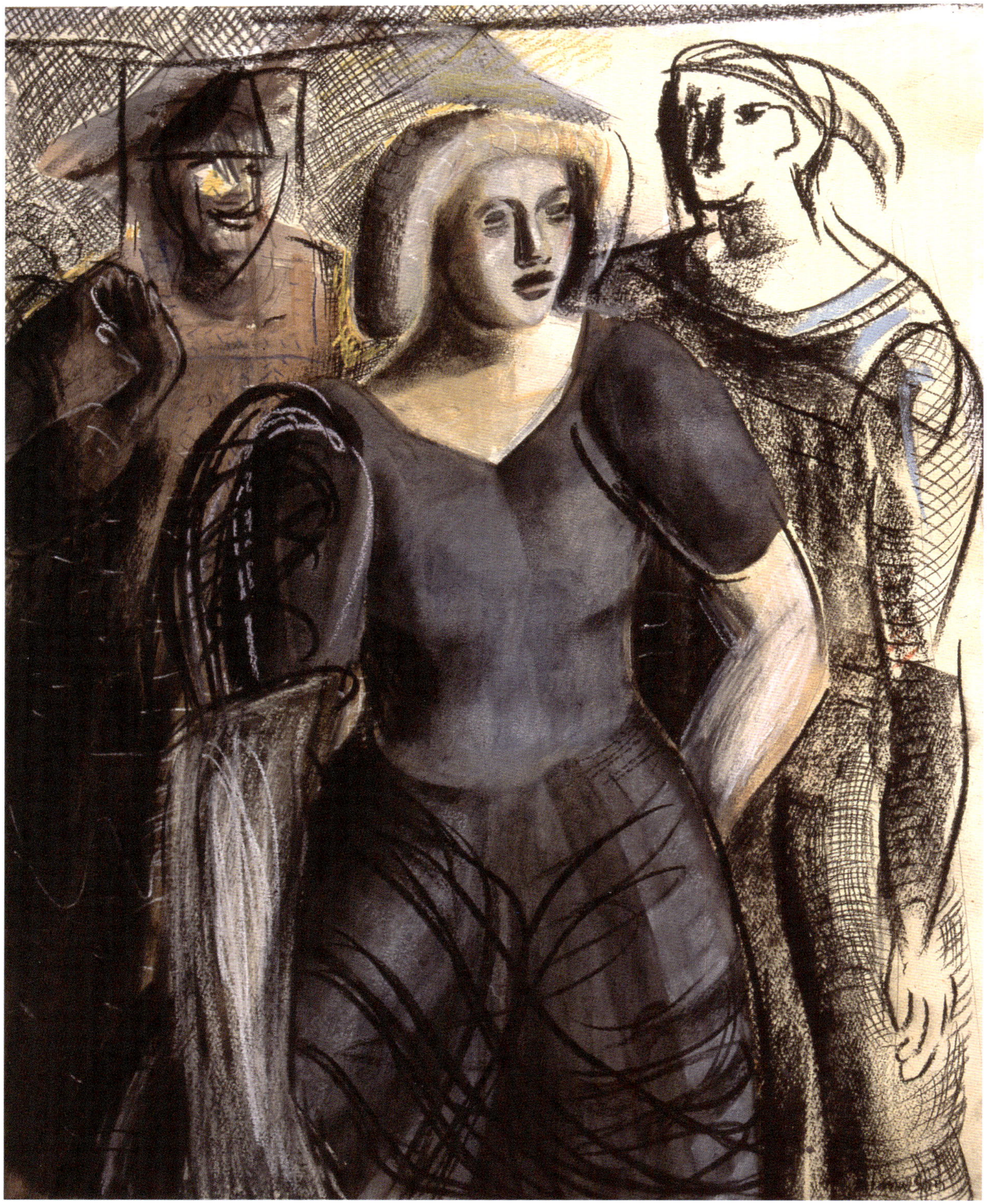

Actors III 1989, charcoal and watercolour, 98 x 60 cm

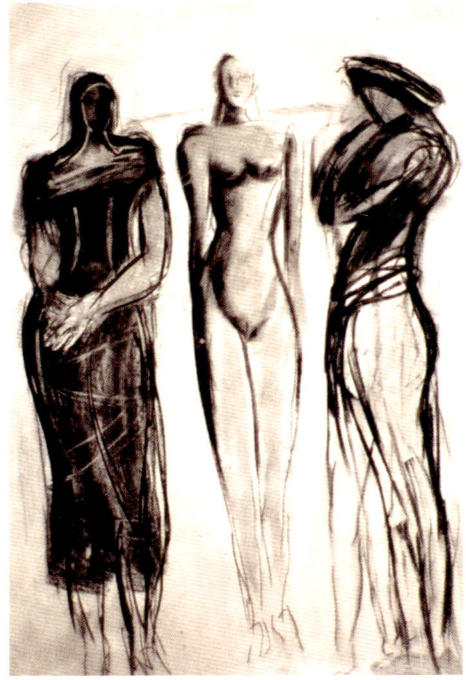

Three Standing Figures 1994, mixed media on paper, 96 x 71 cm

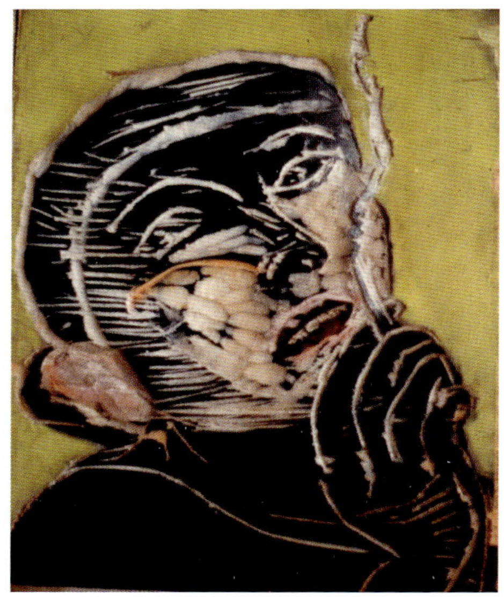

Man with Cigarette 1997, wood and oils, 23 x 20 cm

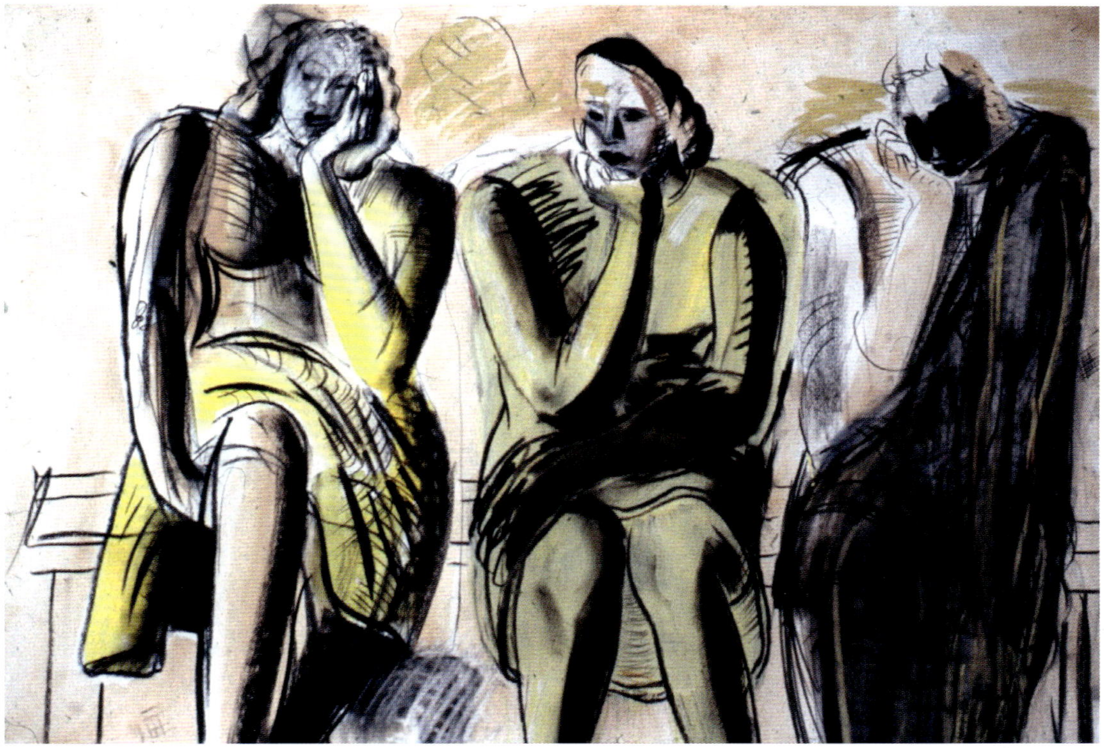

Three Seated Women 1993, charcoal and watercolour on paper, 81 × 108 cm

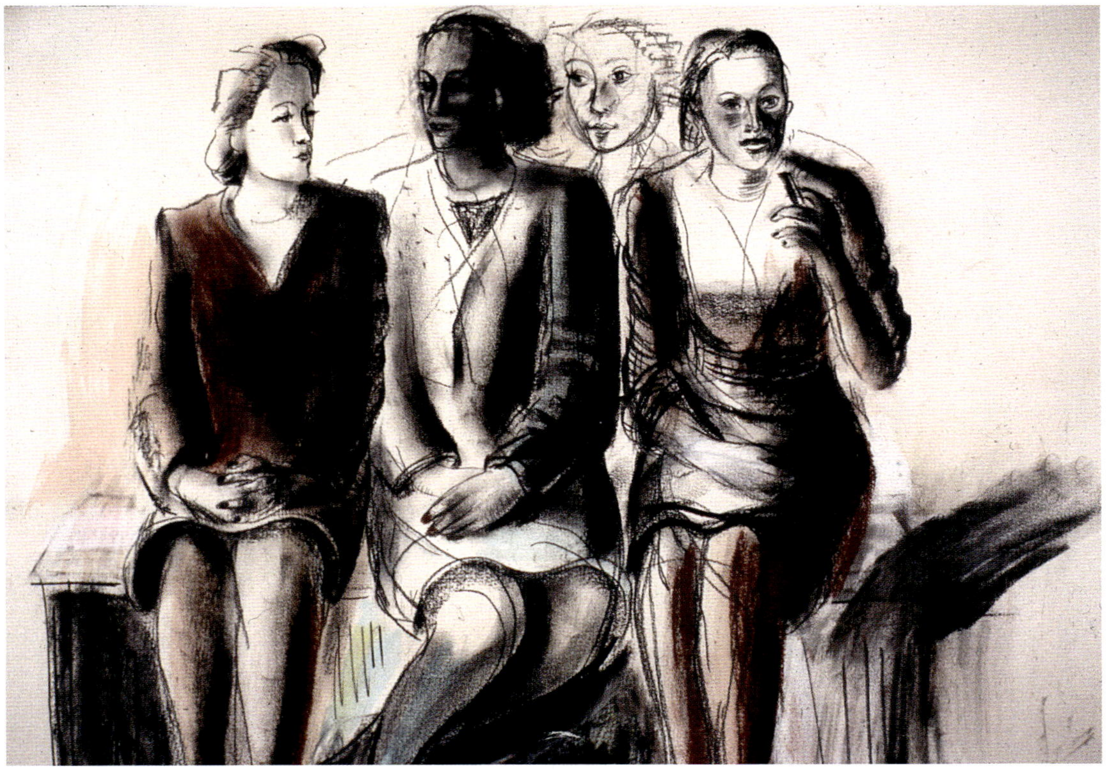

Four Friends 1993, charcoal and watercolour on paper, 81 × 108 cm

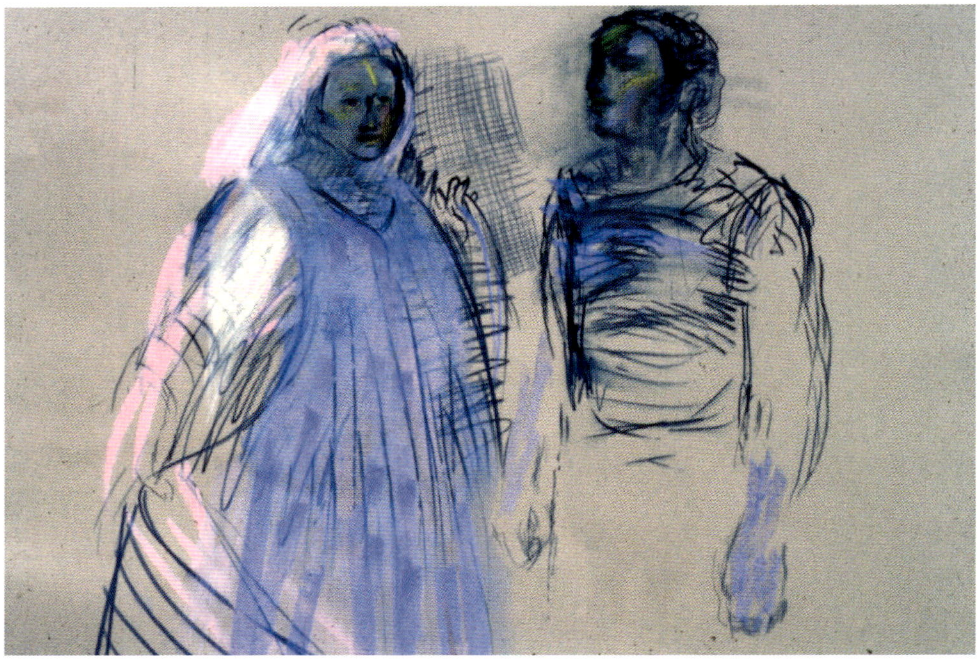

Man and Wife 1993, charcoal and watercolour, 52 x 60 cm

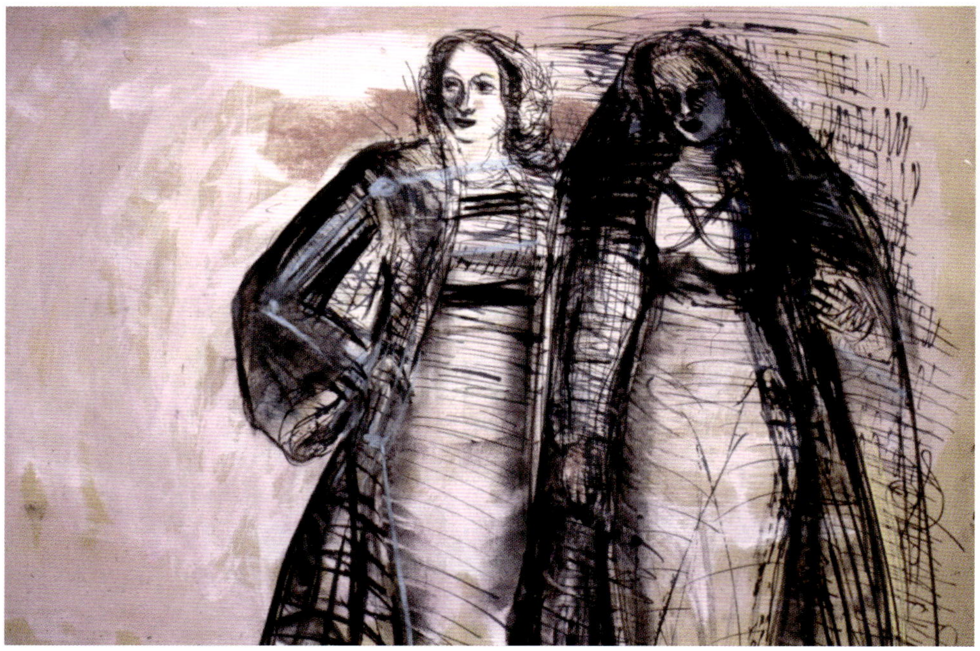

Two Spanish Women 1995, pen and ink, 58 x 78 cm

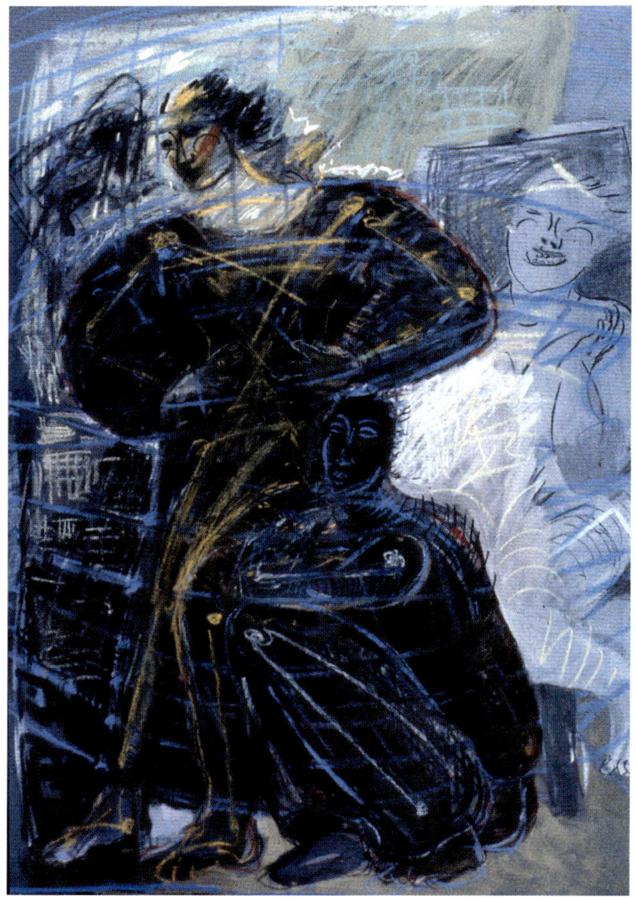

Actors I 1987, chalk and gouache, 98 x 60 cm

Chapter 7

> … whether the tree is made
> To speak or stand as a tree should
> Lifting its branches over lovers
> And moving as the wind moves,
> It is the longed-for, loved event,
> To be by another aloneness loved
>
> From 'Hilton Abstract' by W. S. Graham

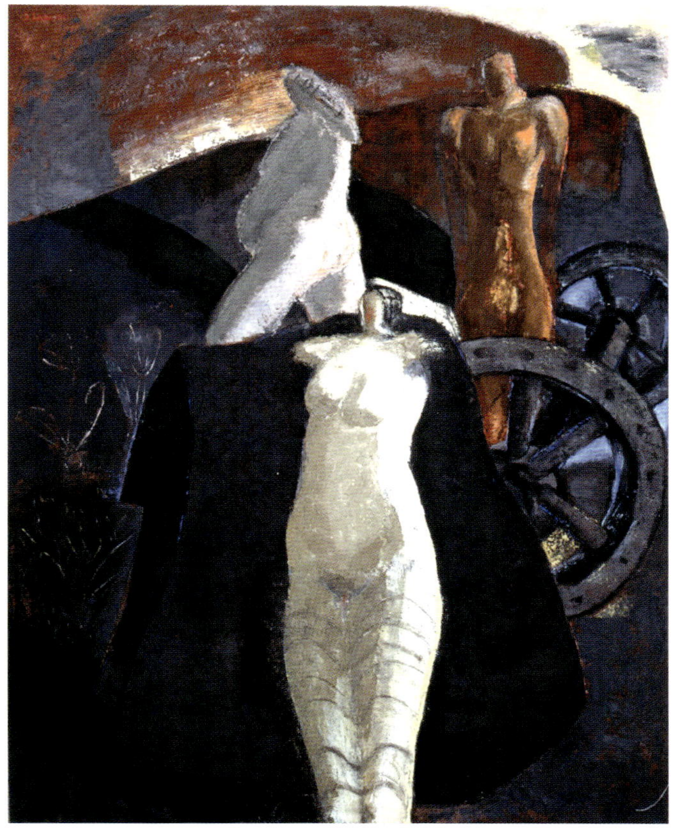

Upon the Great North Road 1992, oil on canvas, 153 x 122 cm

There was no question that, to begin with at least, the time and energy involved in looking after her mother full-time did have a serious impact on her painting – she couldn't even look for any help from her daughter Zoe who, aged 20, was now away at university studying art-history – and there are really only three or four major canvases datable to the years 1990–1991, *Time and*

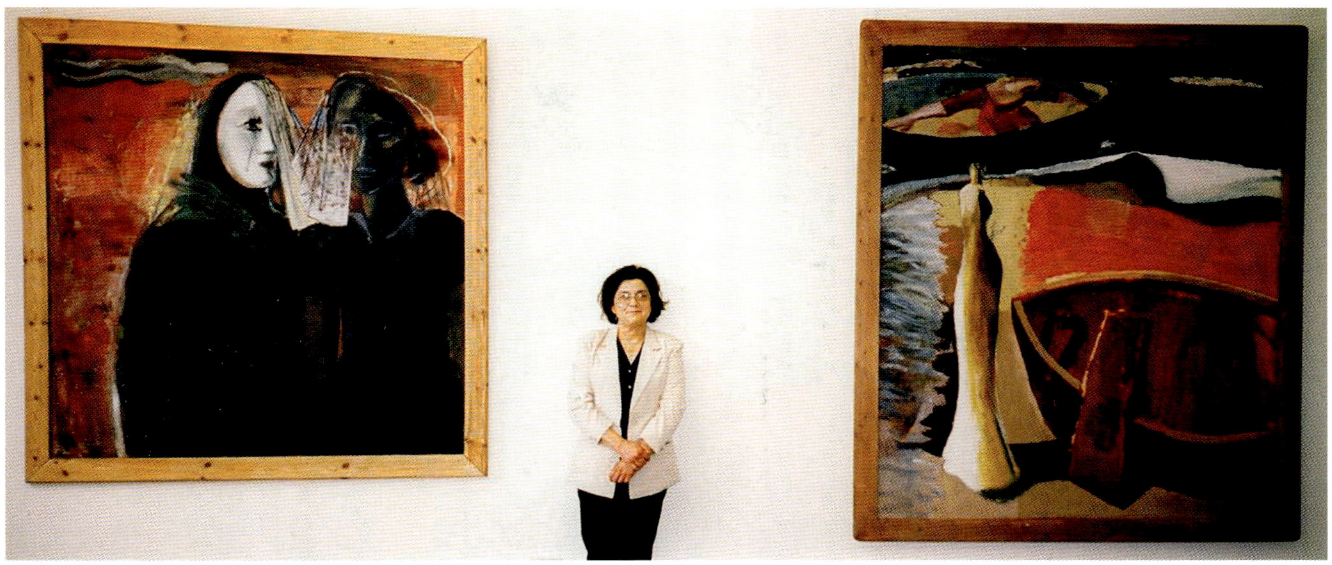

Sonia Lawson at Carlow Arts Festival, 2001, Eire. Solo invited exhibition.
Sonia shown standing between **Grieving Women** (1991) and **Shore** (1994)

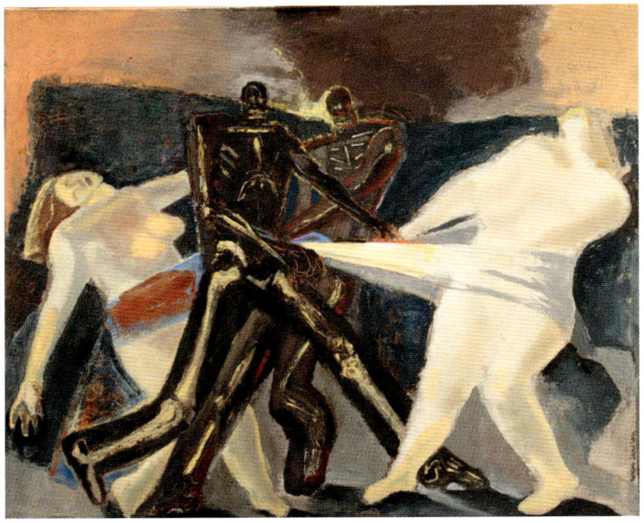

Time and the Maidens 1990

the Maidens (1990), *Boadicea and her Daughters* (c.1991) and *Grieving Women* (c.1991) and one remarkable smaller canvas *Down Among the Empty Boats* (1990). The most immediately striking thing about these paintings is their return, for the most part, to a sombre, almost monochrome colour range – essentially blacks, blue-greys, whites and earthy-browns with brief flashes of yellow and blood-red – and the greatly simplified compositions of weighty, monumental figures, for the most part female, set against the most minimal of landscape or even just plain backdrops. In this they pick up from the single or double studies of female figures she had started in the late 80s, though with the colour range now much reduced and the painted mark rather firmer and fiercer, the whole mood of these paintings changes utterly, the sensation of dreaming and reverie now being supplanted by an altogether harsher, almost more primitive and hierarchic quality that is, at times, not so very far removed from her 'humanitarian' paintings of the late 60s and early 70s such as the *Untitled Anti War* canvases.

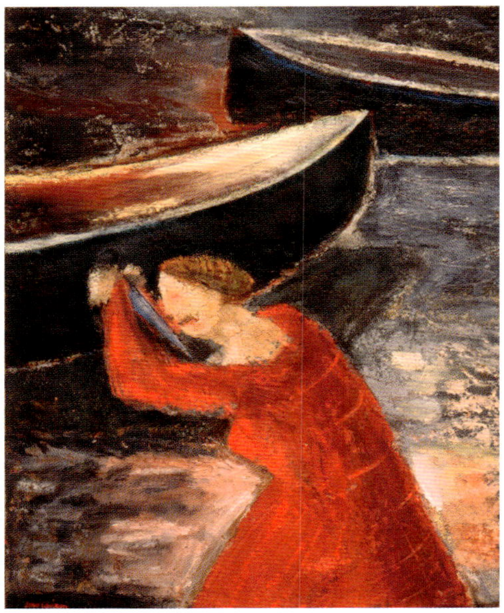

Down Among the Empty Boats 1990

In *Time and the Maidens* (1990), for example, two skeletal giants – their bone structure showing through their black-brown robot-like frames – haul two naked women mercilessly towards them with sheets in a violent, diagonally symmetrical, composition. It is a subject one of Sonia's particular heroes, Munch, once painted, though this bears little if any relationship to that work, being much closer in feeling almost to a medieval wall painting than anything else one can think of. The choice of subject matter is interesting too, seen in autobiographical terms perhaps as a realisation of her beloved mother's now increasingly imminent death. That realization certainly contributes to the feeling of despair that pervades the much smaller but equally ferocious little oil *Down Among the Empty Boats*, Sonia's own recent comments about it conveying as well as anything something of the complexities and levels of feeling that lie behind it: 'When people are *in extremis* they do dramatic, melodramatic things, but they are usually alone. The boats are empty – there is a hollowness about it all. An emptiness to do with loneliness and despair. Also there is a personal aspect. I knew no-one would buy it; it reflects a personal sense of despair one has at times. I like the sharpness of the white blade, small but vital. There is an intimacy between the dagger and the one who despairs. As in Millet's *The Pig Killers,* the knife is small but a savage light glints from it. The pig is dragged towards it yet somehow senses the potential violence of the small keen blade resting on the lip of the butcher's slab.' Its psychological honesty is uncompromising and universal, taking it well beyond being a statement of the simply personal as its inclusion in Ron Brown's 2001 book *The Art of Suicide* only confirms. Meanwhile something of the same dark atmosphere carries over into *Boadicea and her Daughters,* its ferocious, warlike mood underlined by the iron-grey landscape backdrop while the splashes of blood-red around the women's pudenda, suggesting sexual violence as well, are echoed in the glimpse of sky behind. Strong women united against injustice and cruelty is a recurring theme in Sonia's art and this painting should perhaps be seen again as a reworking of this theme in her painting from several decades earlier though here again it is, one senses, underscored also with a sense of personal grief at her mother's suffering.

As much as the subject matter itself, a fusion of personal, intellectual and historical associations, there are some significant developments now taking place in Lawson's work artistically as well, not just in the way it was painted, as has already been noted, but also in the now greatly simplified and powerfully sculptural forms of the monumental female figures. Sonia had always been greatly interested in sculpture – she had made a group of *ciment fondu* heads and abstract forms as a student at the Royal College (see Chapter 2) – and had spent a good deal of time in her student days, and since, studying in the British Museum, in particular the Egyptian Department. In this particular instance though, with their powerful sense of profound, weighty humanity the influence would seem to be more strongly from Cycladic and Archaic Greek standing figures and it gives to this composition an overriding sense of stillness, like great statues in a landscape, that is very much in contrast to the violence of the movement in *Time and the Maidens.*

Already though, by the time we get to the third in this group of paintings from 1990/1, *Grieving Women* (1991), you begin to feel Sonia working her way towards a creative resolution of the despair and frustration she had felt at her mother's helplessness and the problems it posed for her ability to continue painting at full stretch. There is, still, in the harsh redness of the background against which the two

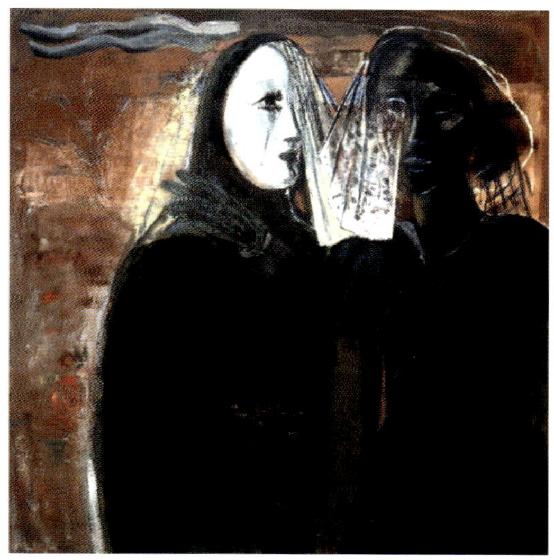

Grieving Women

women stand a strong suggestion of bloodstaining, some terrible event that is the cause of their grief. Equally though there is the calm dignity of the women as they grieve together, one in pale, mask-like semi-profile, the other in shadow, 'gazing into their own distances' as one critic aptly put it, conveying a powerful sense of presences wreathed in serenity. It is a painting which has, understandably enough, attracted a good deal of critical praise over the years, William Packer for example, writing about the painting in his review of the 1991 John Moores Liverpool 17 for the *Financial Times*, considering it 'the best thing in the show, positively Picasso-esque in its expressive symbolism'.

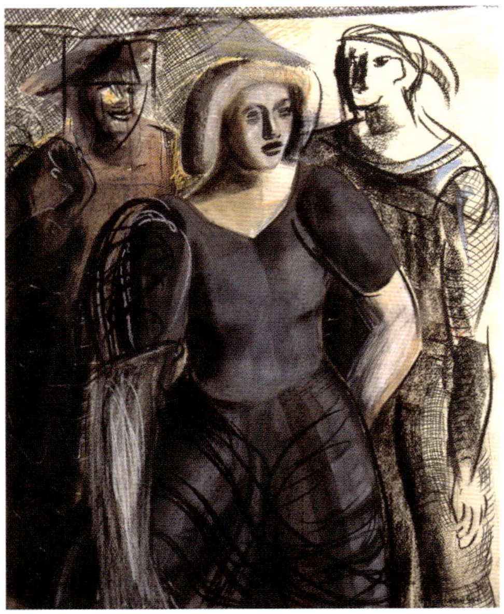

Actors III

Packer's comment about its Picasso-esque qualities also draws attention, albeit indirectly, to the other crucial aspect of this work, the now rather more obviously apparent influence of Sonia's drawing practice in her finished, exhibited work. Drawing had, of course, always been a crucial underpinning of all her major compositions since Royal College days but it was, for the most part, always simply a means to that end. As we have seen however, she had already started making a sequence of substantial pen or charcoal and watercolour, chalk and gouache or mixed media drawings towards the end of the 1980s and now, with less time and energy to take on major sequences of paintings, such drawings were to become, in themselves, an increasingly important expressive vehicle in their own right, works that could stand alongside her paintings on equal terms. Comparatively large in scale (for example 2'6" × 3'), they usually consisted of single as well as double and triple figure groups of women sitting and standing in, for the most part, companionable co-existence, for example *Ladies and Uninvited Time* (1992), *Three Seated Women* (1993), *Three Friends* (1993), *Three Standing Figures* (1994), *Actors III* (1989), *Seated Woman* (1997) and *Standing Girl* (1997). She was to write in 1995 in *Arts Review* 'I feel strongly about drawing. It stands like the mountains, the rest is like passing weather' and this captures well the unmistakably monumental and sculptural qualities of this series of drawings, Picasso-esque maybe but also living and breathing figures powerfully expressive of feminine solidarity in a way also far removed from Picasso.

There is apparent, too, both in these drawings of powerful, dignified women, as well as in *Grieving Women,* a distinct shift in her art as, once again, she absorbed the now hugely changed physical and emotional circumstances of her life and then began to find within them the grounds and need for a radical revision, not only of her subject matter but also for tackling certain pictorial and technical difficulties that she had become increasingly aware of towards the end of the 1980s.

In terms of the subject matter the now daily contact with her mother, though fraught with practical and emotional difficulties, above all the fact that her mother could not now walk, speak or look after herself, would seem nonetheless to have engendered a deepening of the always close mutual feeling between them. As her own daughter Zoe recorded in her catalogue essay on Muriel Metcalfe (2002) 'the two were able to share laughs together' while a doctor, visiting her for the first time 'said, with candid warmth "a wonderful spirit shines through her disability".' It seems to have become, at the same time, a period of profound inward reflectiveness and contemplation for Sonia and this is mirrored in the subject matter of many of the paintings and mixed media work of these years (1990–94) that now followed on from *Grieving Women*, for example, *Atlantic Watch* (1992), *Figure at the Prow* (1993), *Northern Shore* (1994), *Shore* (1994) and *Homage to Blake* (1994) and *Lone Figure Looking out to Sea* – all essentially depicting statuesque, solitary figures on desolate sea-shores. They are, in an obvious sense, about isolation and loneliness. In the catalogue introduction to her 1995 Boundary Gallery exhibition, Edward Lucie-Smith observes how 'she talks a lot about loneliness – about the death [1994] of the mother she cared for for many years and about her daughter growing up and leaving home' but as he also, quite rightly, warns that to 'see them as emblems of isolation alone would … clearly be simplistic'. For him they also 'have the air of being creatures from another world … products of the long-established British mystical tradition which descends from Blake himself …' Lucie-Smith takes that tradition right up to the present day, to Cecil Collins and Craigie Aitchison, while at the same time being careful to exempt Sonia from what he sees as some of the technical shortcomings of that tradition – primarily a lack of expertise in handling materials and a lack of energy in the forms themselves. That is a bold assertion perhaps but it does begin to get at the core of the other key problem for her work that Sonia was now attempting to address, namely the 'content' of the painted mark itself.

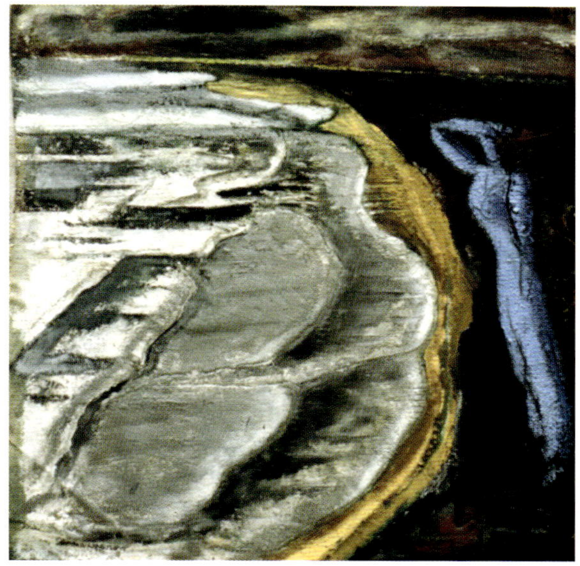

Atlantic Watch

Behind this concern lay a problem common to many contemporary figurative painters, namely the viewers' ineradicable obsession with reading these elements either as narratives or metaphors. Though neither in itself is a bad thing, it is just that they can tend to distract people from arriving at the much richer understanding of her art that derives, above all, from the intrinsic character of the painting process itself. Talking to Agi Katz of the Boundary Gallery for the catalogue of her same 1995 show there, she saw her latest work, with its figures wearing robes or shrouds, acting as 'symbols of people' which thereby freed the viewer and the work from what she, very bluntly, termed 'the tyranny of narrative appearance and the bonds of storytelling'. These were ideas very much at the forefront of her mind at this time as, a year later, writing at the time of her Dean Clough retrospective (1996), she went on to develop them with great lucidity, essentially outlining the programme that lies behind much of her work from 1992/3 onwards: ' My interest is to solve the problem of using recognizable

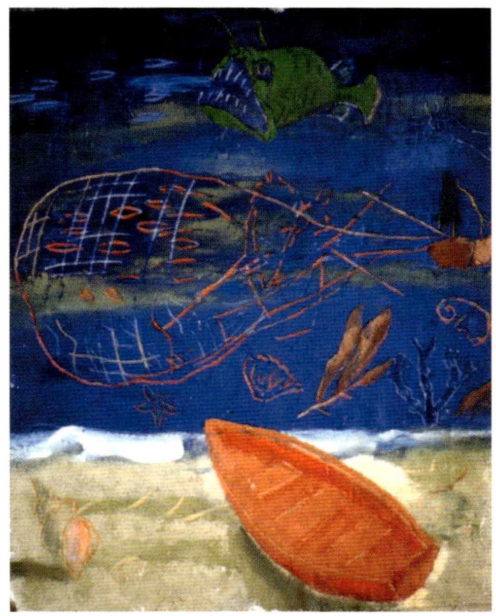

Little Red Boat 1999, oil on canvas, 55 x 40 cm

imagery, yet having the freedom of abstraction, evading the strictures of narrative, yet still using, say, a boat, a tree, a figure if I want to, and if I use them it is important to simultaneously try and break the bonds of familiarity. It makes credible why the German painter Georg Baselitz turns his paintings upside down – it is to escape the spectator's demand for an explanation – he's found his solution, I have to find mine. I don't want the figures to have an identity. I want them to be of no particular time or place and to be anonymous so that there is only an emotion or drama on the canvas.'

Quite apart from the robes and shrouds in which she now wrapped her figures, making them into hieratic, sculptural forms, Sonia started to apply this more generalizing, abstracting tendency to every element of the picture: a boat, as in *Figure at the Prow* (1993) for example, becomes an abstract curved triangle shape, in *Boats and Solitary Figure* (1994), a hollowed ellipse – or the sea, as in *Atlantic Watch* (1992), great semi-circular curves of green and yellow or, in *Lone Figure Looking Out to Sea* (1995), a rippling fan-shape of deep blues and turquoise green. It is interesting in this context to read Linda Saunders' record of a conversation with Sonia about this group of paintings in a *Modern Painters* article of 1996, which 'started off …just from the "emotion" of the sea and the sky' – 'when I realized what they were about – my mother and my aunt crossing the Styx – I put the figures in.'

Meanwhile, crucial also to these new, abstracting developments, had been the steady evolution of her painterly technique which had, by now, long since abandoned the loose, flickering quality of her 1980s work for a much denser, broader brushstroke. The effect is to help simplify the images, giving them in the process a much denser, more textured character or, as she put it to Agi Katz at the time, 'a wrought certainty of surface that is satisfying in itself', the result she was aiming at 'a compression like vegetation becoming coal, a tough, simple parcel packed with pent energy.' This sense of the materiality of the surface now increasingly took on an almost literal character as she started to mix wood dust, sand and other materials into the paint, allowing her to build up surfaces in an increasingly sculptural way. This is first apparent in her work from 1993 on, notably, the extraordinary little landscape oil, *The First of England* (1993), in which, in a play on the Pre-Raphaelite Ford Madox Brown's *The Last of England,* Sonia depicts the White Cliffs of Dover as a sequence of solid rectangles and sharp triangles in light and dark colours. She also starts to score heavily and rhythmically into the heavily-worked surfaces with the end of her paintbrush which, with their now heavily textured surfaces, take on the character of chalk and stone blocks. It was to become over the next few years a technique she would develop and expand to an increasingly complex degree and on paintings of much greater scale.

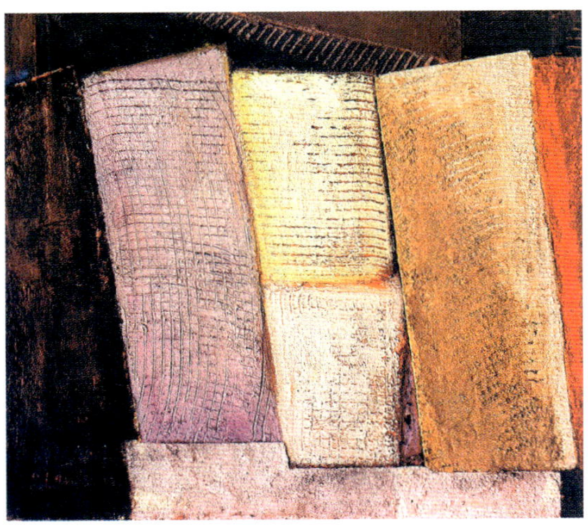

The First of England

The other significant effect of these new techniques becomes apparent in her approach to the painted mark and to colour which now take on a much weightier role than ever, no longer simply just part of the narrative description or, as she put it in an article in *Arts Review* in 1996 'not just for its own sake, which isn't enough, but as a potent integral aside.' Such thoughts, it would seem, had been on her mind since the end of the 1980s, when she had seen Kieślowski's *A Short Film about Killing* (1987) for, in this same *Arts Review* article, she goes on to reflect how she had 'always looked on Bergman's *The Seventh Seal* (1957), shot in black and white, as holding all the weight of passionate colour. I now see Kieślowski's film [*A Short Film about Killing*], shot in colour, as holding all the strength and intensity of black and white. Both directors succeed in engaging us so thoroughly by their characteristic minimalism. Their vision is what counts …' It was a revelation of enormous import for everything that has followed in her work up to the present day, freeing her up so that colour, texture and, through the process of incising into the paint, all her drawing had now become seamlessly and powerfully integrated in one increasingly powerful and flexible expressive whole. In an article for *Galleries* magazine in July 1996 I wrote how I felt that what had been happening in this recent work was 'a digging inwards into deeper layers of personal experience and memory, loss and pain, and an eruption outwards of more highly charged colour, more abstract form and, above all, a greater trust in the expressive possibilities of paint itself.' You only have to look at a painting like *Boats and Solitary Figure* (1994) with its icy blues and astringent lemony yellows set against rusty reds, velvety blacks and purply browns and you know intuitively what the painting is about with its Giacometti-esque figure standing by the ramp into the waiting boat as the dark waves role shoreward.

There was yet another outcome from these pictorial transformations in Sonia's work – it enabled her to achieve her effects on a much smaller scale than at any other previous point in her career. As she admitted in an article by Mary Sara in *Contemporary Art* (1996) that 'she had thought she could not paint small' but, as Sara shrewdly observed 'their comparative simplicity is deceptive. Her large canvases are places of possibilities; portals disclosing events; arenas for action – and feeling. The recent small works with their gritty compressed surfaces are sites of hard-won certainties; statements not questions.' Certainly these smaller canvases worked well for her when she had her second show at the Boundary Gallery in 1995, selling well, and they certainly formed a sizeable proportion of the works on show at her Dean Clough retrospective the following year. That show, with its remarkably strong and favourable critical reaction, proved an important moment in which, having made these huge changes to her working method, she considered her way forward. Where to take her hard-won discoveries?

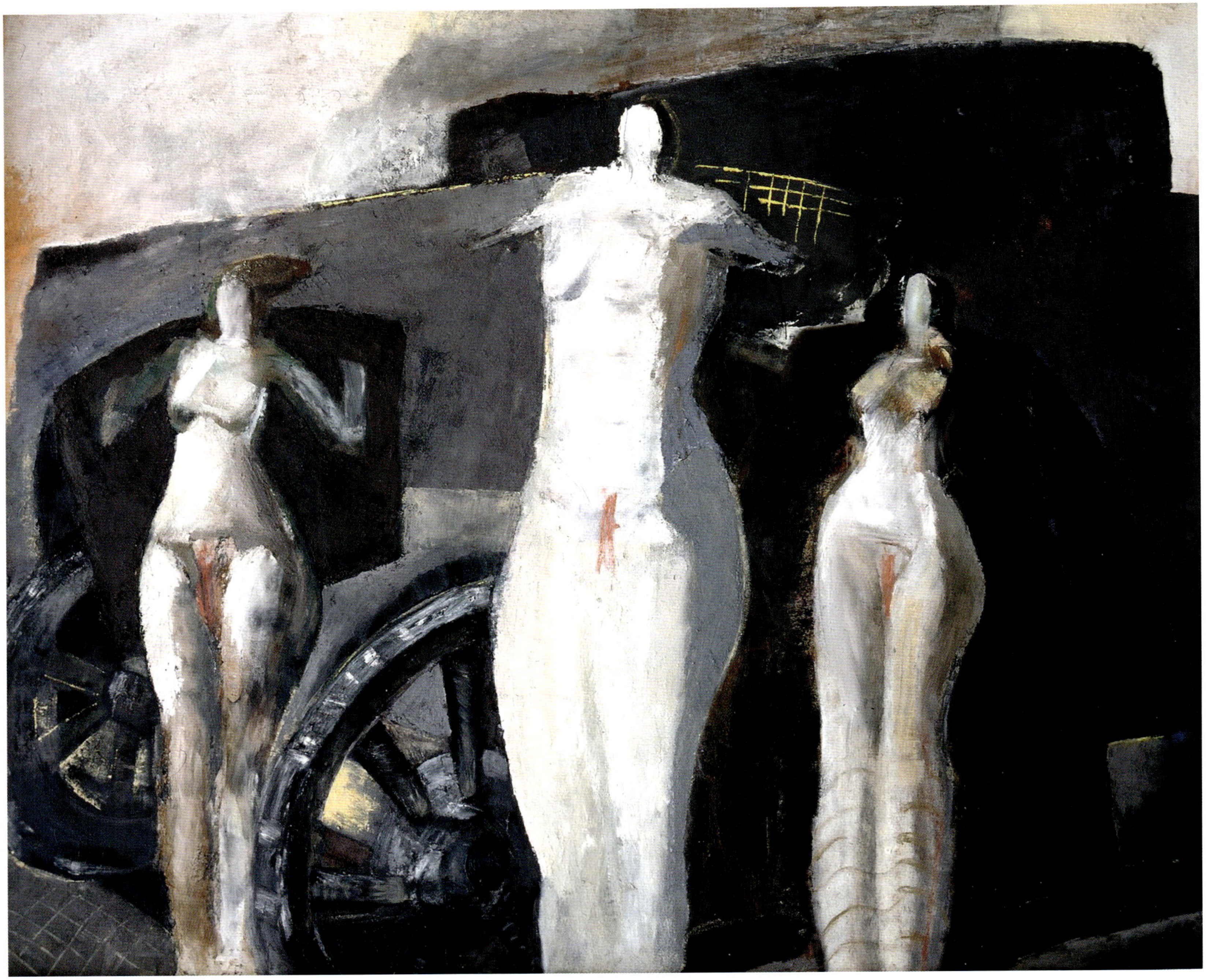

Boadicea and Her Daughters 1991, oil on canvas, 122 × 152 cm

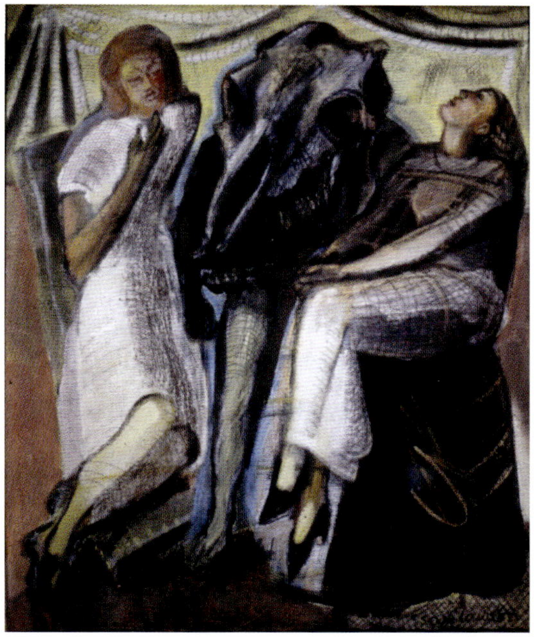

Ladies and Uninvited Time 1992, mixed media on paper, 82.5 × 70 cm

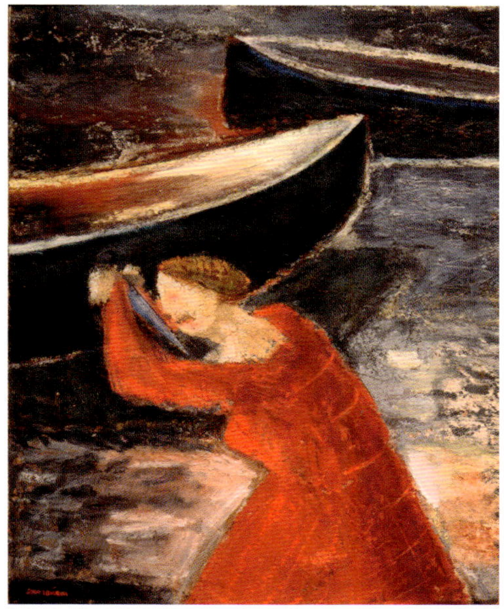

Down Among the Empty Boats 1990, oil on canvas, 46 × 36 cm

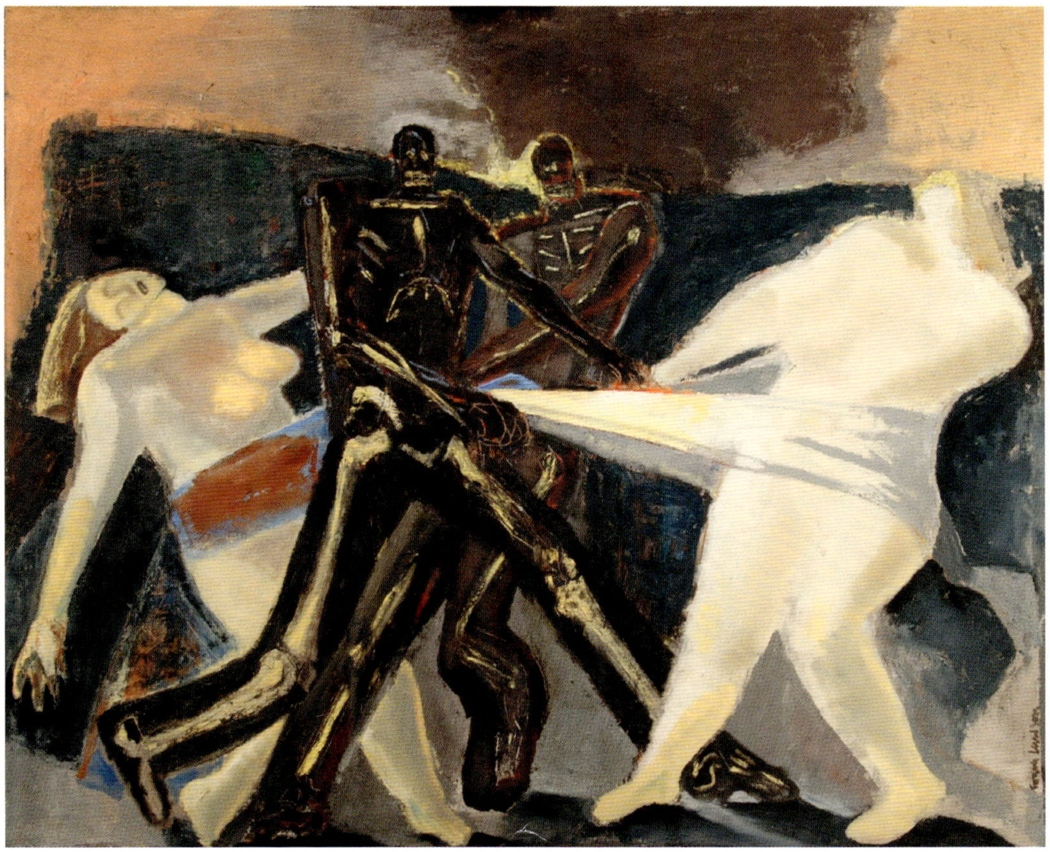

Time and the Maidens 1990, oil on canvas, 122 × 152 cm

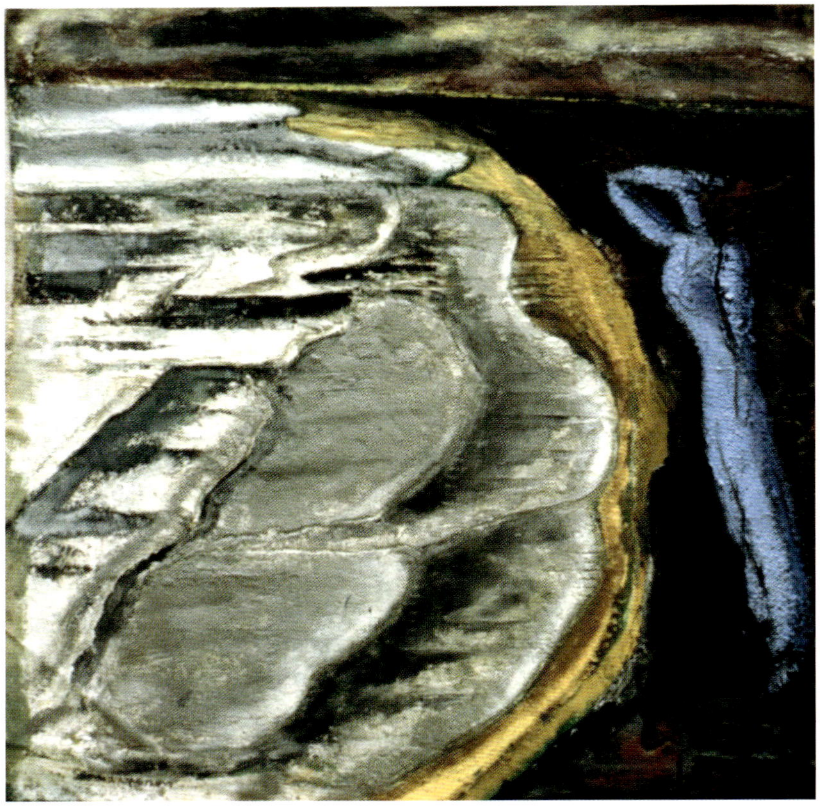

Atlantic Watch 1992, oil on canvas, 48 × 48 cm

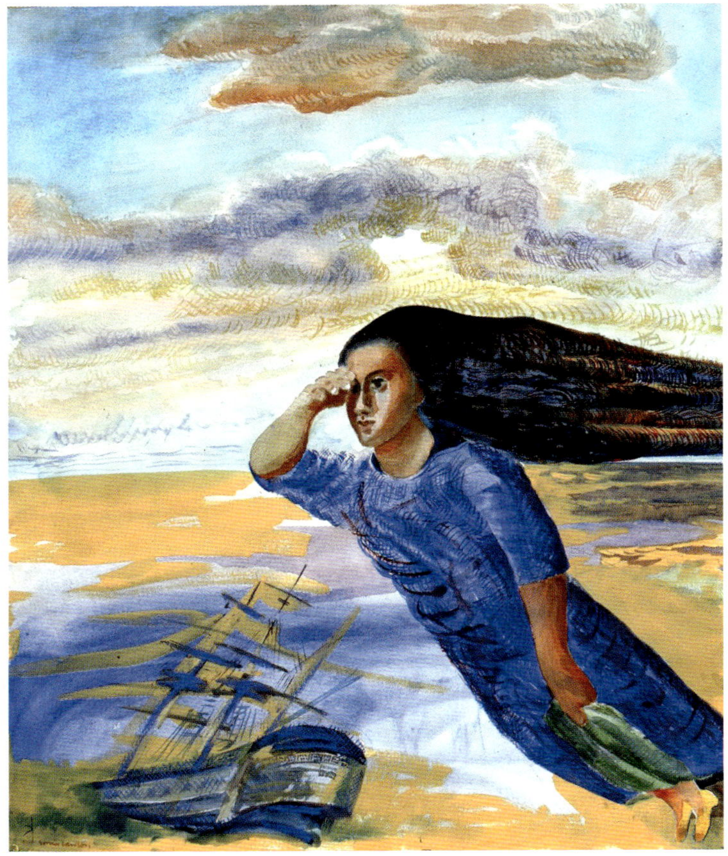

Lost Figurehead 1986, watercolour on paper, 60 × 50 cm

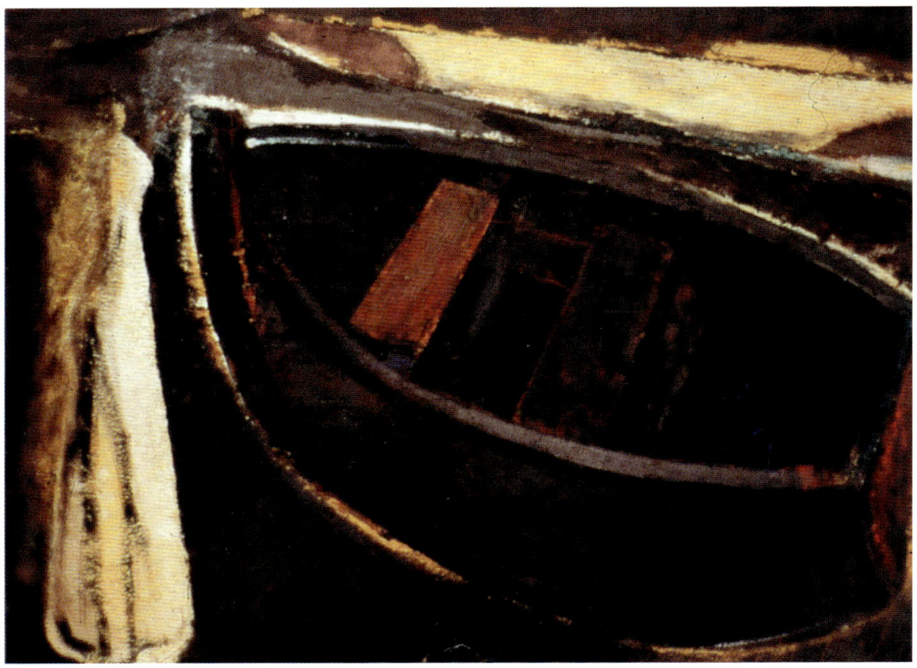

Northern Shore 1994, oil on canvas, 71.1 × 91.4 cm

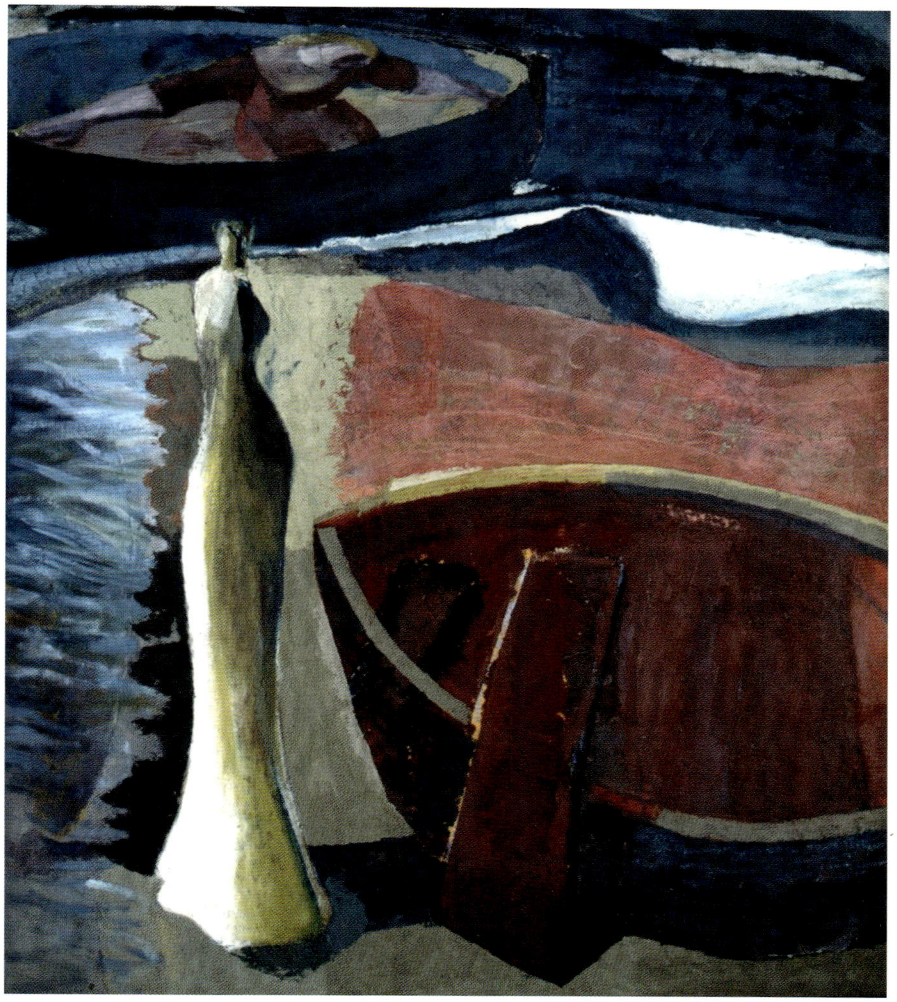

Shore 1994, oil on canvas, 189 x 169 cm

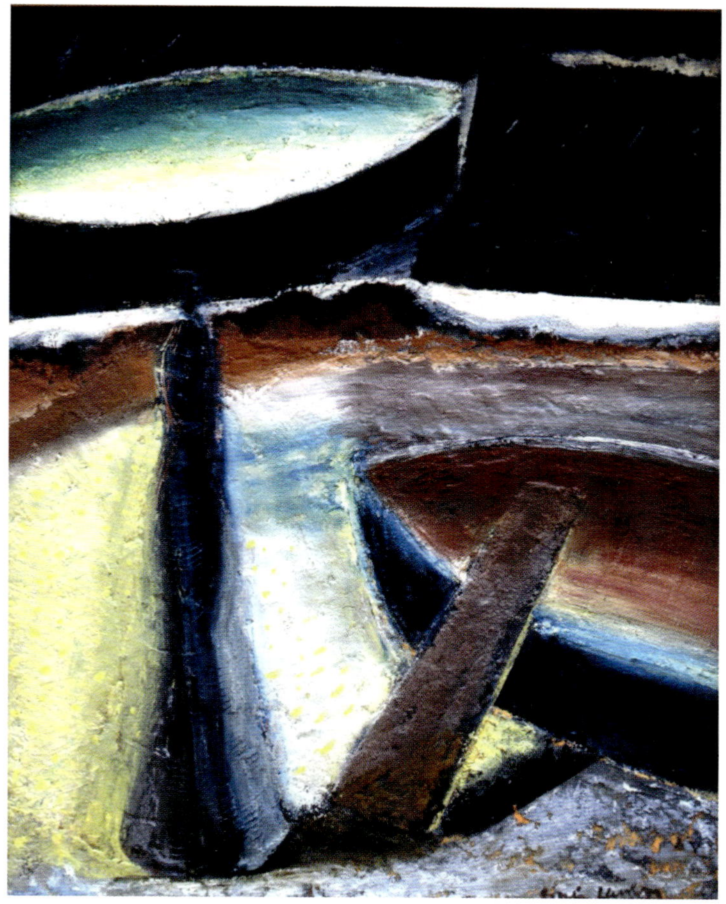

Boats and Solitary Figure 1994, oil on canvas, 61 x 51 cm

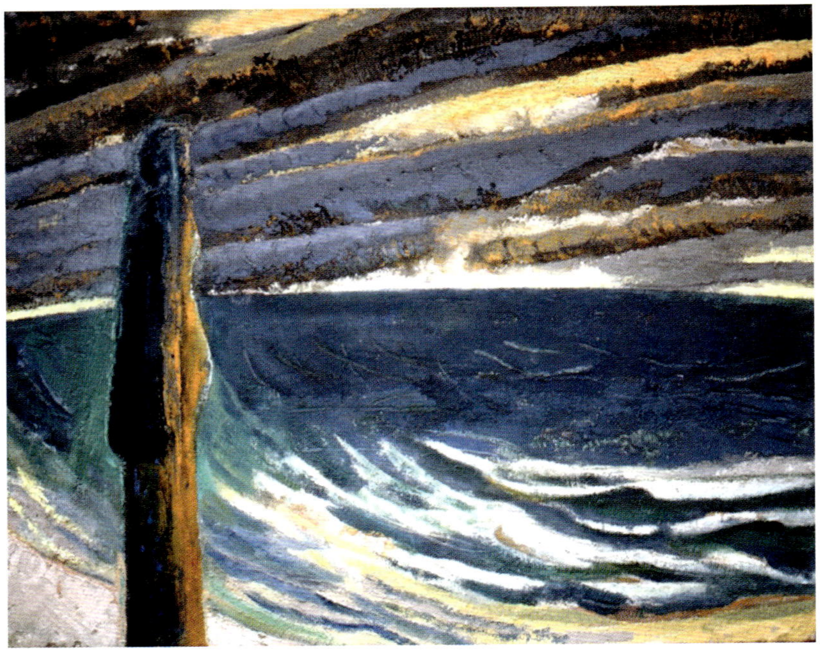

Lone Figure Looking Out to Sea 1995, oil on canvas, 53.3 × 70 cm

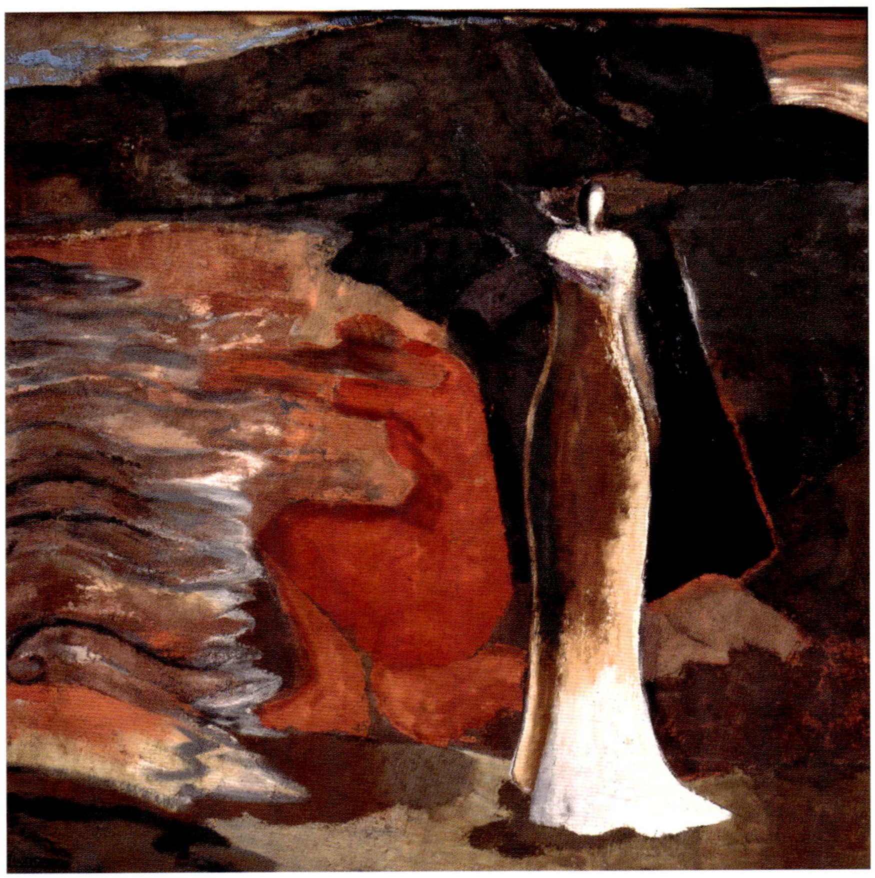

Homage to Blake c.1994, oil on canvas, 173 × 180 cm

Two works which flank the staircase, University Centre, Birmingham

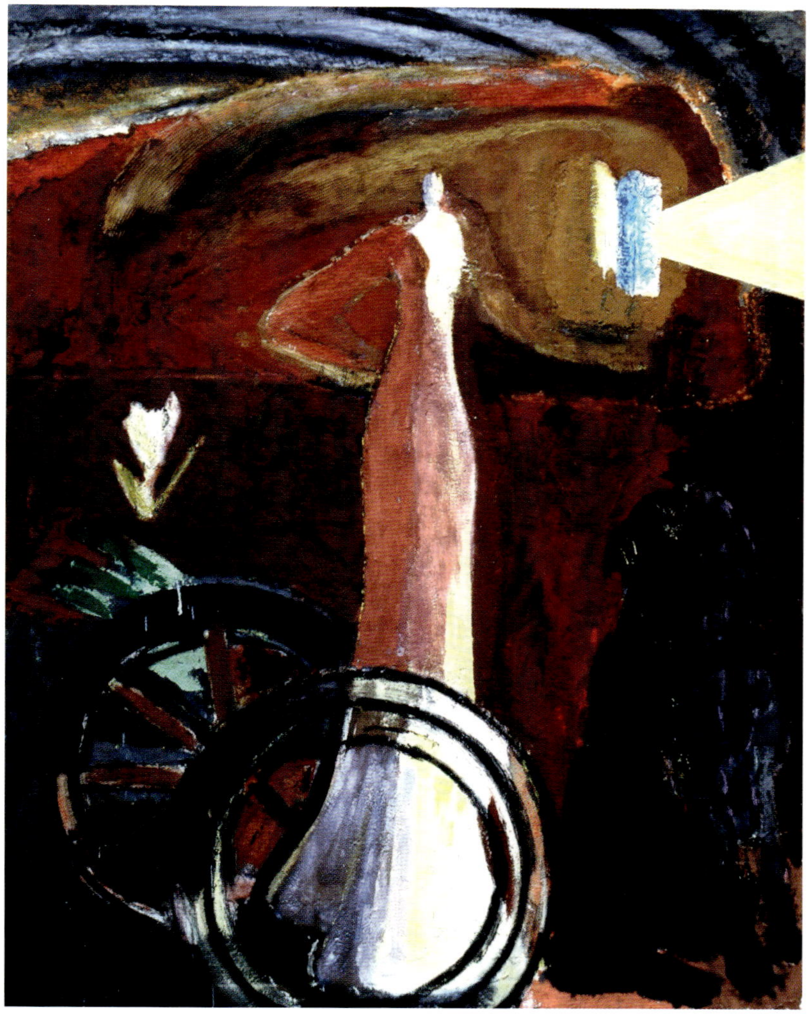

Guardian I 1994, oil on canvas, 152 x 124 cm

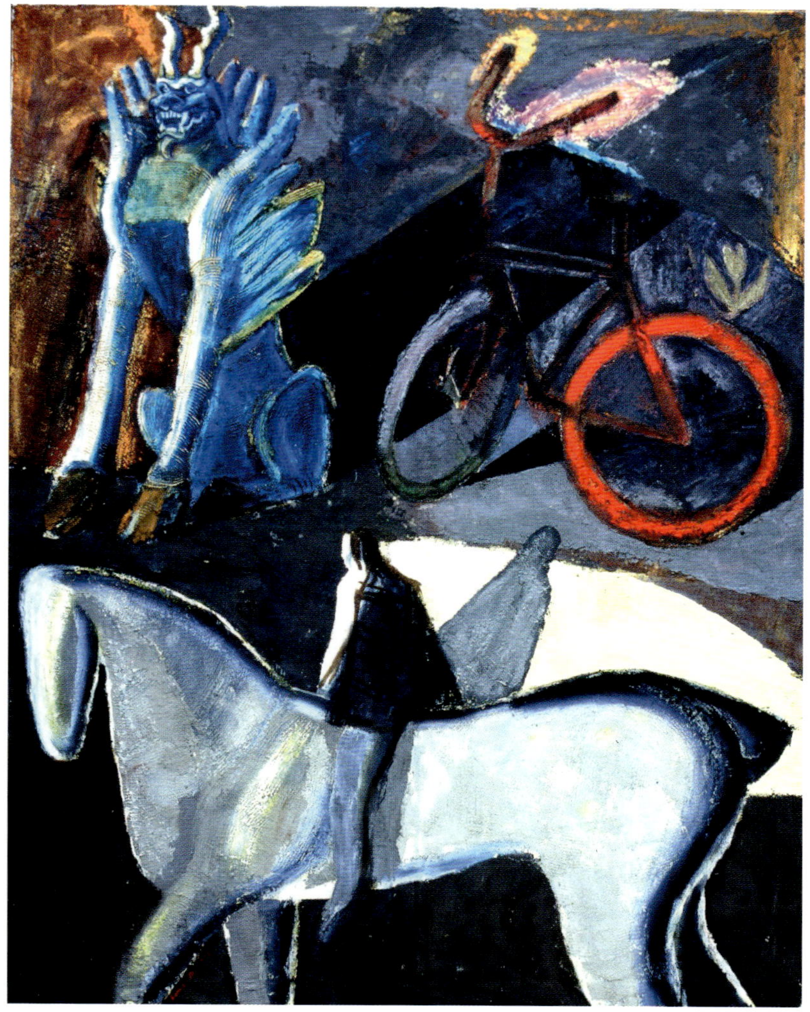

Guardian II 1994, oil on canvas, 152 x 124 cm

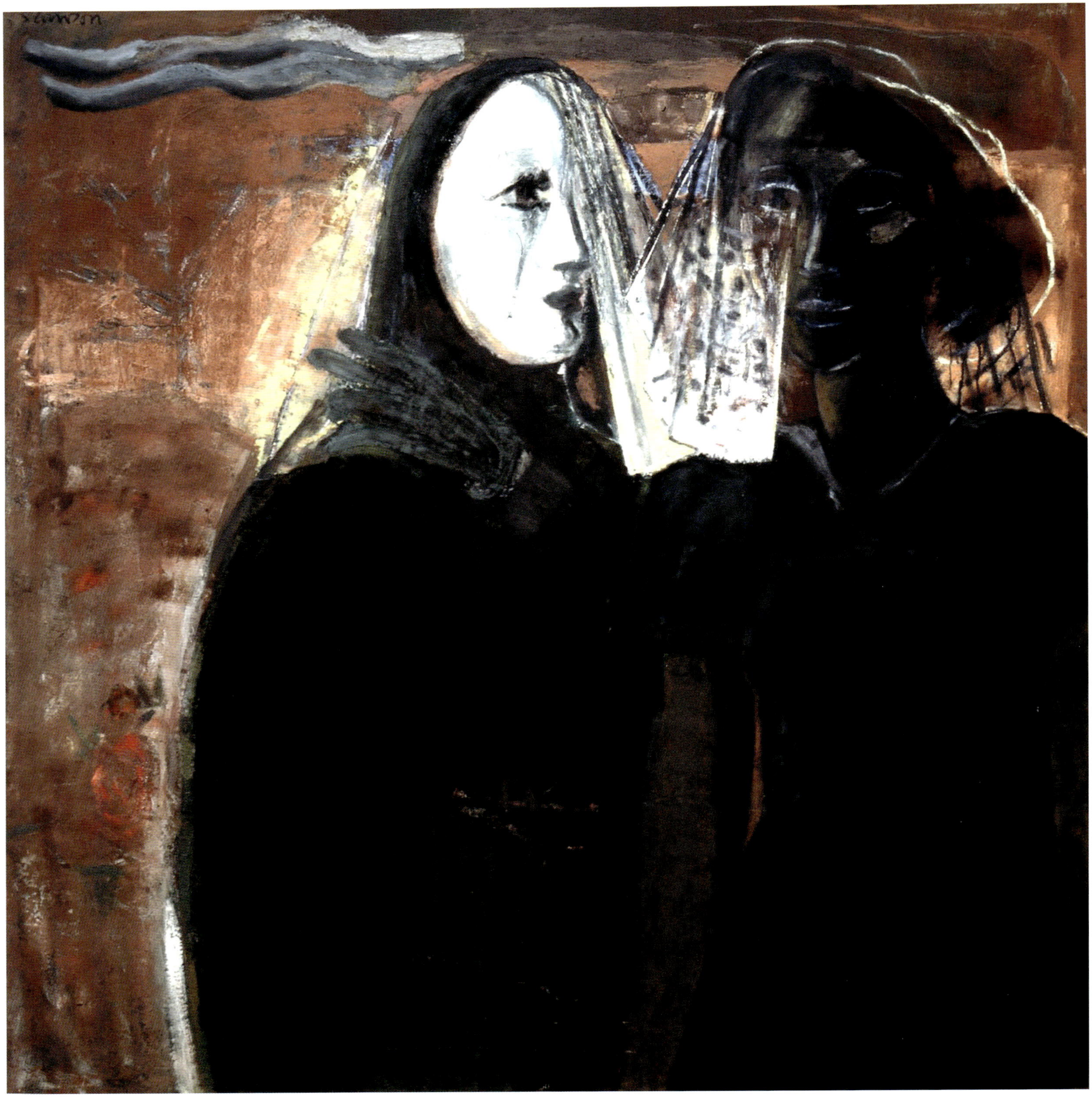

Grieving Women 1991, oil on canvas, 153 × 153 cm

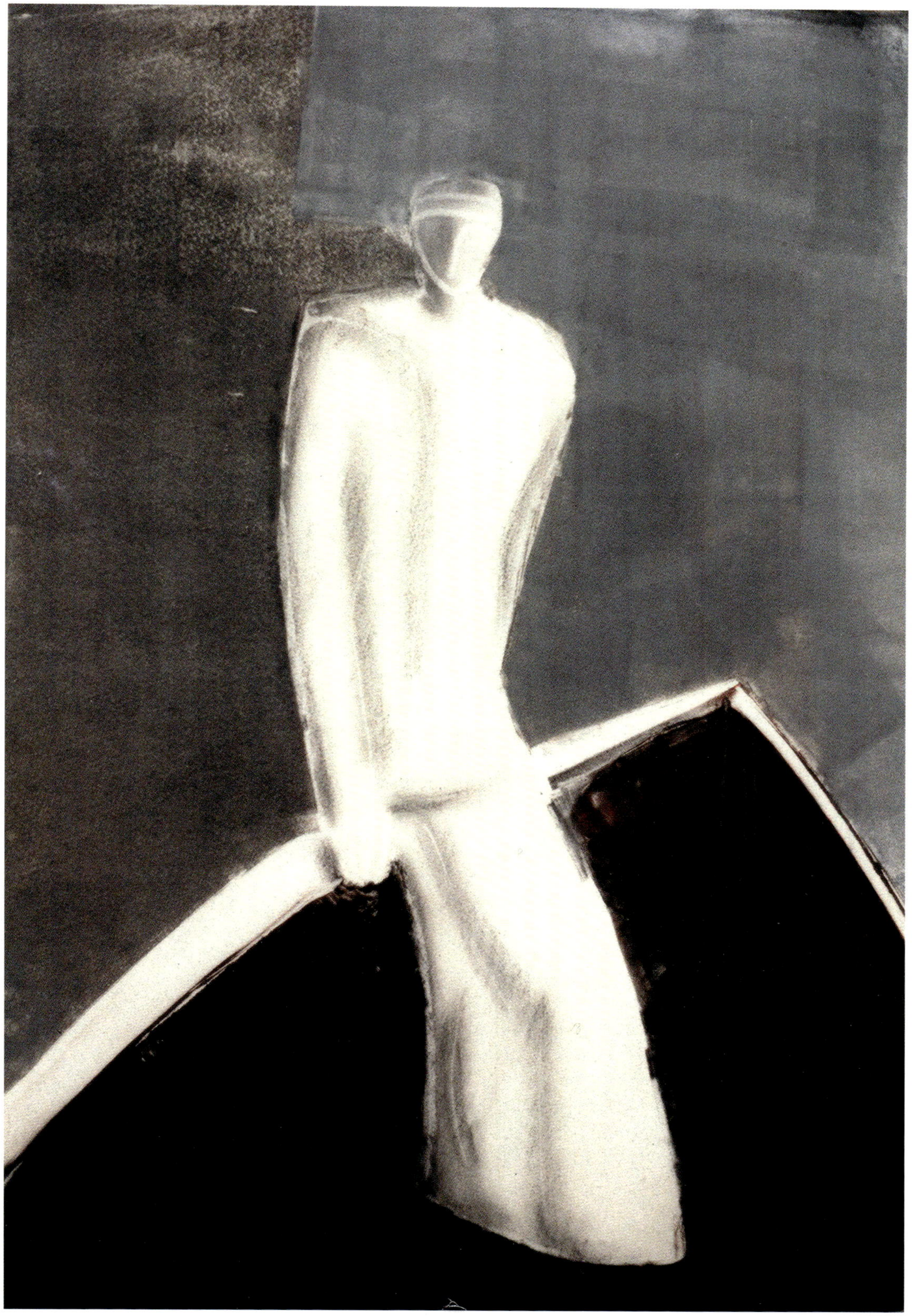

Figure at Prow 1993, mixed media on paper, 50 x 42 cm

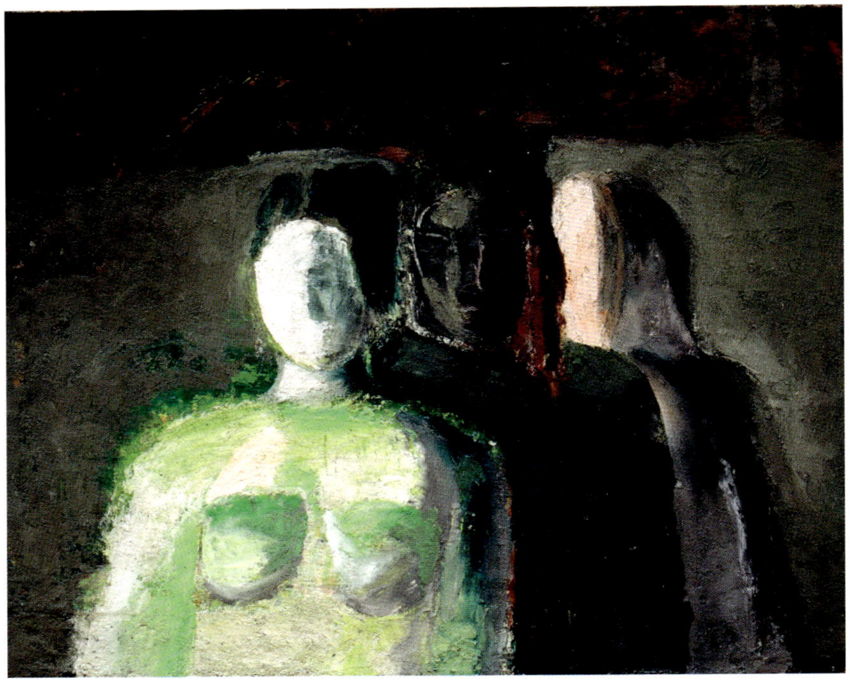

Three Woman 1993, oil on board, 62 x 78 cm

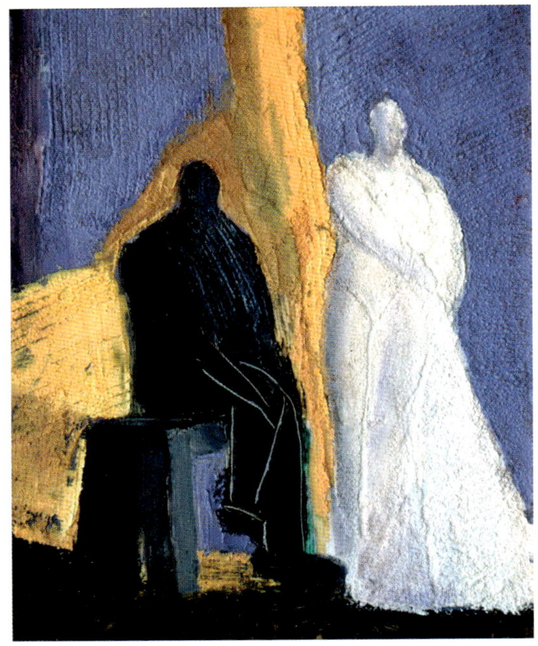

Dark and Light Figures 1995, oil on board, 33 x 26 cm

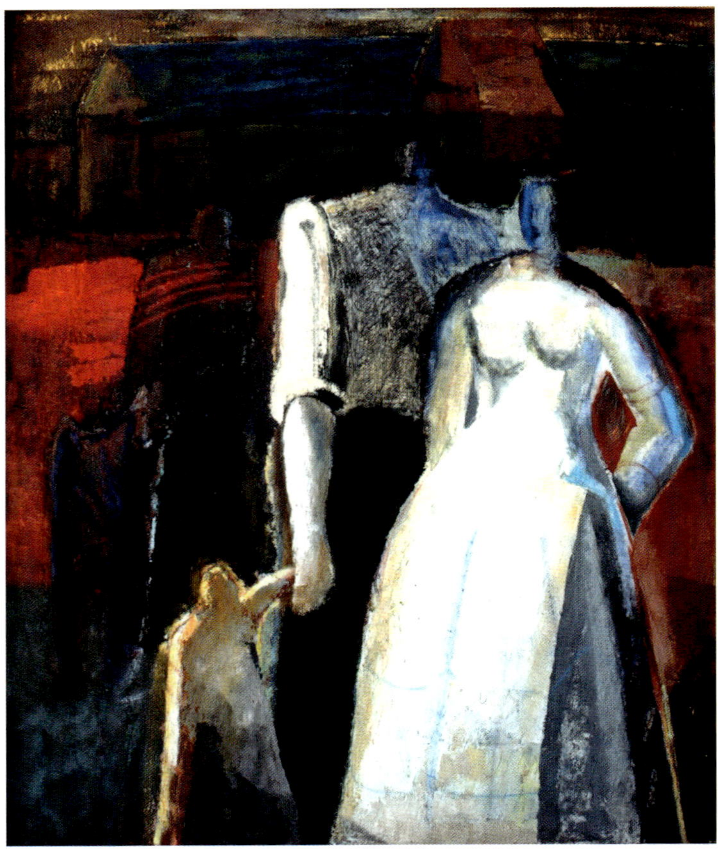

Small Family 1993, oil on canvas, 142 x 124 cm

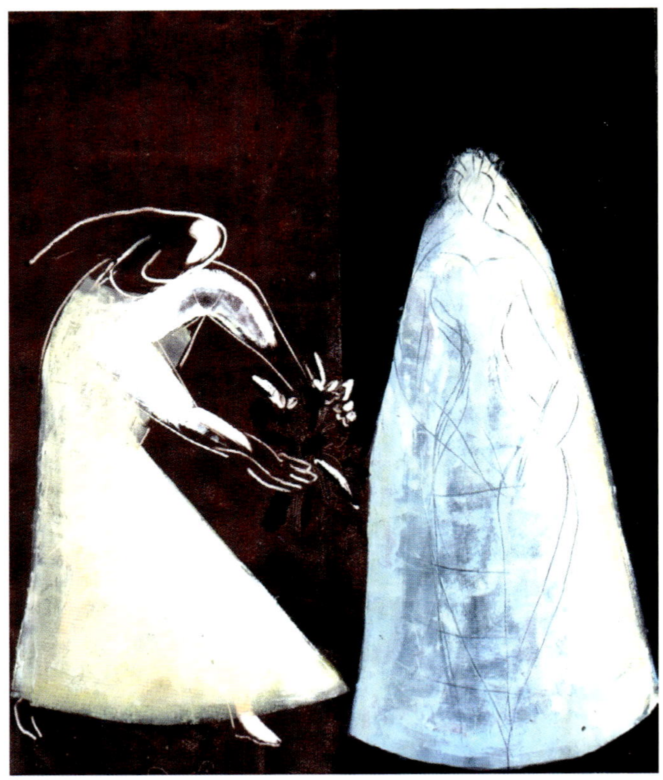

Bride and Bridesmaid 1994, mixed media on paper, 58 x 50 cm

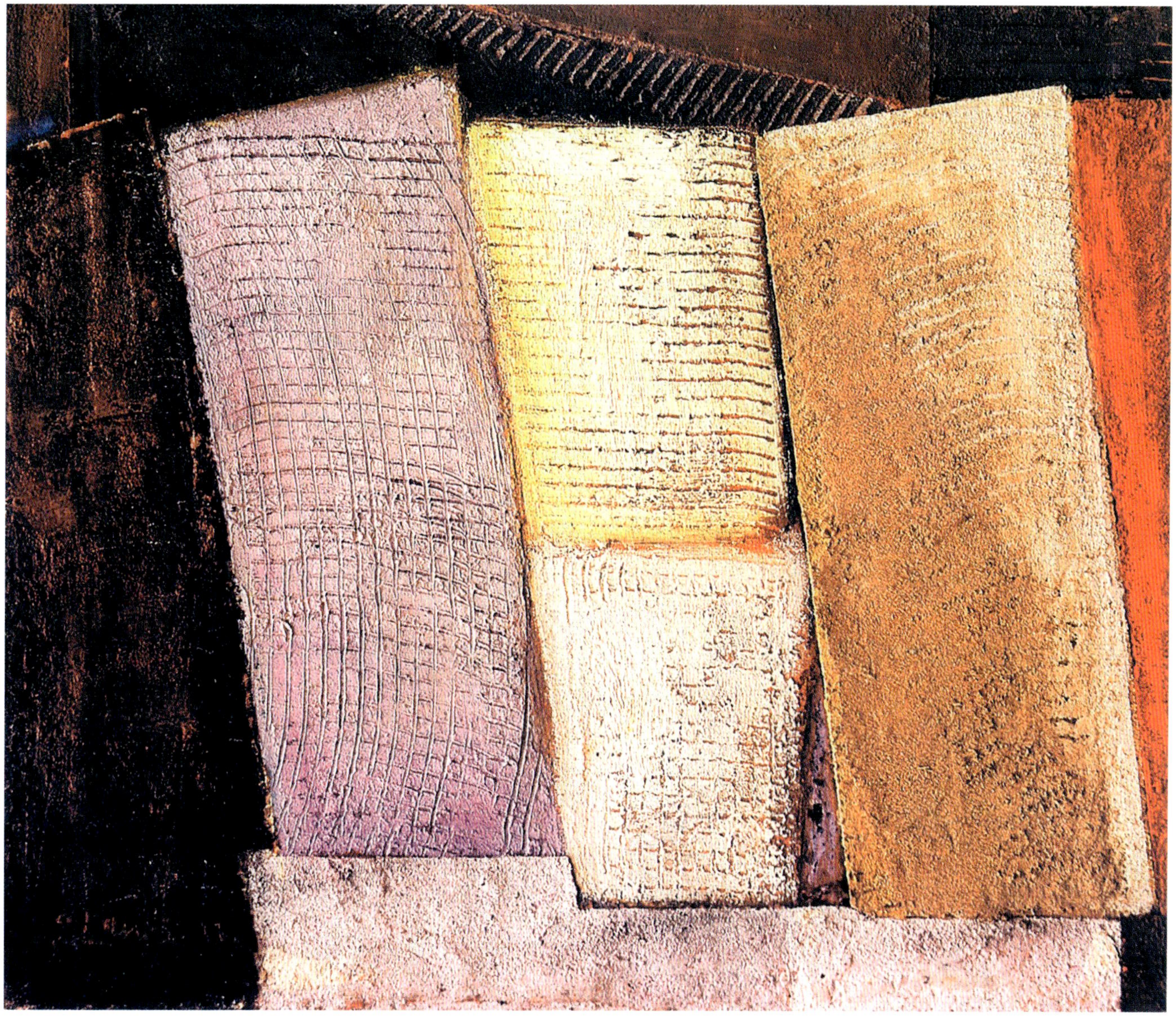

The First of England 1993–94, oil on canvas, 35.5 x 36.5 cm

Chapter 8

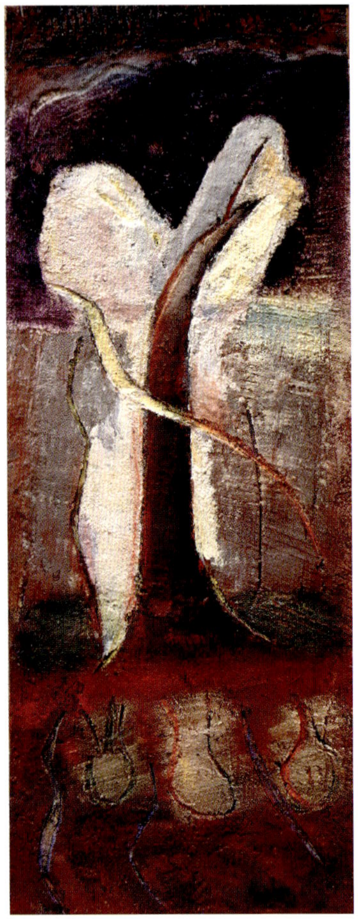

Spring Tree and Bulbs

> I know the Dales grit of my upbringing, landscape, weather, castles, abbeys, the sense of passing history yet the sense of the everlasting through these surrounding hills. Indelible influences making me what I am for good and ill.
>
> Sonia Lawson – from a letter to Nicholas Usherwood, November 1996

If the 60s and 70s had been a period when she had seen herself as an artist of conscience and accountability, the 80s a time for the exploration of a more personal and inward narrative, about family and the nature of creativity, and the early 90s a search for more formal and symbolic emotional archetypes, the decade or so that now follows, up to the present day, would seem to be one that looked to find a way of working that stylistically fused and emotionally satisfied all of these clearly integral elements of her artistic personality. In terms of both her personal life and her art this was now very much a time when she could finally start to make such a significant reappraisal; her mother had died in 1994 and, as full of grief as the moment must have been for her, you get the very strong sense also, from the course the work had taken through the early 90s, that Sonia had done something of her grieving before that moment and that there was, even by then, a range of ideas and techniques forming and being experimented with that would provide the basis for this next shift of direction.

The other key event in this process was, of course, the substantial retrospective show she had at the Dean Clough Gallery in Halifax in the late summer of 1996. Covering the whole of her career to date, judiciously selected, and with a perceptive biographical essay by the distinguished curator and art-historian Norbert Lynton, the first, remarkably, ever to attempt such a comprehensive overview of her work, the show achieved, for something taking place outside London, a very high level of critical coverage, all of it hugely favourable. Many of the substantial articles on her work already referred to in this book, notably Linda Saunders in *Modern Painters* and Mary Sara in *Contemporary Art*, were written in relation to this show while Ian Gale, in a warm and thoughtful review in *The Independent*, places her in a tradition that stretches back to the vengeful God of Blake and Palmer, through Turner, to the British neo-Romantic painters of the 1940s – Piper, Vaughan and Nash. He goes on to refer to her as an important and increasingly collected artist who has matured into a painter of outstanding ingenuity and originality, the work occupying an important position in the history of twentieth-century British Art, making a plea for Tate to use this occasion finally to buy a work of hers for the collection, a plea echoed over the years by other critics but, to date, always studiously ignored.

It was, in short, a good and positive moment in which to take stock and it was as an important part of doing just this that she and her daughter Zoe, now back from her studies and travels and starting to work in her father's business, took a trip together to Pompeii, Herculaneum and Paestum in the spring of 1997. Always interested in history and archaeology since her first visits as a student to the British Museum, the sight of the extraordinary remains at Pompeii with their intensely moving traces of human life cut suddenly short and, above all, that vivid life expressed in the exquisite murals, had an immediate and profound impact on her work. 'Going to Pompeii and seeing the streets and places intact, can allow a fellowship with these people, something one suspected but could not prove. Then suddenly a revelation and proof that this was life even 2000 years ago; such a joy. Wanting to do something that is an extension of this, to get that warmth into it, something alive' was her description of that moment, confirming to her that the technical direction she had started to take before her mother's death, namely the incising of drawn lines into the dense, rich pigments of her painted surfaces – a plump vigorous minimalism as she termed it – was absolutely the direction she now needed to take. She had already begun to see, too, how she might adapt this way of painting to the kind of much larger-scale work she now wanted to take up again. Many of the paintings she had completed since c.1993, the more experimental pieces particularly, like *The First of England, Boats and Solitary Figure, Three Women* and *Blue Rider,* had been on a comparatively modest scale, approximately one or two feet square. As we noted earlier, she herself had always been impressed by how well these smaller pieces held their own at the Royal Academy Summer shows but, for all that, they could not begin to contain the range and scope of ideas she now envisioned for her work. As a consequence, from 1996 on, she embarked on a series of large-scale works of a character quite unlike anything else that had gone before in her work, paintings that would draw together all the varied threads that had run through her work over the decades.

The passage from the letter to the author in November 1996 quoted at the head of this chapter provides something of the programme for this new series of paintings –

the landscape, weather, castles, abbeys, the sense of passing history and the sense of the everlasting in the surrounding hills of her beloved Wensleydale. Going on from that, there is the thoughtful recognition of the truth that places change us rather more than we can ever hope to change them and that that change is embedded in us as memory – not as nostalgia – in the way in which we give meaning to our experience of the physical world as sensate beings. She was well aware too she had in fact found a wonderfully apt pictorial metaphor for these kinds of themes, of history, archaeology and even geology, in the way she had started to incise into the paint itself, delving down to reveal something that comes to the surface as if it had held out against time and 'invites us into the circle' was how she put it to me recently.

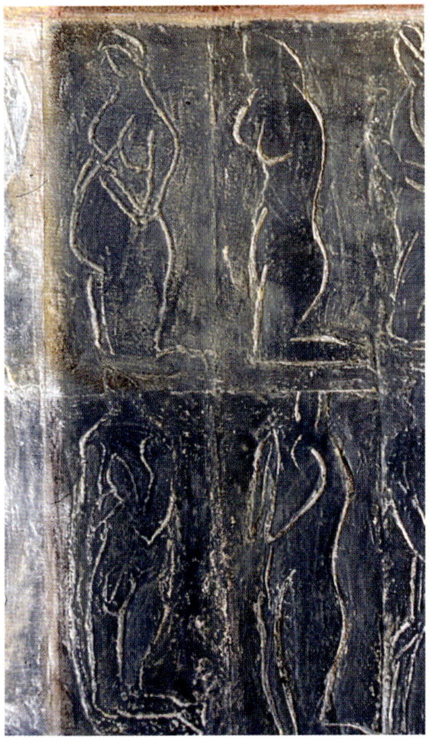

Detail from **Begging and Praying**

Equally important though was the need to find an overall compositional structure which could contain all these jostling, exuberant signs of human life and history and, again, Sonia quickly seems to have evolved a weighty and monumental compositional structure, one that, similarly, seems to embody the themes of landscape and the layering of human histories with a powerful degree of metaphorical and poetic resonance. *Herd* (1996) and *Begging and Praying* (1997) are the two key early canvases in this process, being made up of a series of rectangular, interlocking blocks of dense pigment of varying sizes and proportions into which are incised sequences of figures and animals, made either with the brush handle into the surface of the paint or cutting into the thick layers of pigment with a knife. Whichever technique, it is, in any meaningful sense, drawing and no longer drawing simply as an underpinning, vital though it has always been to the clarity and force of her work, but as an expressive element in its own right on equal terms to colour and surface.

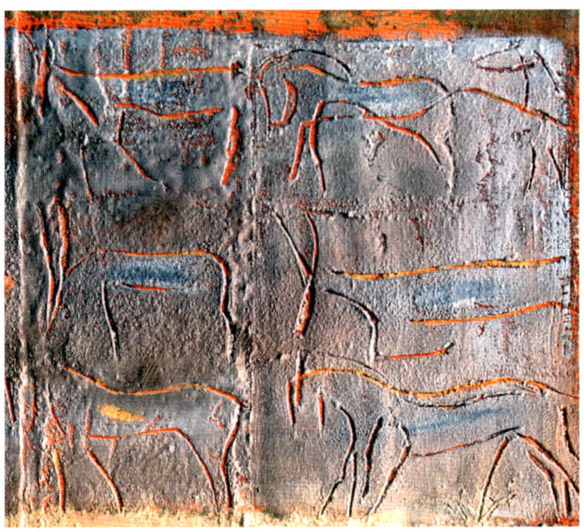

Detail from **Passing Animals (frieze)**

Talking to her at the time of her 1998 show at the Boundary Gallery about *Begging and Praying* she too was in no doubt that this scoring of the built-up surface with a brush-handle was very akin to drawing and done purely to carry a drawing on across the 'page' *ad infinitum* and to enjoy the involvement of the technicalities of surface build up. Making runes was her term for it and it is an apt phrase since the final effect in these two initial works and the stream of monumental works that now followed – *Passing Animals* (1998), *Stealth Warriors* (2000), *History Book II* (2000), *Verona I* (2002) and *Winter Solstice* (2002) – is to conjure up images that convey a feeling of enormous antiquity, not only of Neolithic cave paintings but Assyrian stone reliefs and Egyptian carvings too. And, paradoxically, in conveying the unmistakable sense of passing time, their surfaces almost seem to hum with life. That said, the sheer scale of these paintings can often make these quite delicate incised lines difficult to read in comparatively small-scale book and catalogue reproductions but something of their effect can be gained by the illustrations of small areas of surface detail that are

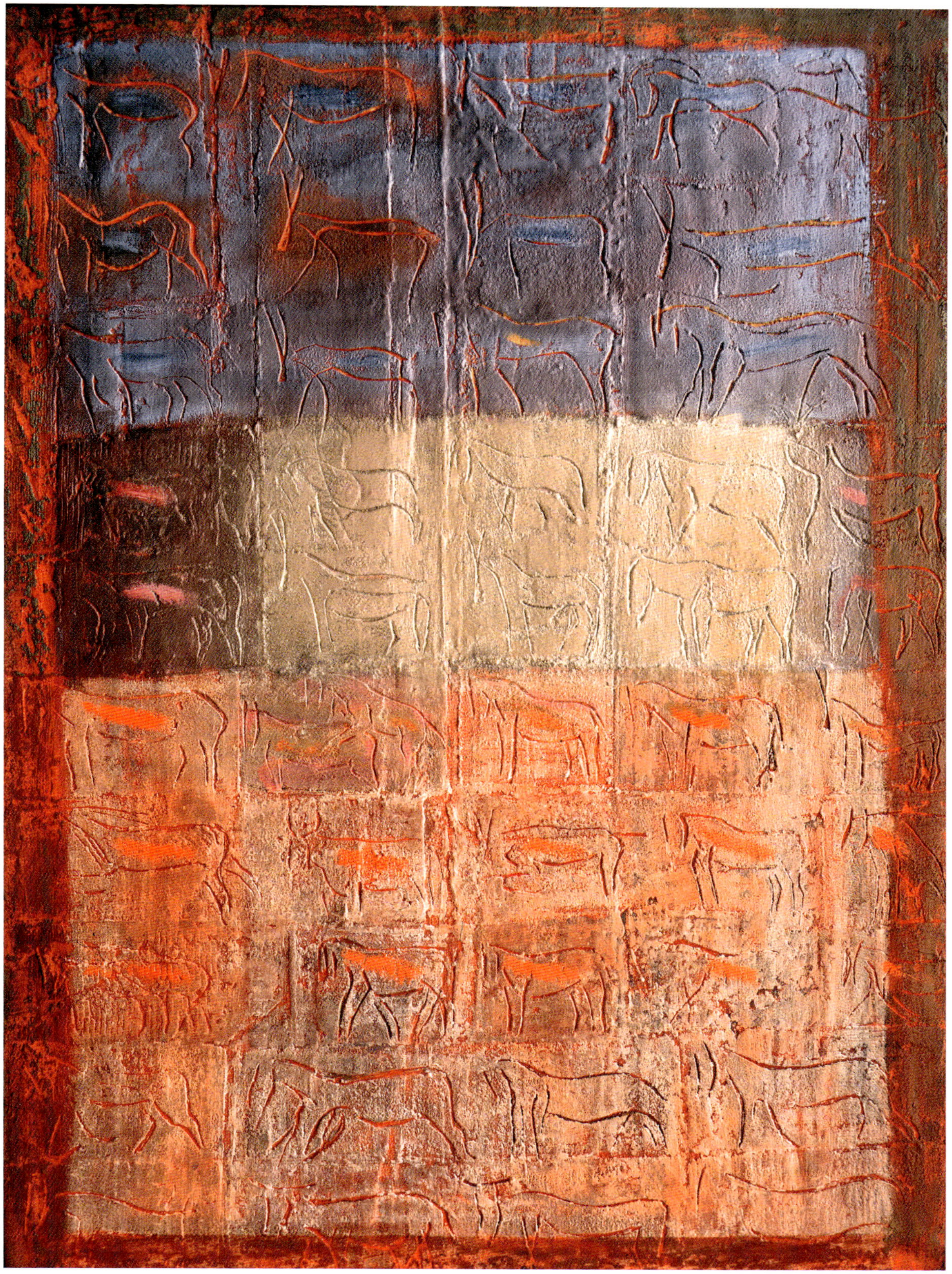

Passing Animals (frieze) 1998, oil on canvas mounted on board, 102 × 76 cm

shown here alongside some of the paintings from which they are taken. Notably, for example, from the top right-hand corner of *Passing Animals* where, with its roughly textured surface (again stone dust and other materials have been mixed in with the pigment) the feeling is that for a moment, you are almost looking at a detail from the walls of Lascaux or Altamira. And suddenly we become aware that we are back in Sonia's early childhood as well with those memories of snuggling up to the cows and other animals on her uncle's Wensleydale farm. Time in these paintings becomes circular rather than linear, not unlike the Native American idea of time as a deep, round, sacred lake.

It is precisely this ability to see how these continuities of feeling, the human march as she calls it, run through time, particularly her own time and experiences of it, as one history among many other human histories, that prevents these paintings and the flood of major canvases that have followed over the last decade from becoming dry, historicizing essays or studies in stylistic formalism. Her gift for then being able to convey those feelings entirely in terms of the process of painting and drawing is never anything short of astonishing. Thus in *Herd,* for example, when painting the great rectangular plates of sombre, steely grey and black metallic paint that form the 'stage', so to speak, for these runic drawings, she found herself remembering the dull sheen of the steam locomotives that used to plough up and down Wensleydale when she was a child. It is just this kind of precise visual focus which transforms them into such powerful artistic statements.

This compositional method was also able to provide a very flexible and fluid compositional structure and, alongside the painting/drawing technique she had now evolved, one that allowed for a wide range of moods and themes, not always so sombre and weighty as *Herd* or as curiously menacing as *Stealth Warrior* (2000). Her final show at Boundary Gallery in 2003, for example, was entitled 'Time Away' by which she was thinking of the human need for 'time away' in many of its manifestations, rest or restless travel, staying at home or meandering abroad and, in a work like *Verona I* (2002) with its friezes of panels in creamy whites, rusty reds and petrolly blues containing incised figures of horses, people and leaf forms, the mood is somehow lighter, the suggestion more of Roman reliefs and Early Renaissance murals than cave painting. The form develops interestingly as well, so that in a painting like *Siena* (2005), the abstract panels of colour bear a much greater weight of descriptive detail as the ranks of flag-bearing horsemen, both men and horses dressed in medieval costume – for the city's Palio – create an altogether more festive and exhilarating atmosphere. *Notes from a Secret Diary* (2005), from the same year on the other hand, is very different again, the sequences of smaller panels in rusty reds and blacks containing repeated motifs of lovers interspersed with leaf and tree forms and figure groups that create an intensely lyrical and poetic atmosphere.

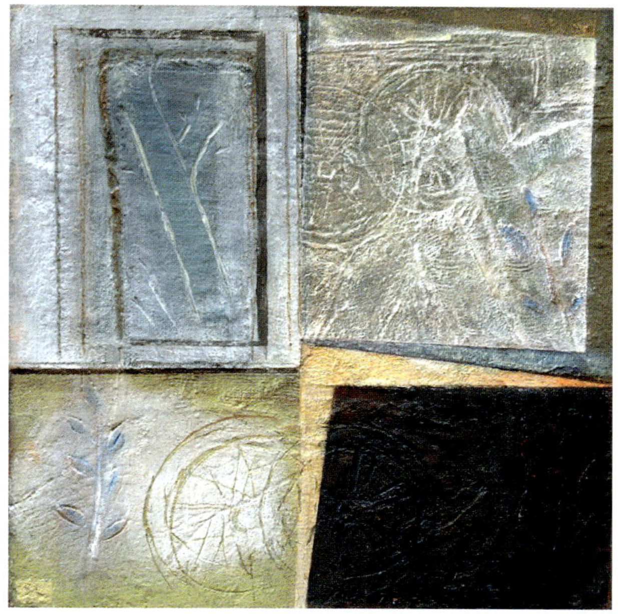

Rural Ride I

The same diversity is no less apparent meanwhile in the smaller paintings that she continued to paint alongside the larger canvases; her 2003 Boundary show contained a vivid diversity of themes and ideas – Pompeian memories of flowers, figures and birds, pale, cool semi-abstract landscapes and small multi-panel pieces – their chief divergence from the bigger works coming in the greater exuberance of colour and heavily-worked surface that their smaller scale made more possible pictorially. Thus, from 2003–2005, her smaller paintings changed again; semi-abstract compositions on landscape and interior themes like *Rural Ride I* (2003), *Rain on the Pane* (2005) and *Sound of Distant Waters* (2005) with heavily textured and incised surfaces in paler tones suggestive of water and rain – blue-greys, greens and creams, again both lyrical and witty in mood.

This mood could, in some ways, be seen as rather against the grain of her life at this moment; just two years before, in 2003, she had had to give up her teaching at the Royal Academy Schools after being diagnosed with Parkinson's Disease but even though the illness was naturally becoming very sapping of her energy for painting, she was still producing a quite remarkable quantity of work on an often very substantial scale like *Siena* (2005), *French Connection* (2005) and *Notes from a Secret Diary* (2005). And, in this same year too, she embarked on a new series of paintings of a rather different character again. Entitled 'River Shallows' and inspired by a book of poems by Linda Saunders (who had written on her work some nine years before for *Modern Painters*) called *She River*, there are four key works in the group – *River Shallows* (2005), *Dark Tarn* (2005), *Pond* (2005) and *She River* (2005). Taking *She River* as representative of a group of works that are stylistically very close in character, Sonia puts together a loose-knit pictorial structure out of two thick and sinuous vertical lines in textured grey-blue paint and a third fainter and straighter one over which she places what feels like a series of diaphanous screens of creamy-yellow, grey-blue and rusty-red horizontal blocks. Held within these webs of colour, shoals of small fish, incised in blue-grey can gradually be discerned as they make their way from one edge of the canvas to the other, as can small tree and plant forms while, over the top of all these layers of watery activity, the more distinct forms of dragonflies flicker and dart in deep, sparkling blues and yellowy-greens. Using an extraordinarily varied range of textured, incised lines and scorings, Sonia builds up quite the most remarkably tangible sensations – and distinctions between – the mediums of water and air that these creatures imply. It is not, in any conventional sense, the rendering of a river-bank but rather takes its cue from the original Saunders poem which opens with the words: 'The river girl has loosed her long plaits –/there she lies. Water does it all, uncoils/uncrimps and parts from where her small head/ crowns the current spreading a teasing weft/of ripples …' The wavy vertical lines thus represent the female form rather than river banks, as the fish which appear all over the picture surface, seem to recognize!

And it is in this dream-like, contemplative evocation of teeming life and sensate experiences of the world that this painting excels, a pictorial sensation that can, to my mind, only be compared to something in Indian or Chinese art, the work that keeps coming to mind above all being that of some of the 'Garden and the Cosmos' paintings from the Rajasthani Court in the seventeenth–nineteenth centuries with their flattening out of complex mental and physical spaces in great rivers of colour and mark, Earth and the Cosmos indivisibly linked in ecstatic pictorial meditation.

It is this quality of the ecstatic which marks out all the work Sonia has done since then and up to the present day. If the pace of production may have slowed over these last few years the intensity and power of the work seems to have grown proportionally stronger. Four main works – *Break of Day* (2009), *Night Drive* (2009), *Portal to Shangri-La* (2011) and *Night in a Private Garden* (2010) – stand out from this time as works which would seem to be a drawing together of so many strands in her work, not just of what had been happening over the previous 10–15 years but going back to the 80s and even earlier. *Break of Day,* the earliest of the series, continues that process of breaking down the more clear-cut blocks of colour begun in the 'She River' series with a flood of golden, almost Turner-esque light pouring down over a landscape filled with animal shapes, dissolving and flattening out everything in its path. Yorkshire, Italy and the great light and colour-filled compositions of the early 80s are all here.

She took this process still further that same year with *Night Drive* which, with its myriad small panels of reds and purple-blacks filled with star-bursts of brilliant light and swirling circular forms across which deer and other animal forms race, begins to take the form of a Persian carpet or tapestry design. The subject meanwhile seems to hark back to long-remembered night-walks back to her parents' house in Castle Bolton as much as it does to Pompeii or the plump minimalism she had begun to explore in the early 90s.

And from this it was only a comparatively short step, compositionally speaking, to the extraordinary pair of paintings from 2010 and 2011, *Night in a Private Garden* and *Portal to Shangri-La.* The second of these, with its outer frieze of panels surrounding a clearly demarcated central block of similar panels, seems half-way between a doorway and an ancient Persian carpet, its richness of scumbled, incised worked surfaces among the most complex she has yet painted, equivalent in its texture almost to the knots and tufts of a woven carpet. It is, in many ways, one of the most abstract paintings she has ever painted, the myriad small panels which cover its surface filled with scored circular discs of golden light against a largely red to reddy-brown base like decorative panels in a door, the only figurative elements the tiny horse-forms which gallop and trot across its surface. Sometimes, in her more cynical moments, she entitles it 'Portal to Shangri-Bloody-La' and has recently described its subject as being supposed to be the gateway to happiness but that she doesn't believe it can exist. It is, in that sense, an enigmatic picture; the colour is fiery, intense and exhilarating, the overall richness of its surface resonant with all the implications of an earthly paradise that one finds in Persian miniatures and carpets but, on the other hand, the portal is clearly firmly shut and seemingly impenetrable, the animals run across it but not through it …

No such ambiguity would seem to exist around its nominal pair, *Night in a Private Garden,* on the other hand with its pair of kissing lovers set against a screen and tree-forms and a rich, bluey-green background seemingly hung with myriad lights with, higher up, star-forms in a darker blue sky and watched over from the sides by standing male and female figures. The panel structure used in *Portal to Shangri-La* is much more loosely treated here, the whole composition more free-flowing giving the picture a more unambiguously ecstatic character and with something of the compositional complexity of her great 1980s compositions.

This is the point from which Sonia, having just celebrated her 80th birthday and been heavily involved with the interviews and preparations leading up to this book, now looks forward to getting back to painting again and, as so often in her career, I believe we will be surprised and amazed by what emerges. What we can say is that, looked at alongside nearly 60 years of painting and drawing, it will be drawing on those same deep and essentially timeless pools of feeling and experience, observation and poetic reference that have allowed the work to develop with such consistency over such an apparently wide range of subjects and themes. A younger painter friend of mine, also from North Yorkshire and also figuratively biased, looking at Sonia's painting, was struck most particularly by how the paint surface in so much of her work seems to describe a process of building up, scratching away and exposing and then folding over again – a building up, a revealing and then a partial covering over again. It seems to me a very apt analogy for the process by which she has quietly examined her life and found the pictorial symbols and the structures to express what she has found there, the metaphorical means through which they can then resonate within us also. That is what a really good artist does.

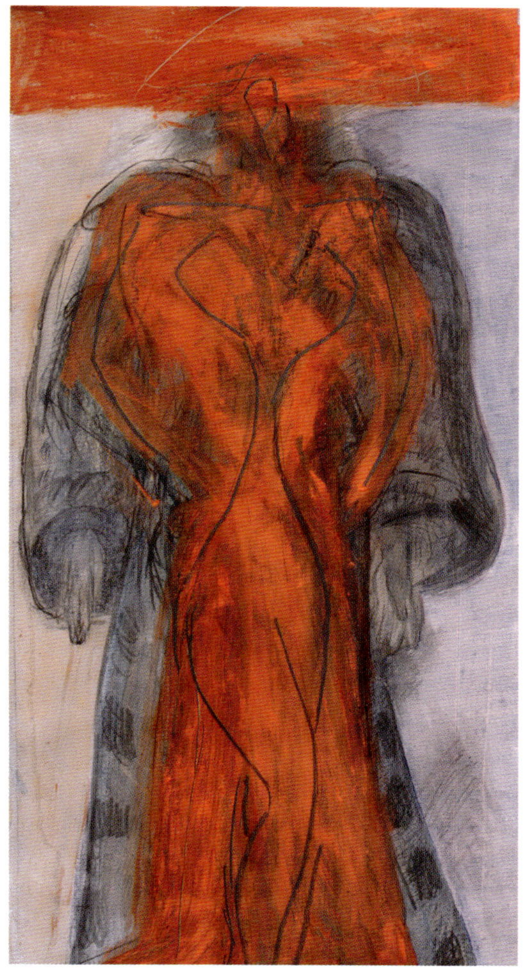

Inner Self 2010, gouache and charcoal, 128 x 75 cm

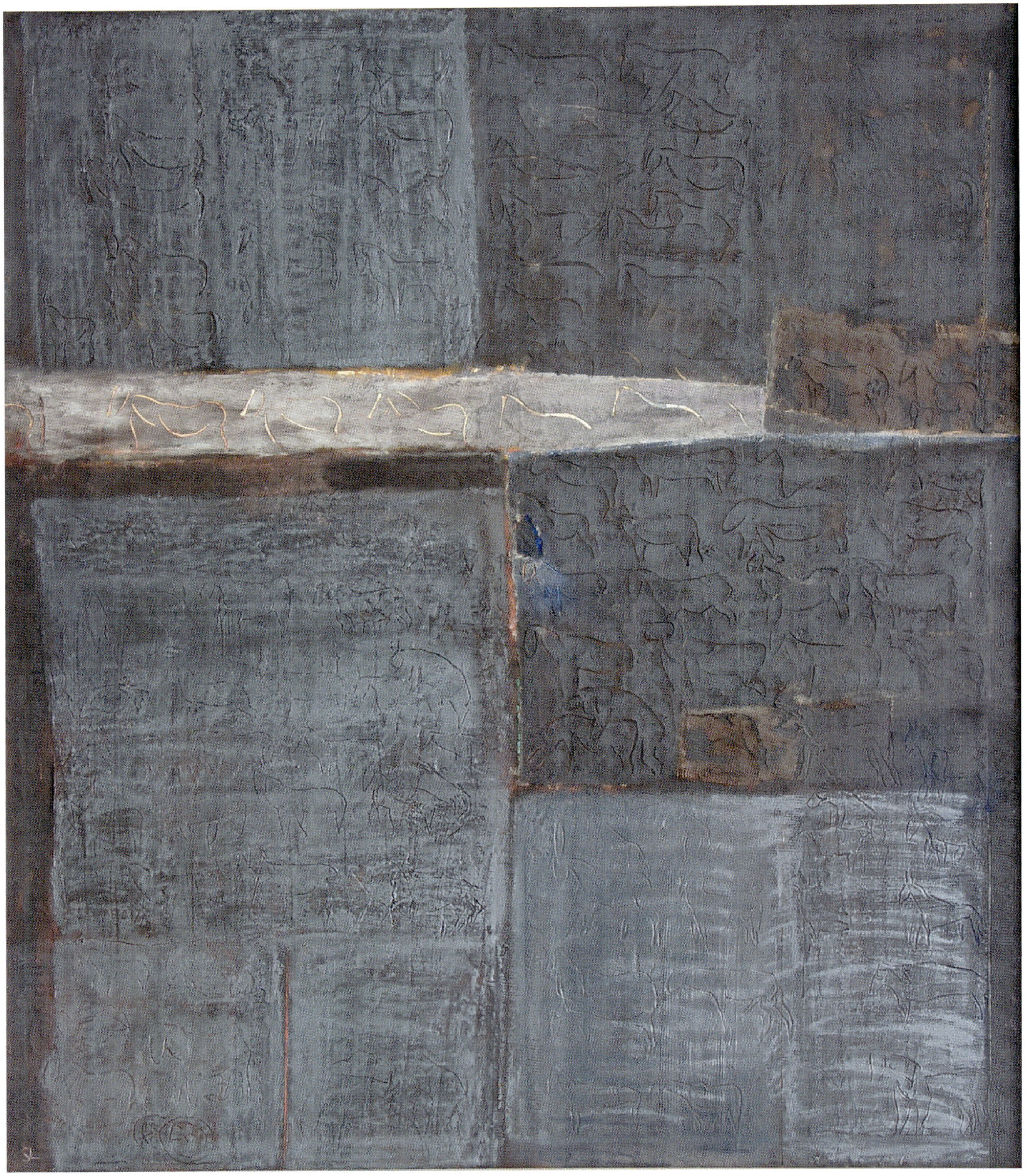

Herd 1996, oil on canvas, 183 × 163 cm

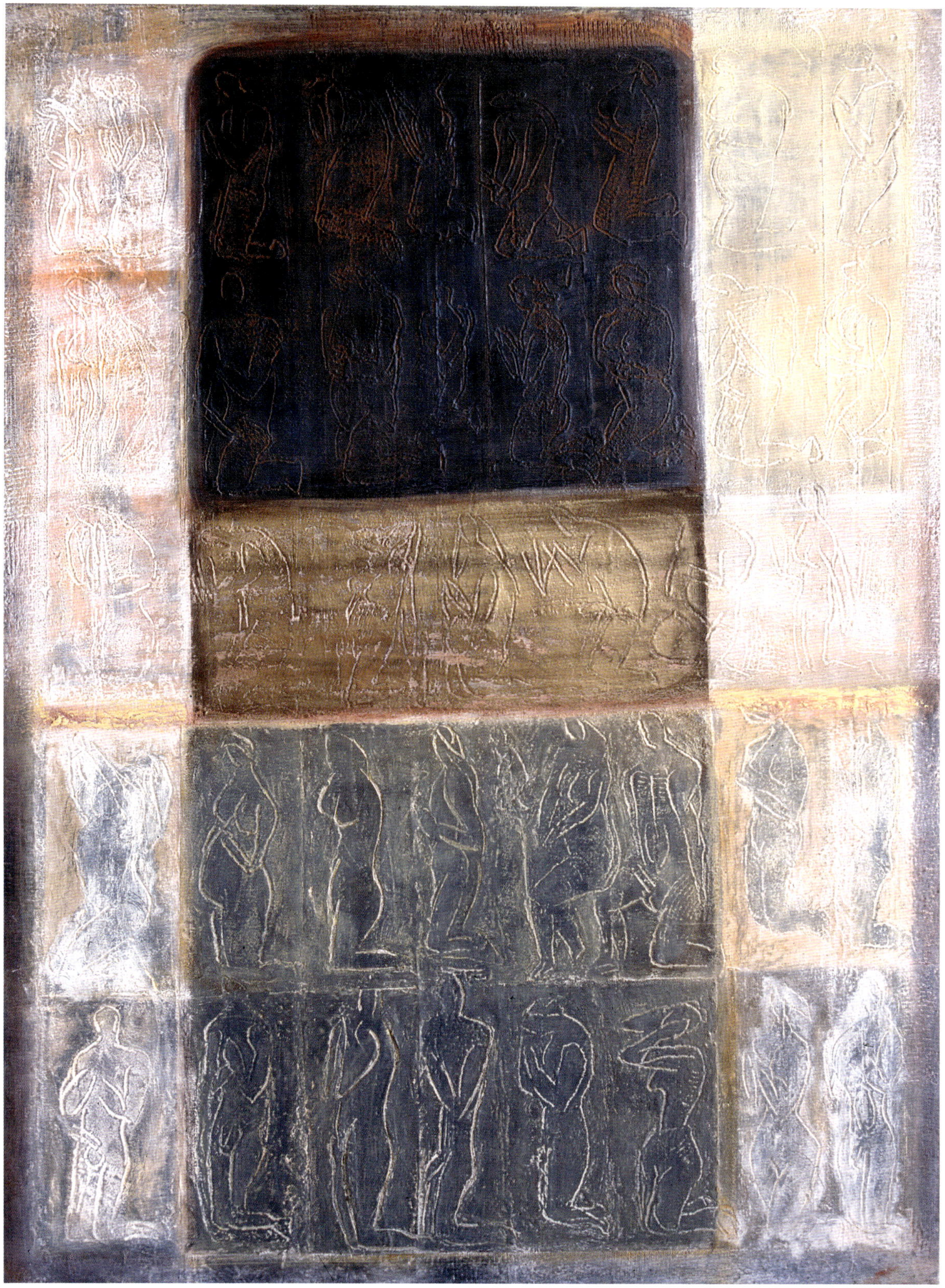

Begging and Praying 1997, oil on canvas, 122 x 91.5 cm

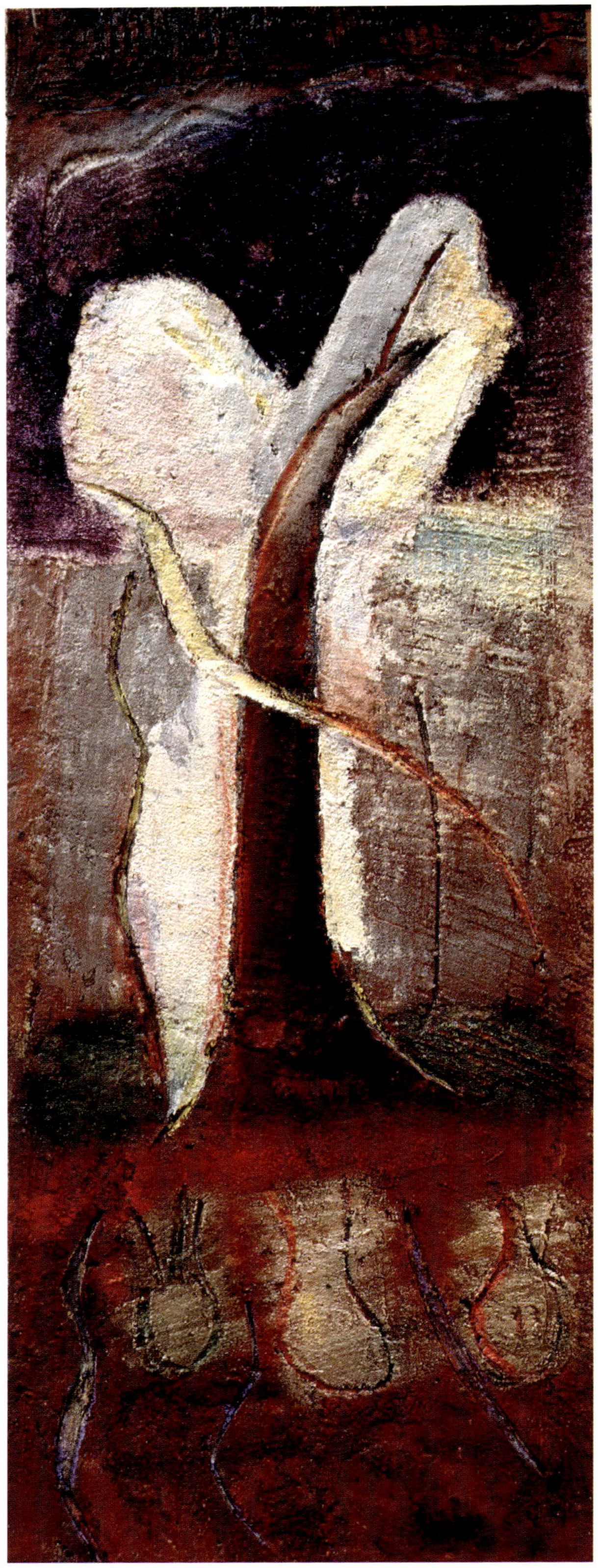

Spring Tree and Bulbs 1996, oil on canvas, 48 x 37 cm

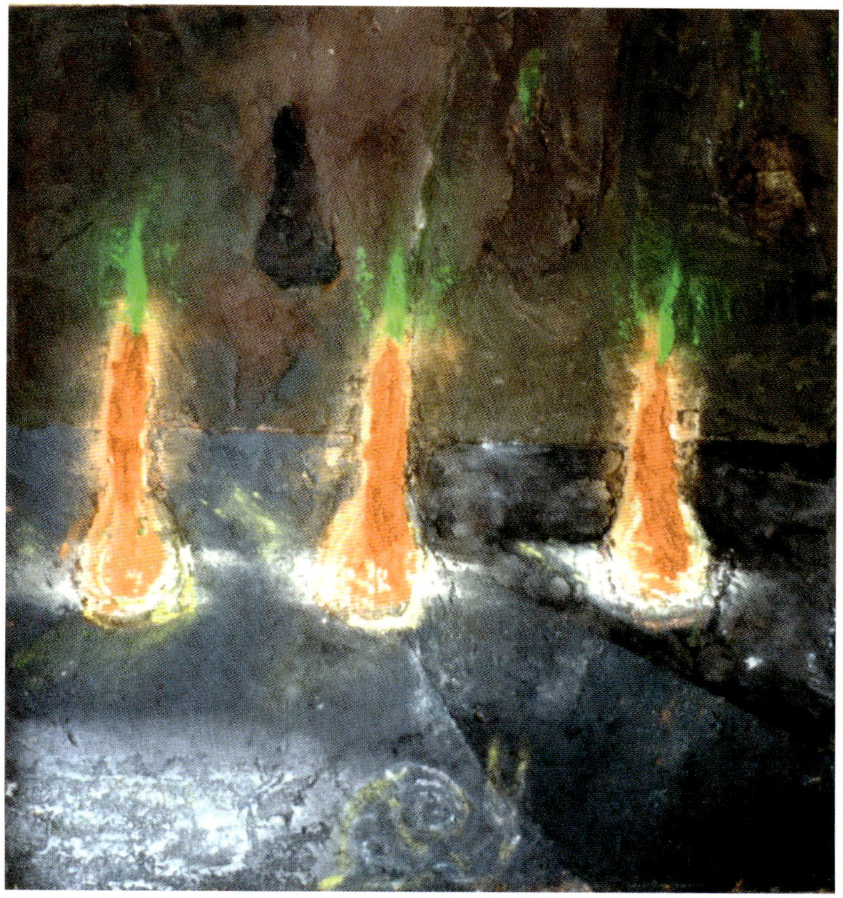

Spring Pricks c.1996, oil on canvas, 49 x 47 cm

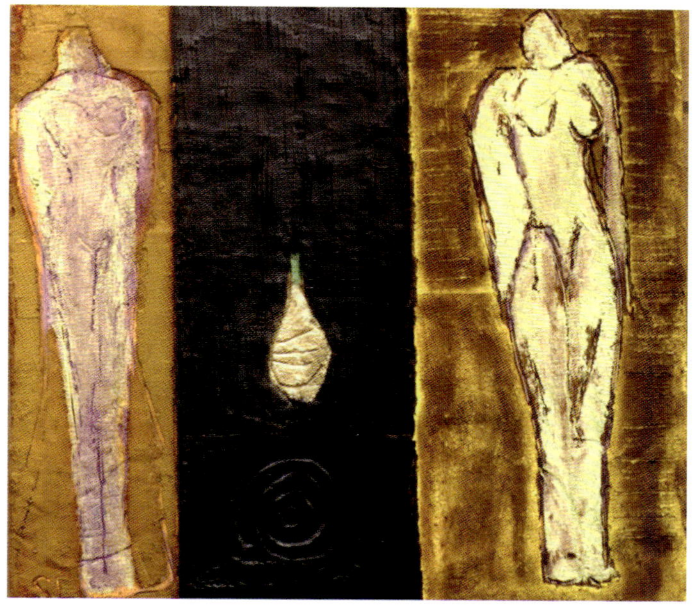

Guardians of Spring c.1997, oil on canvas, 60 x 60 cm

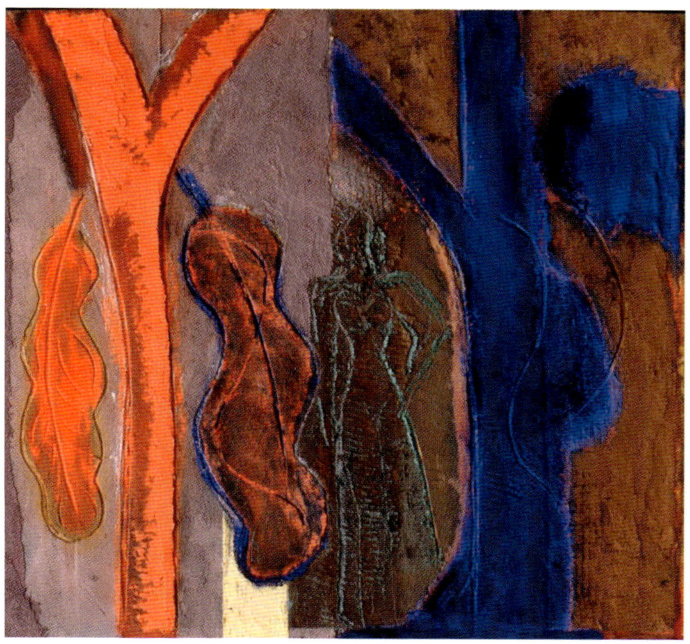

Woman in Woodland 1997, oil on canvas, 48 x 50 cm

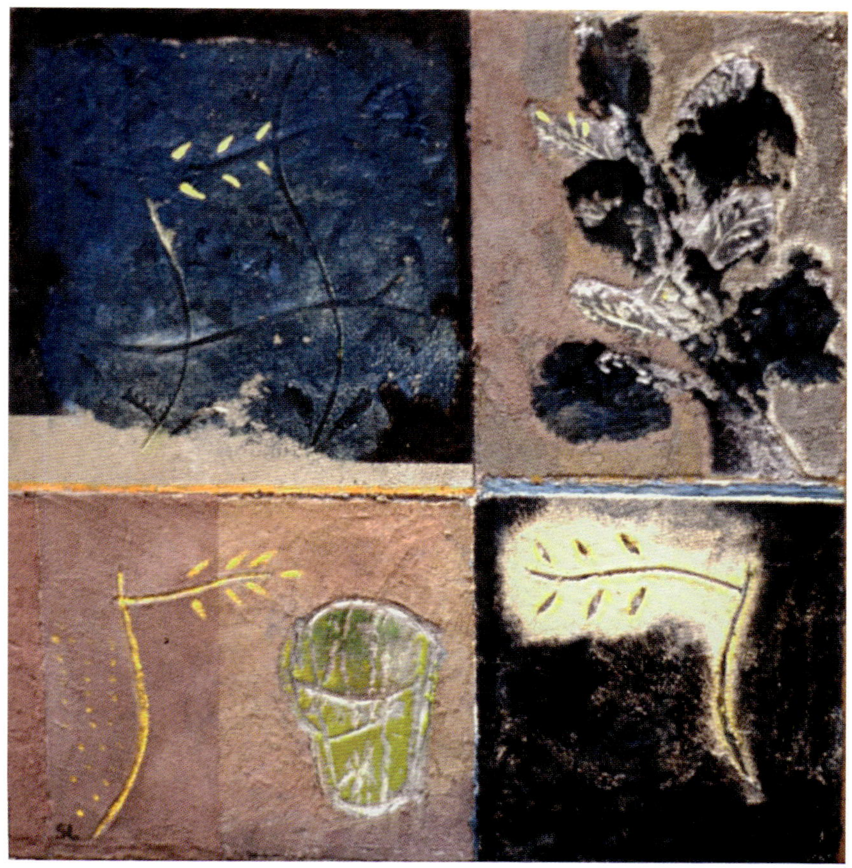

Towards the Land II c.1997, oil on canvas, 32 x 32 cm

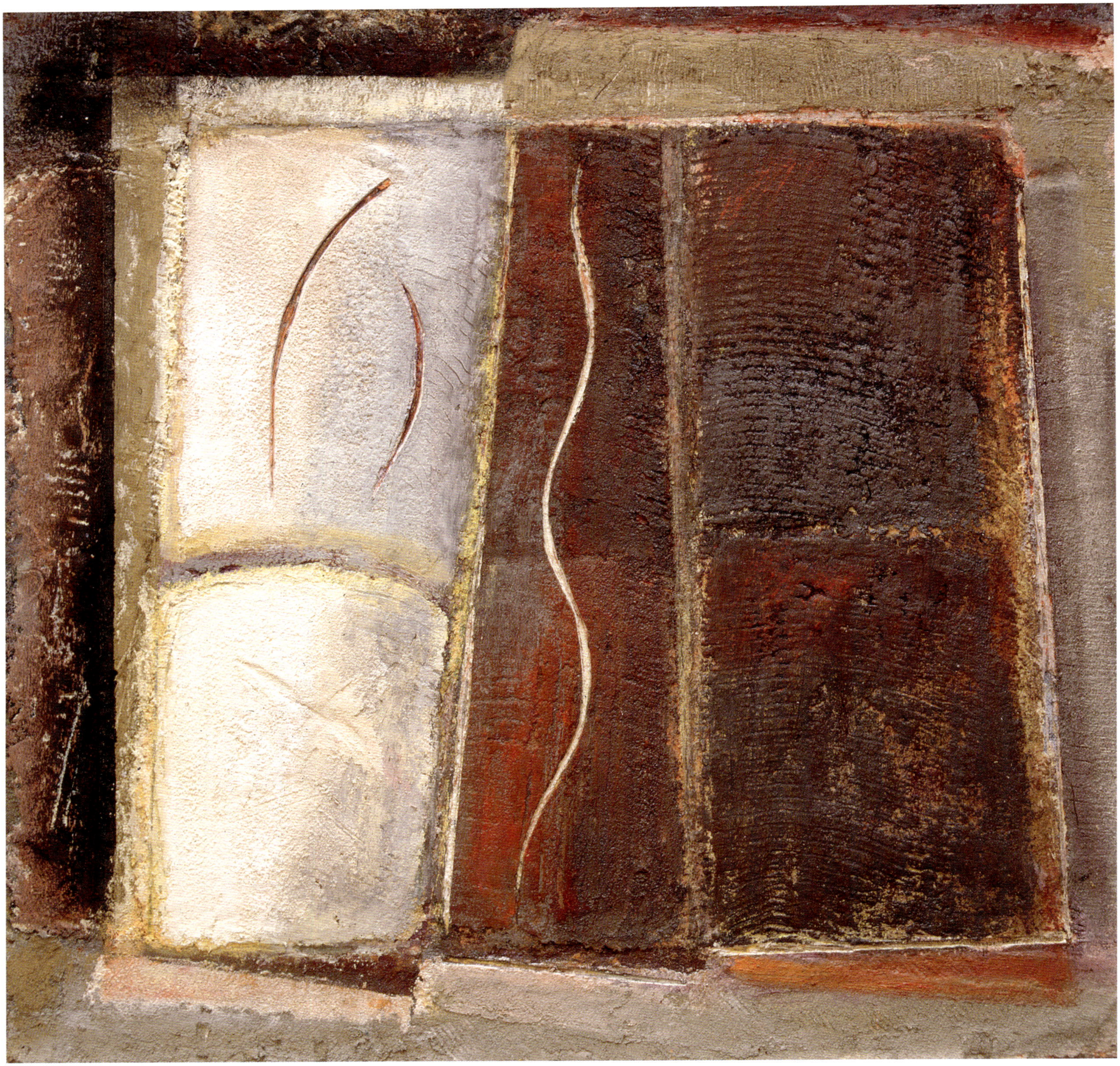

Rune Rock c.1996, oil on canvas, 38 x 27 cm

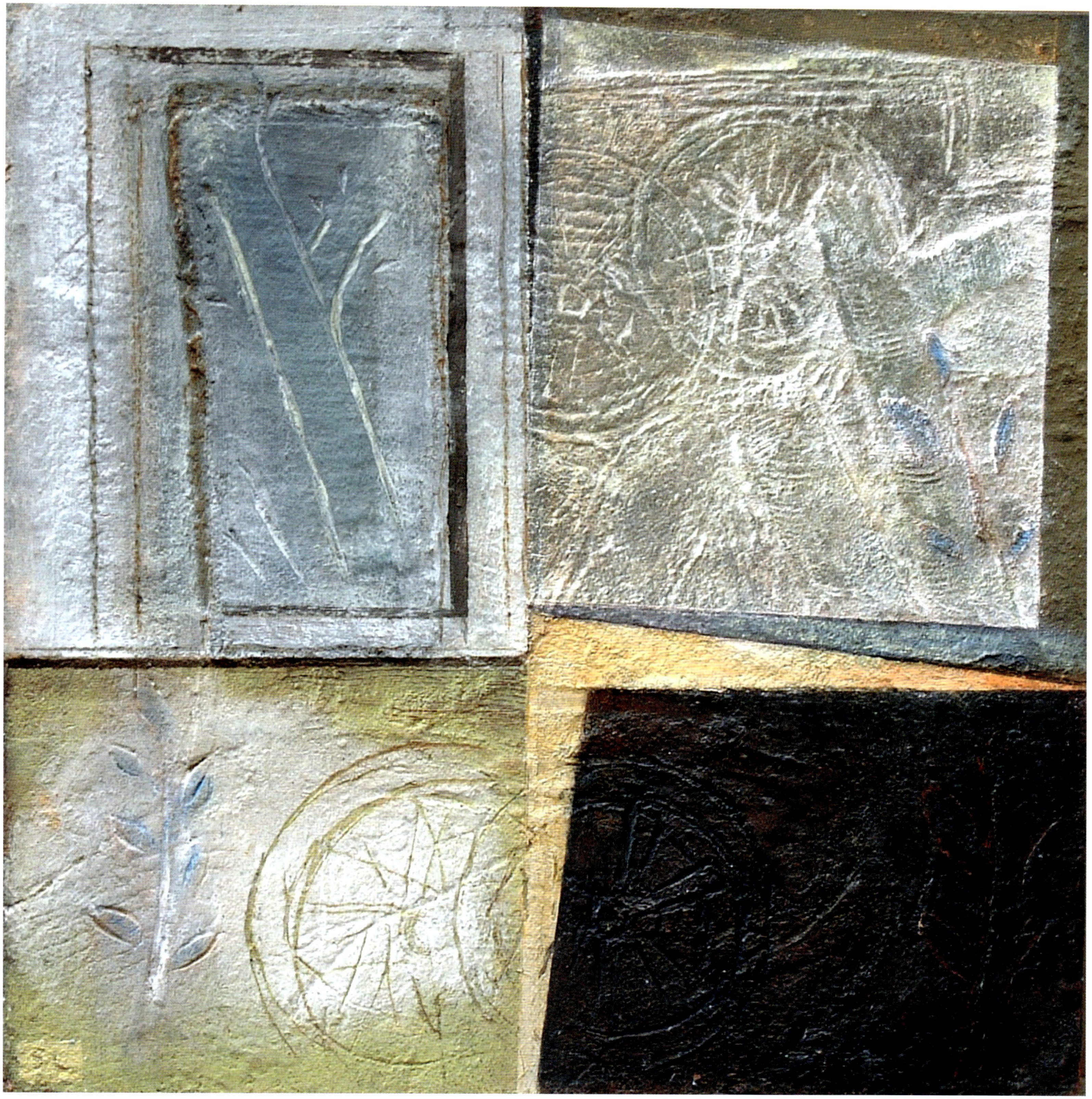

Rural Ride I 2003, oil on canvas, 31 x 31 cm

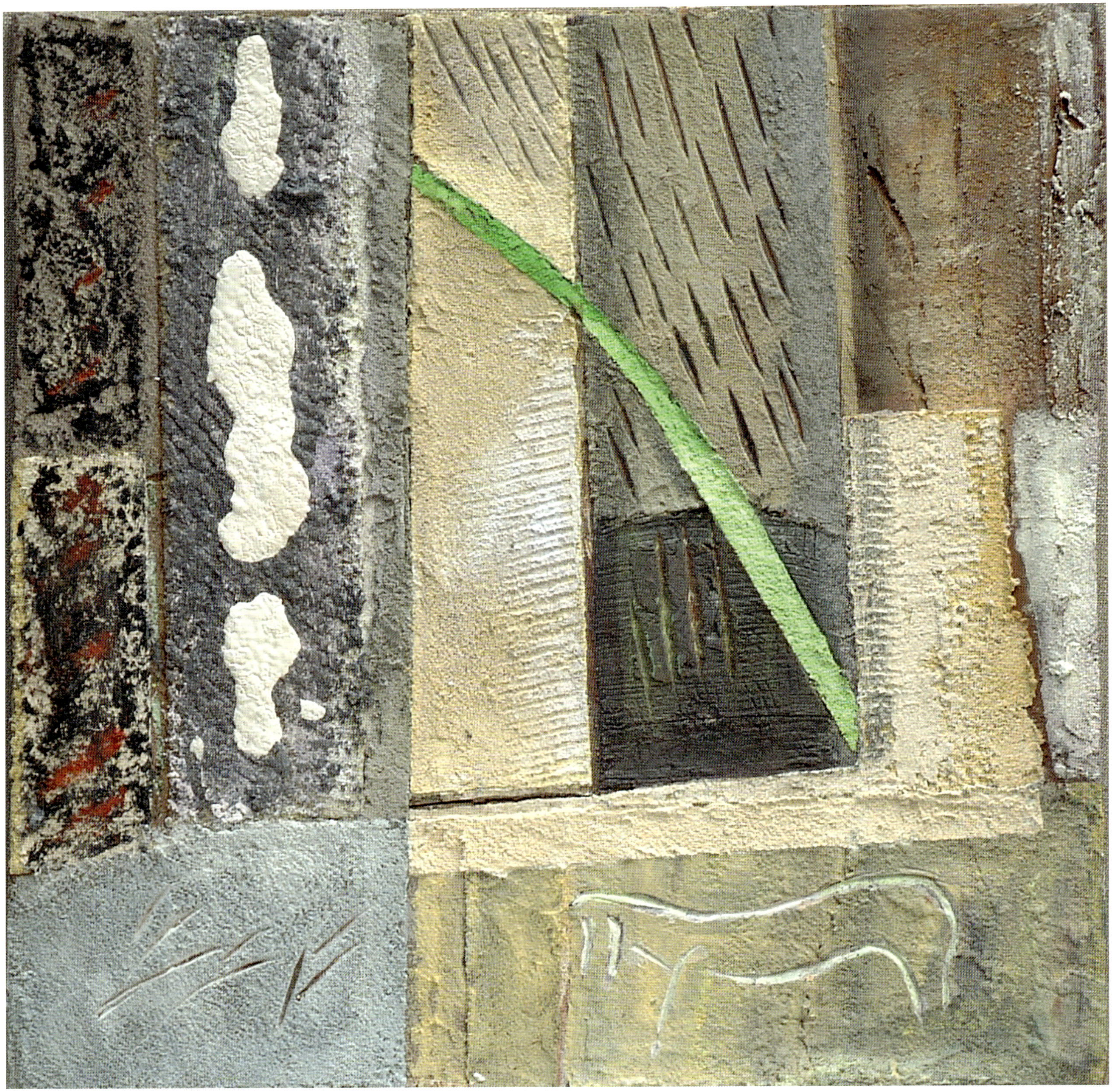

Rain on the Pane 2005, oil on canvas, 30 x 30 cm

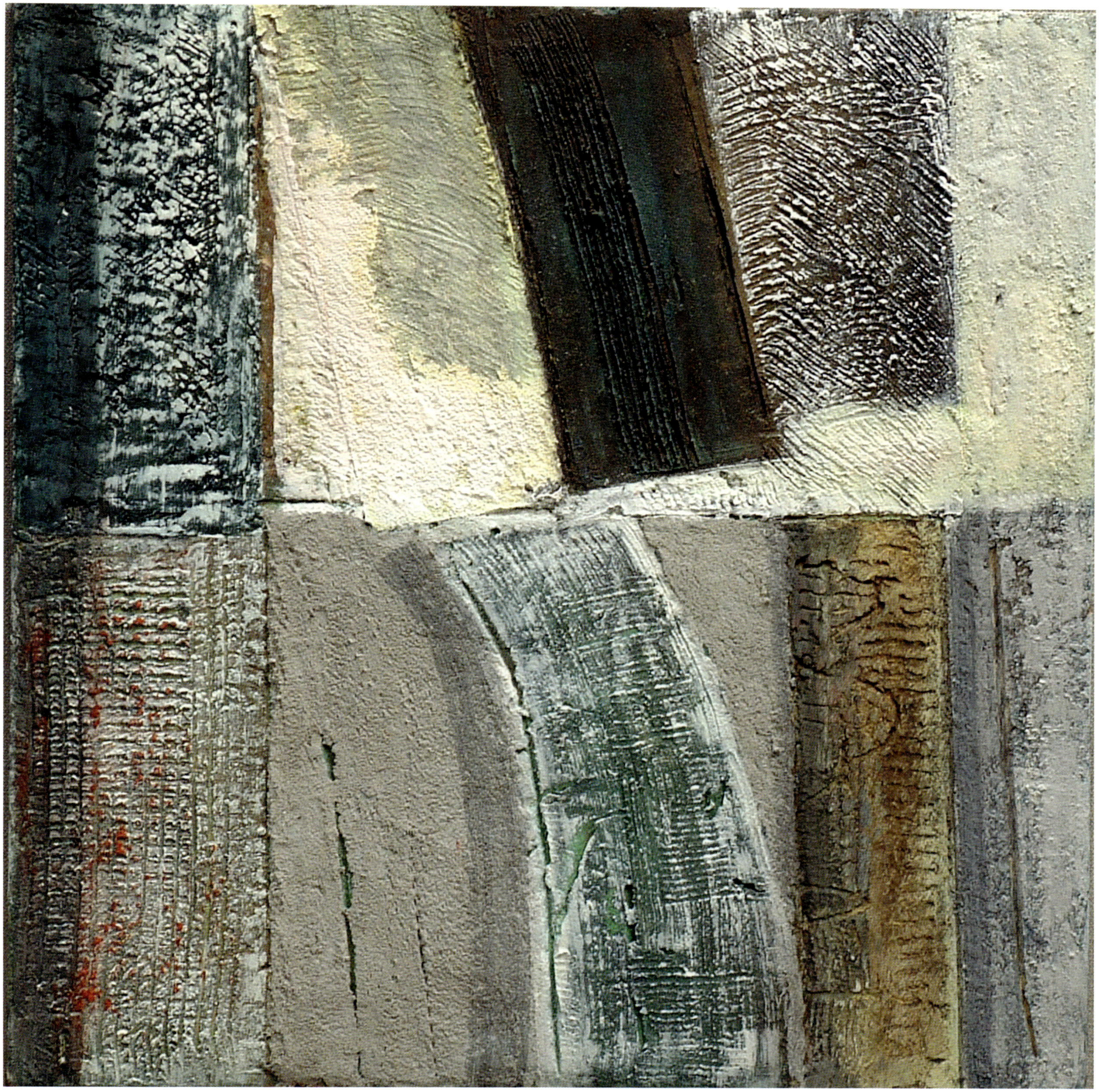

Sound of Distant Waters 2005, oil on canvas, 30 x 30 cm

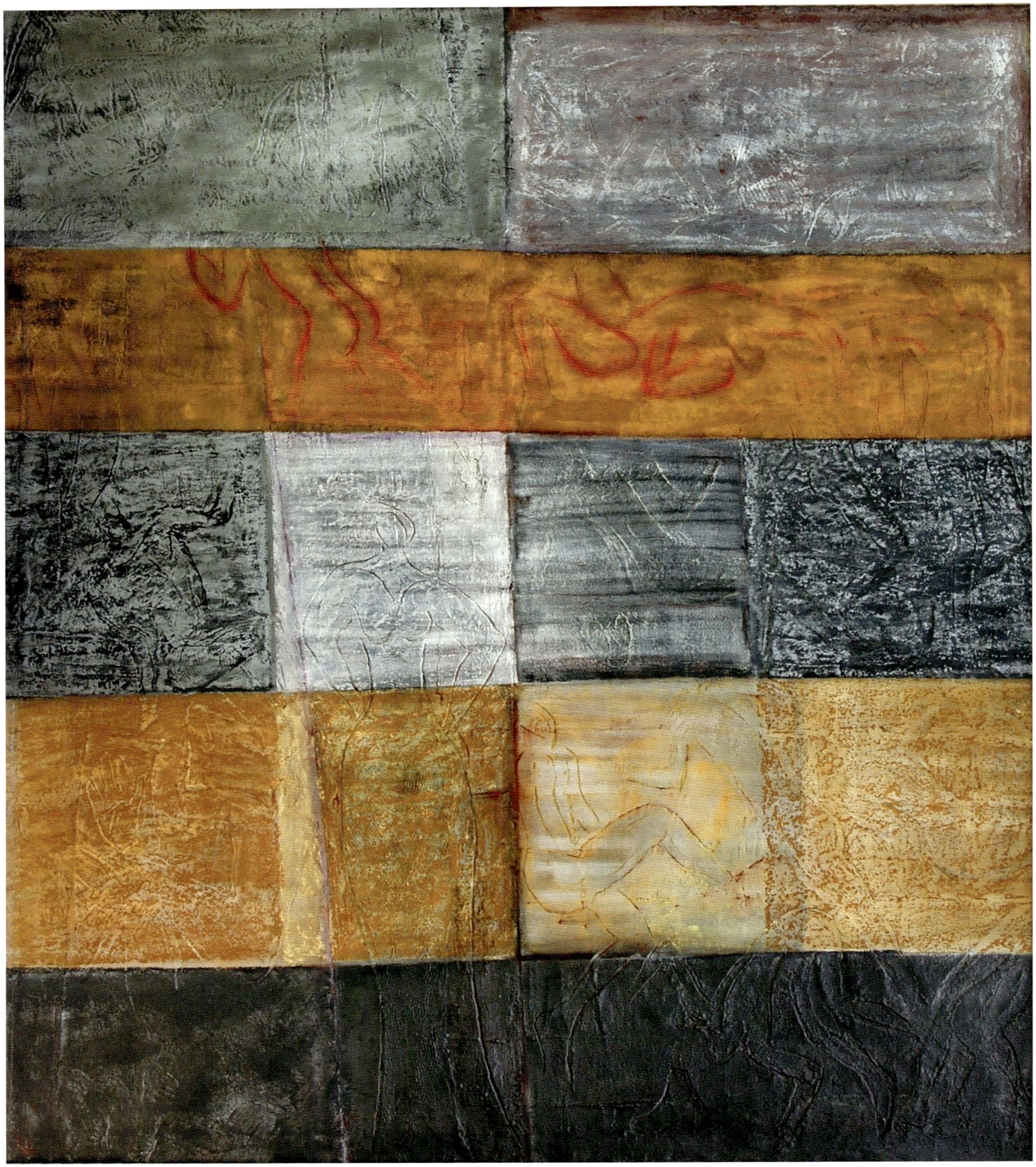

History Book II 2000, oil on canvas, 190 × 165 cm

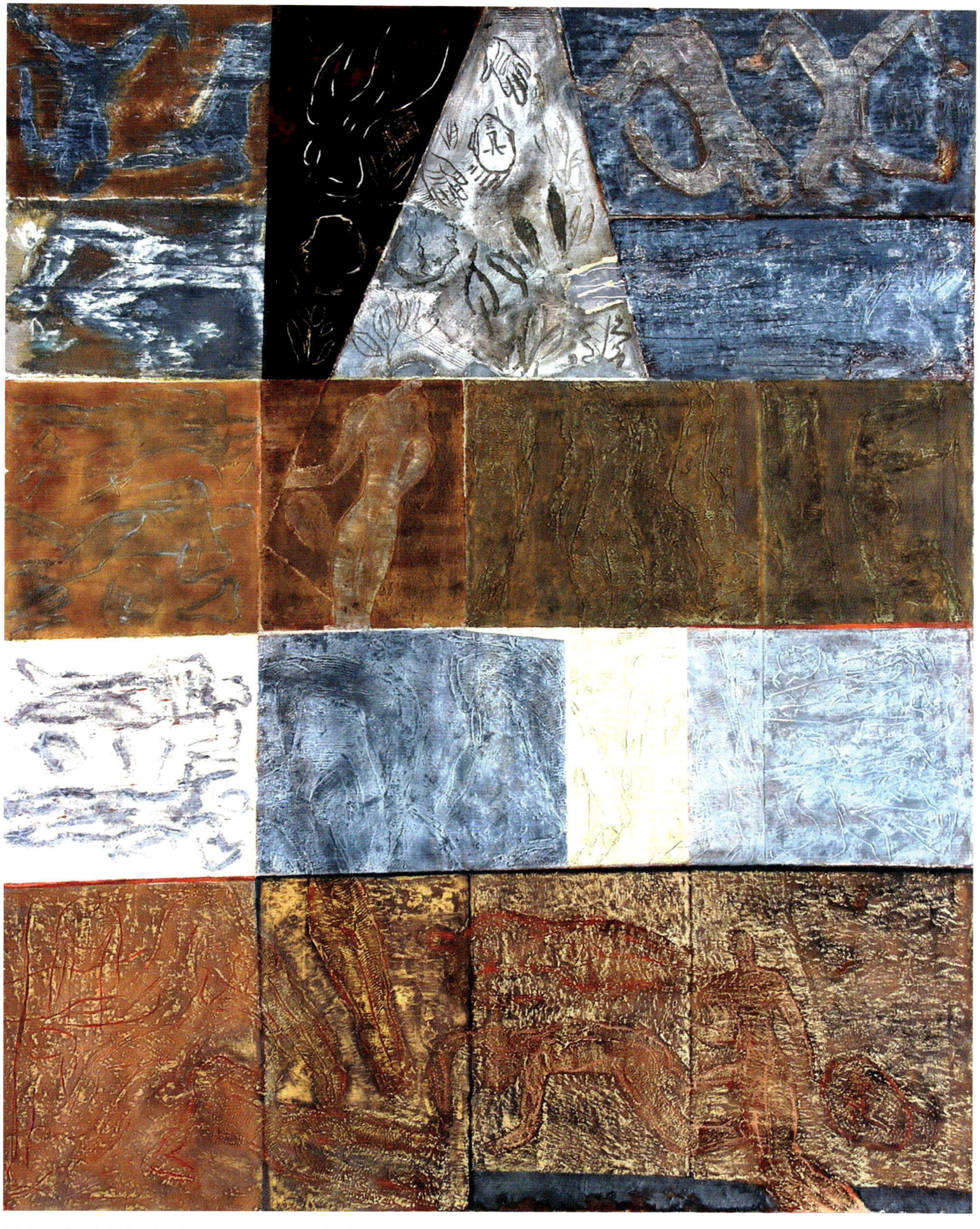

History Book III 2000, oil on canvas, 190 x 165 cm

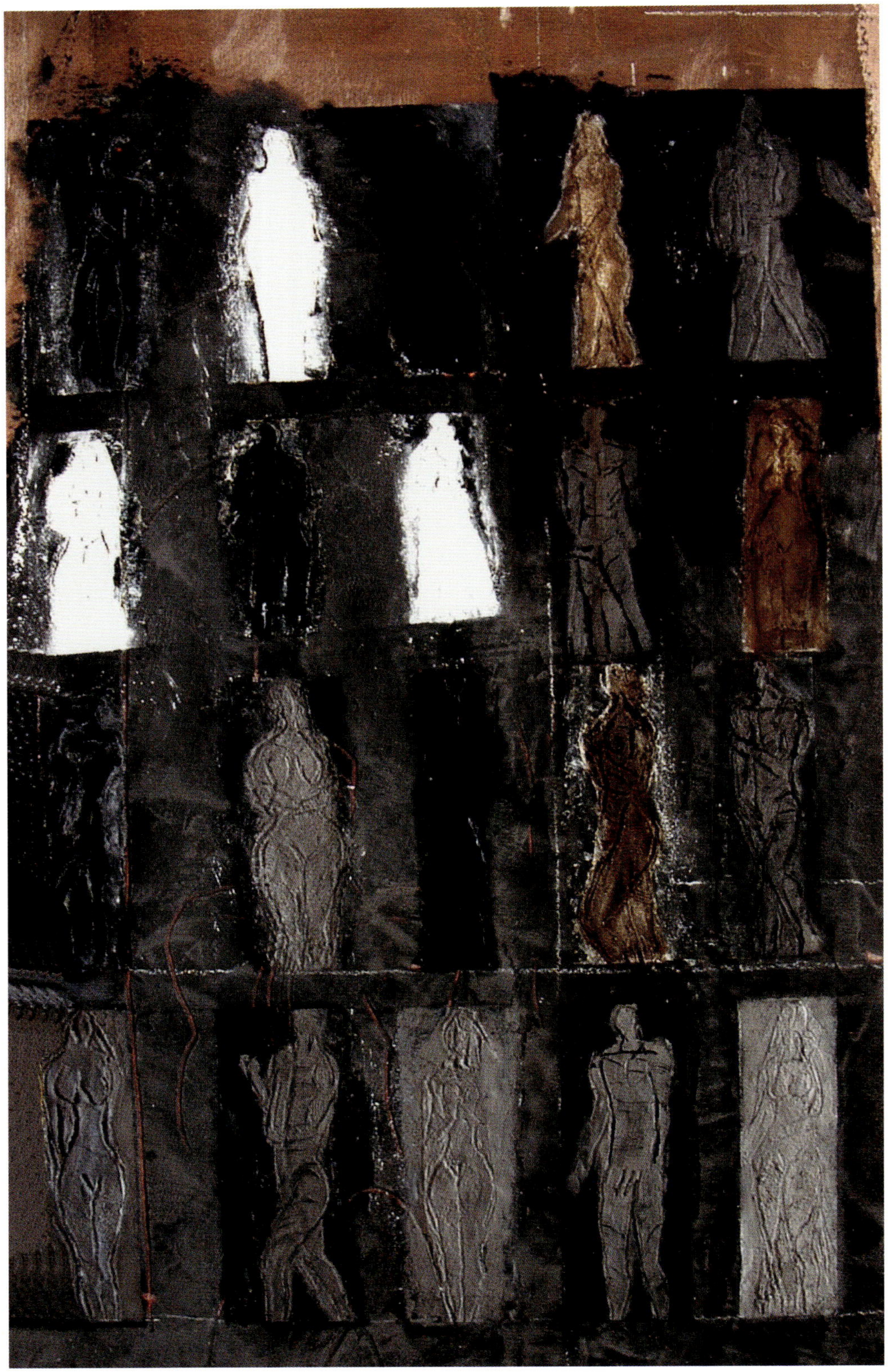

Winter Solstice 2002, oil on canvas, 152 x 122 cm. Detail showing the surface texture and Lawson's trademark scoring into layers technique

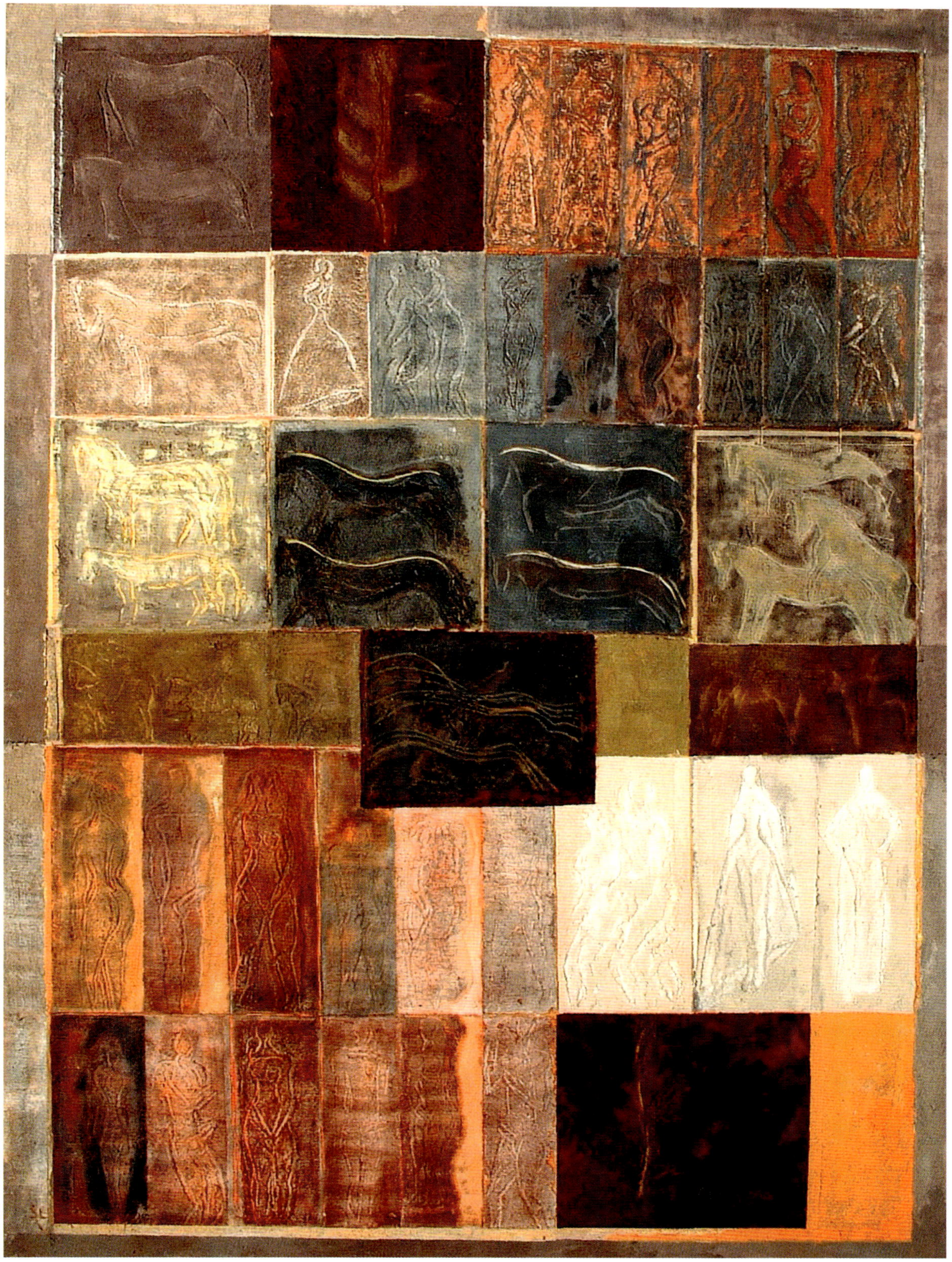

Verona I 2002, oil on canvas, 152 × 122 cm

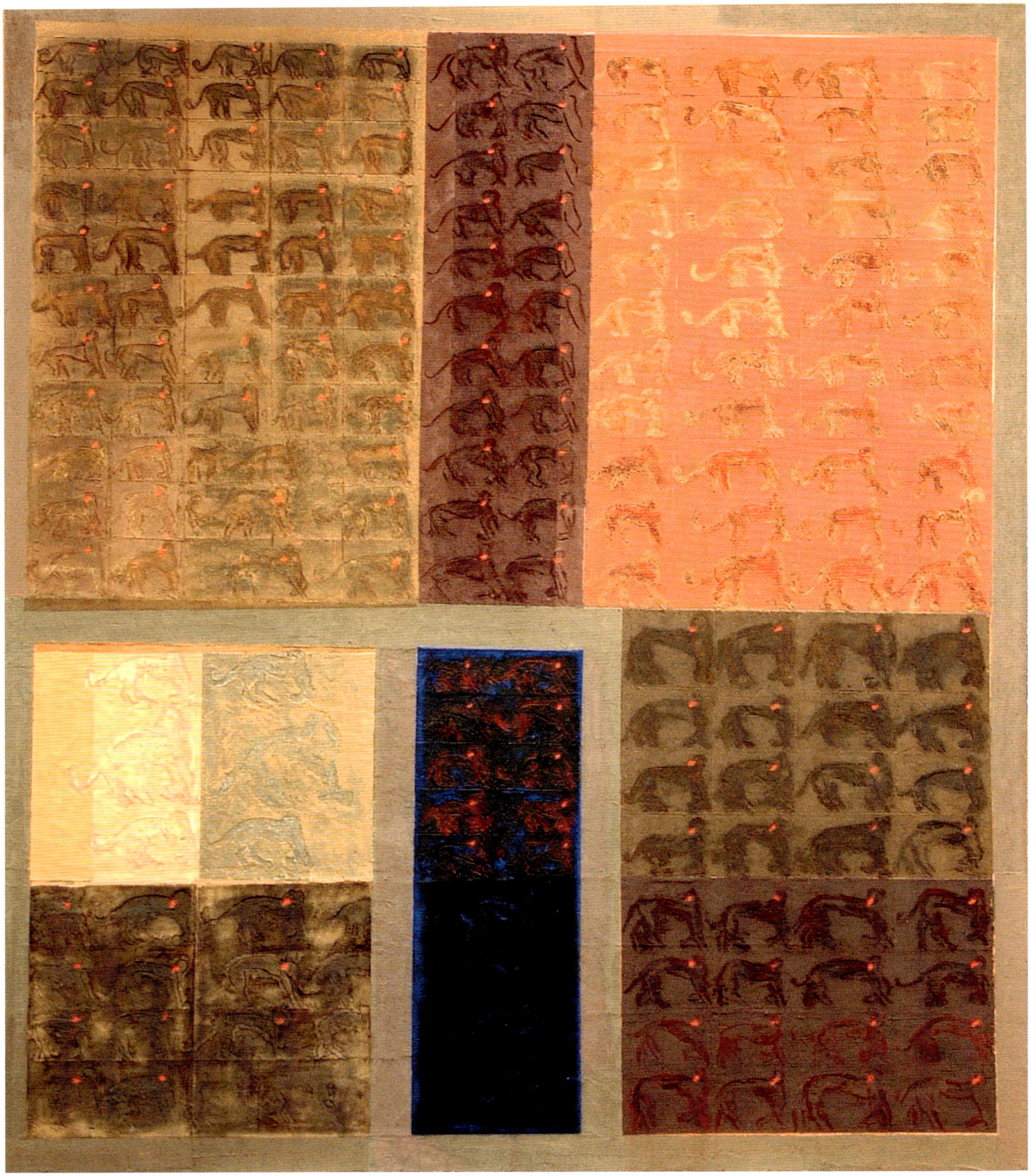

Stealth Warriors 2000, oil on canvas, 190 × 165 cm

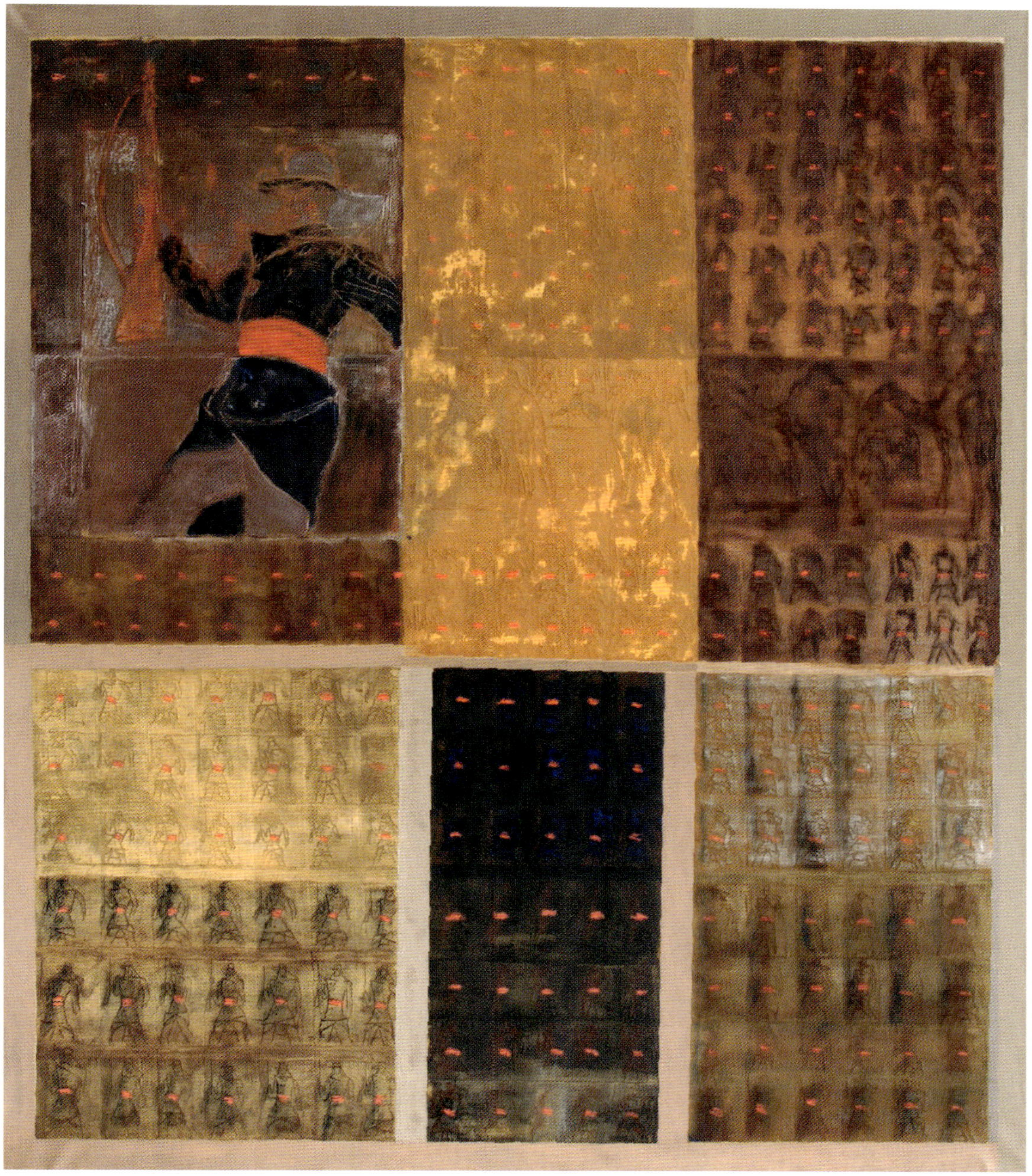

Légion Etrangère 2002, oil on canvas, 190 × 165 cm

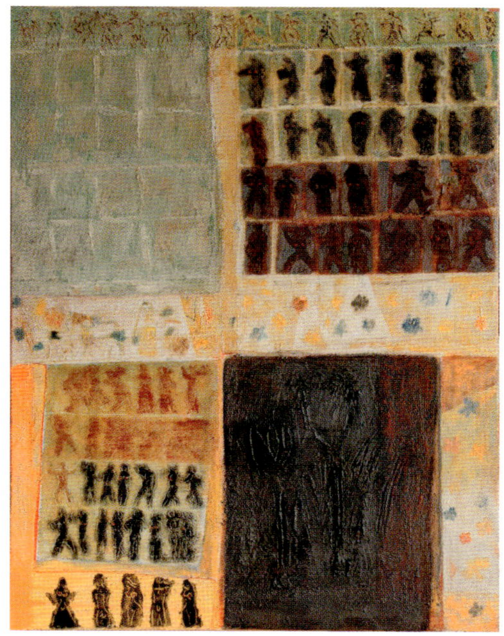

Postcard from Provence I 2012, oil on canvas, 90 × 70 cm

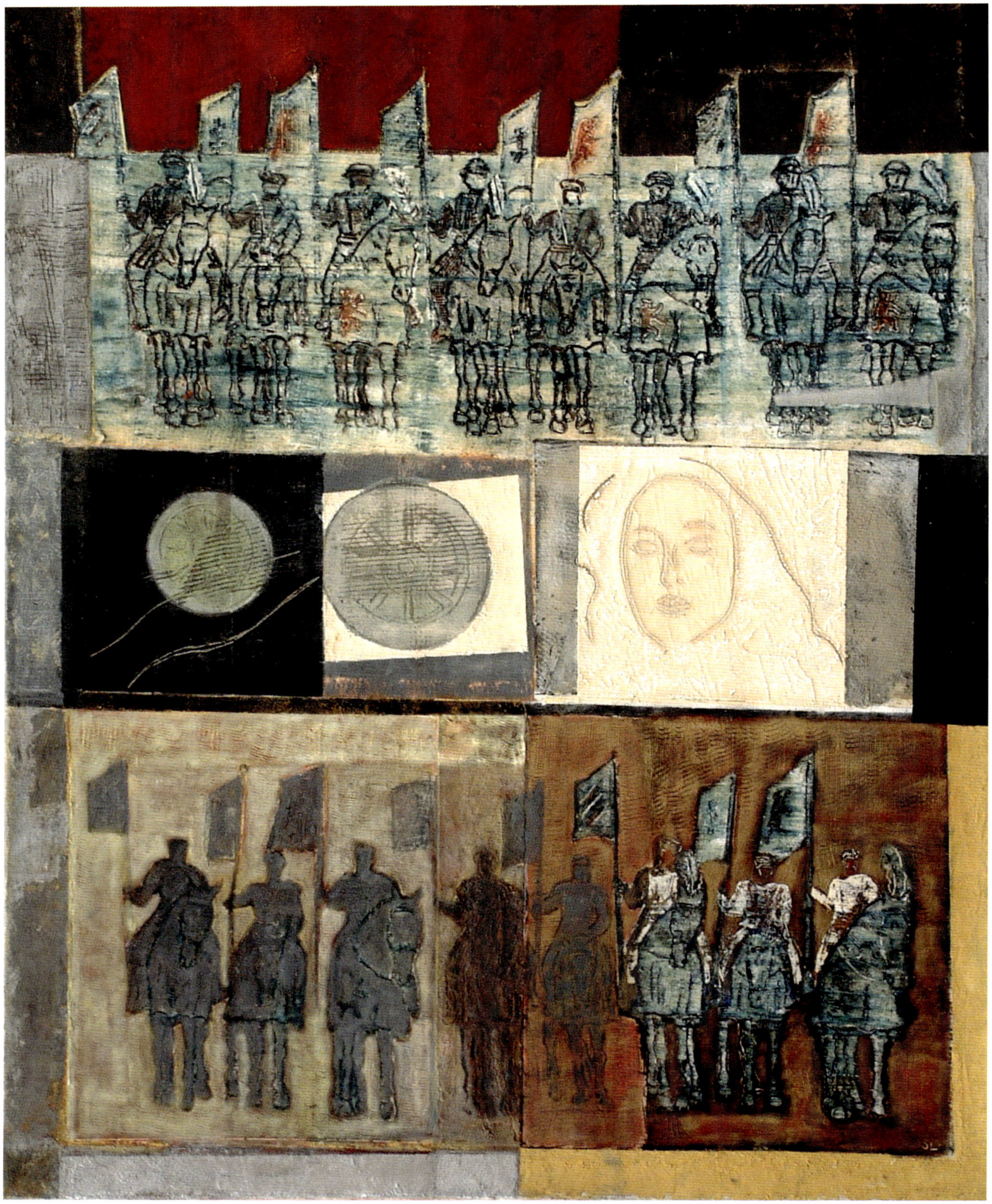

Siena 2005–2006, oil on canvas, 119 x 91 cm

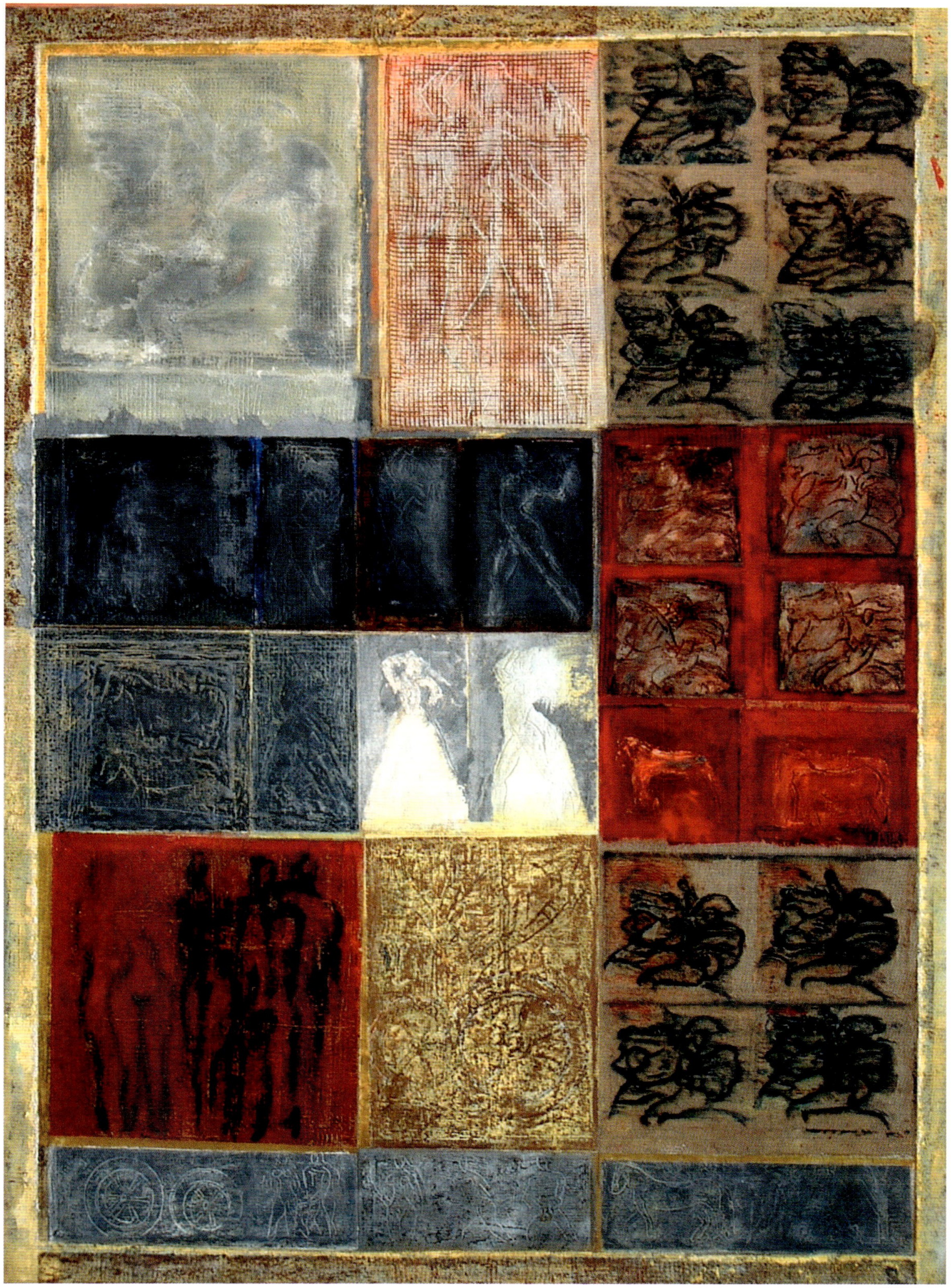

Postcard from Paris 2004, oil on canvas, 163 × 122 cm

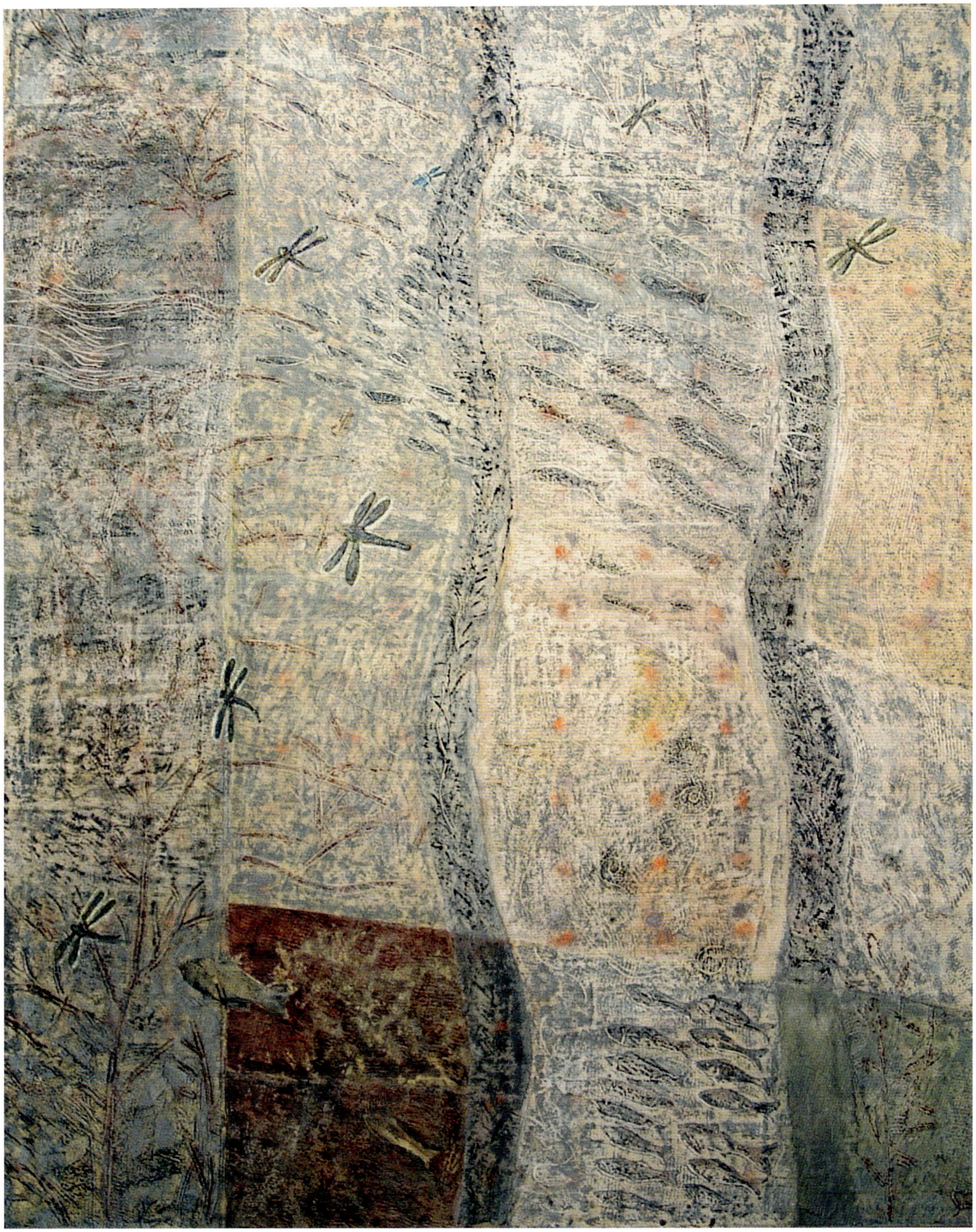

She River c.2005, oil on canvas, 152 × 120 cm

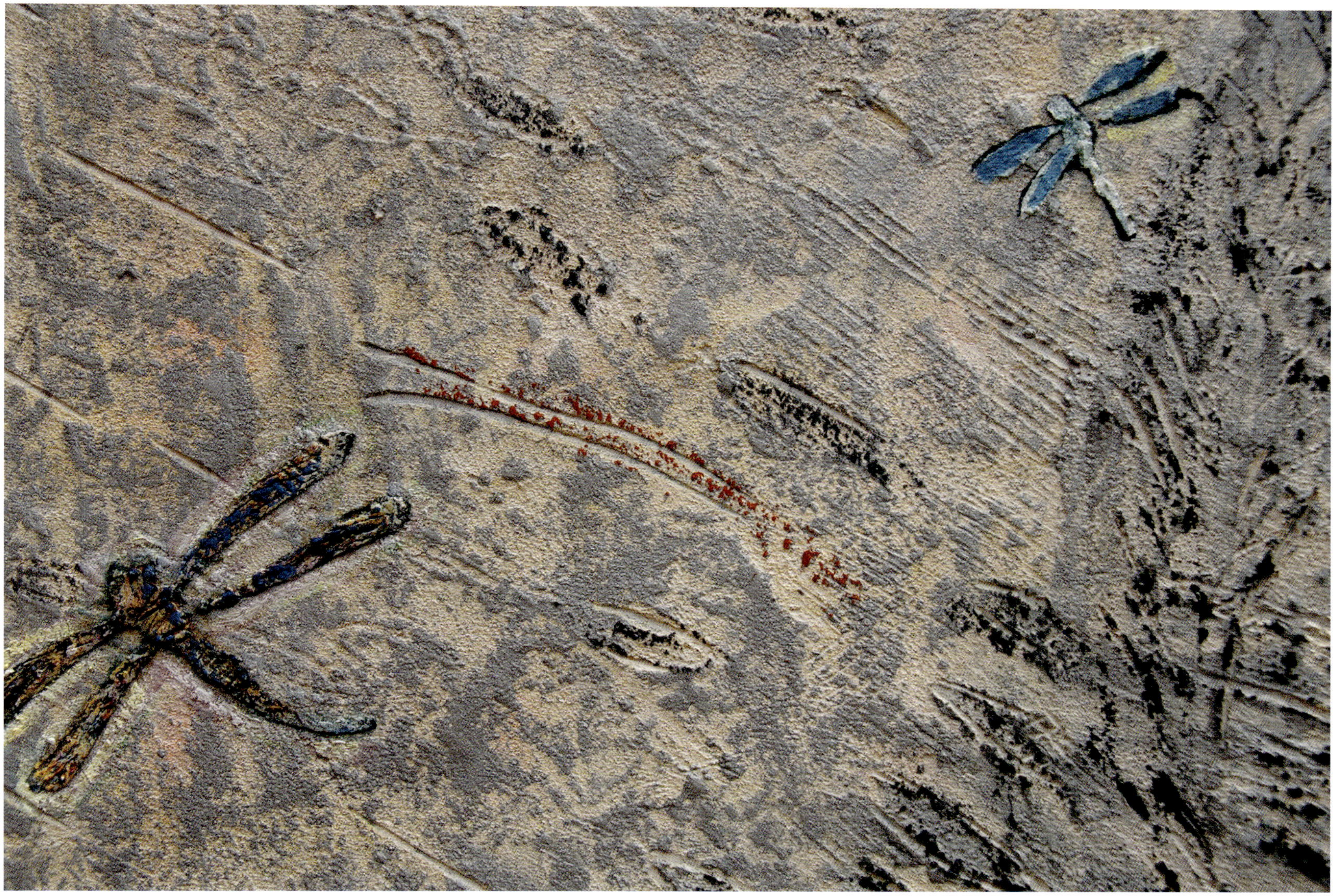

Detail from **She River**

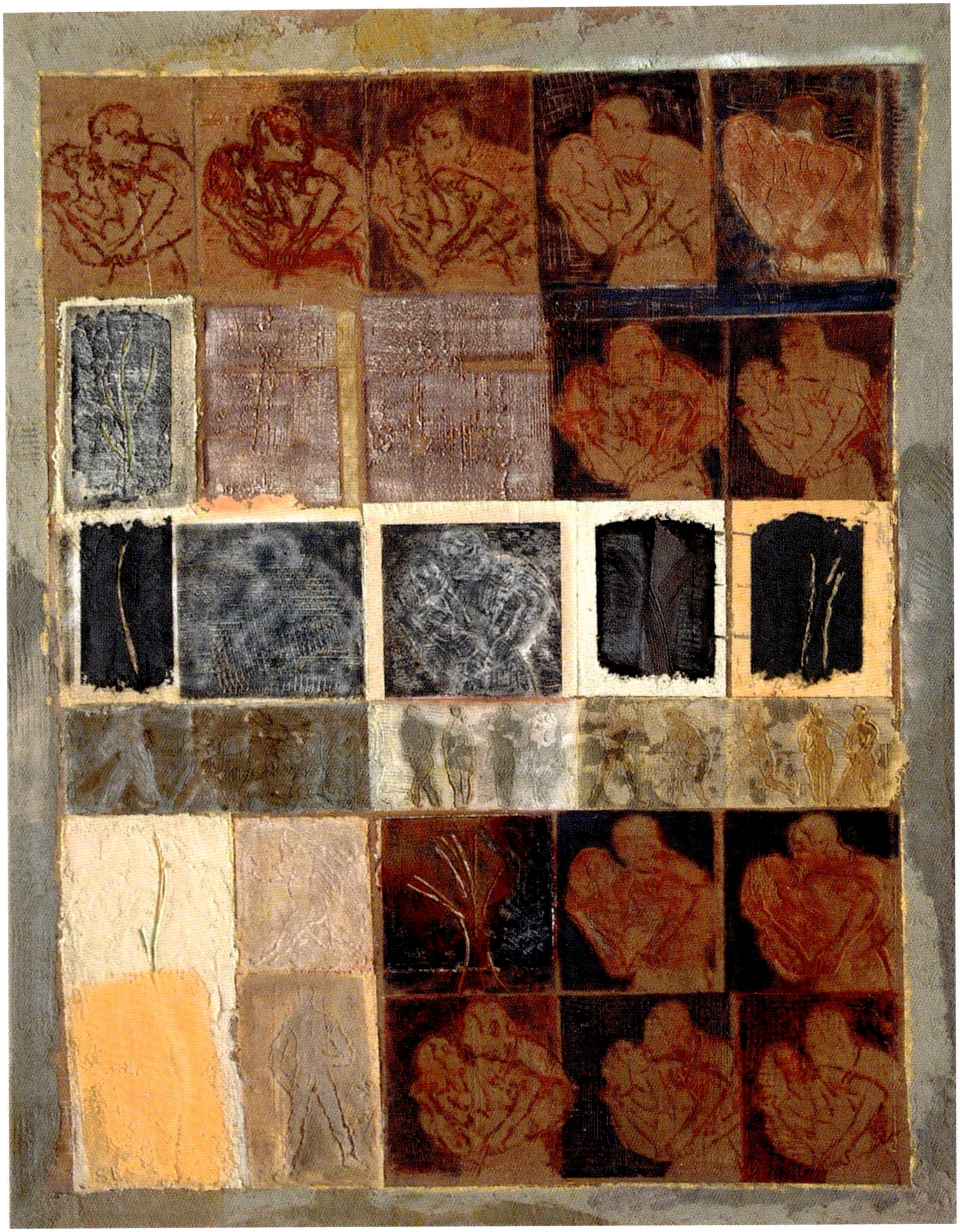

Notes from A Secret Diary 2005, oil on canvas, 91 × 71 cm

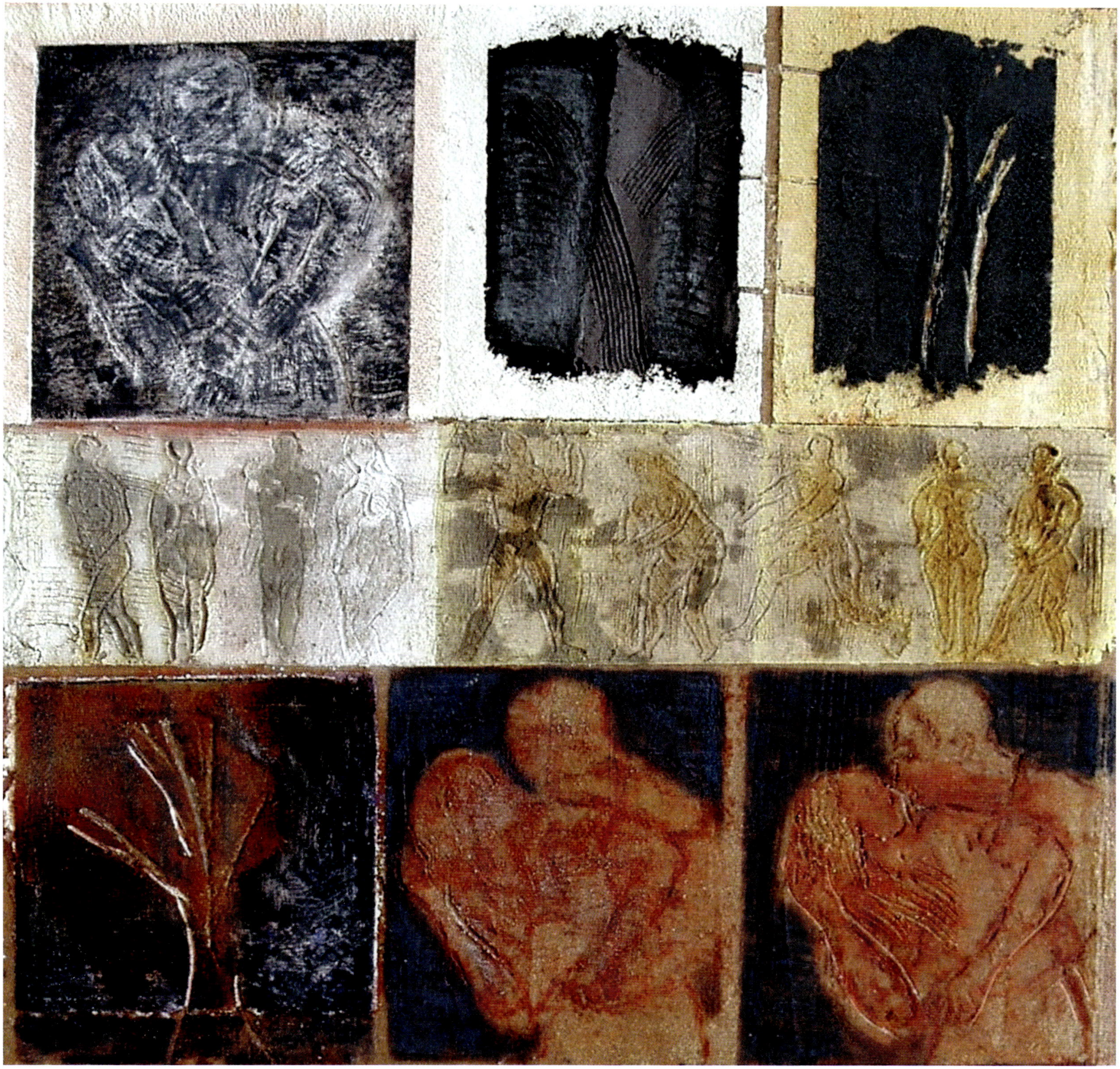

Detail from **Notes from A Secret Diary**

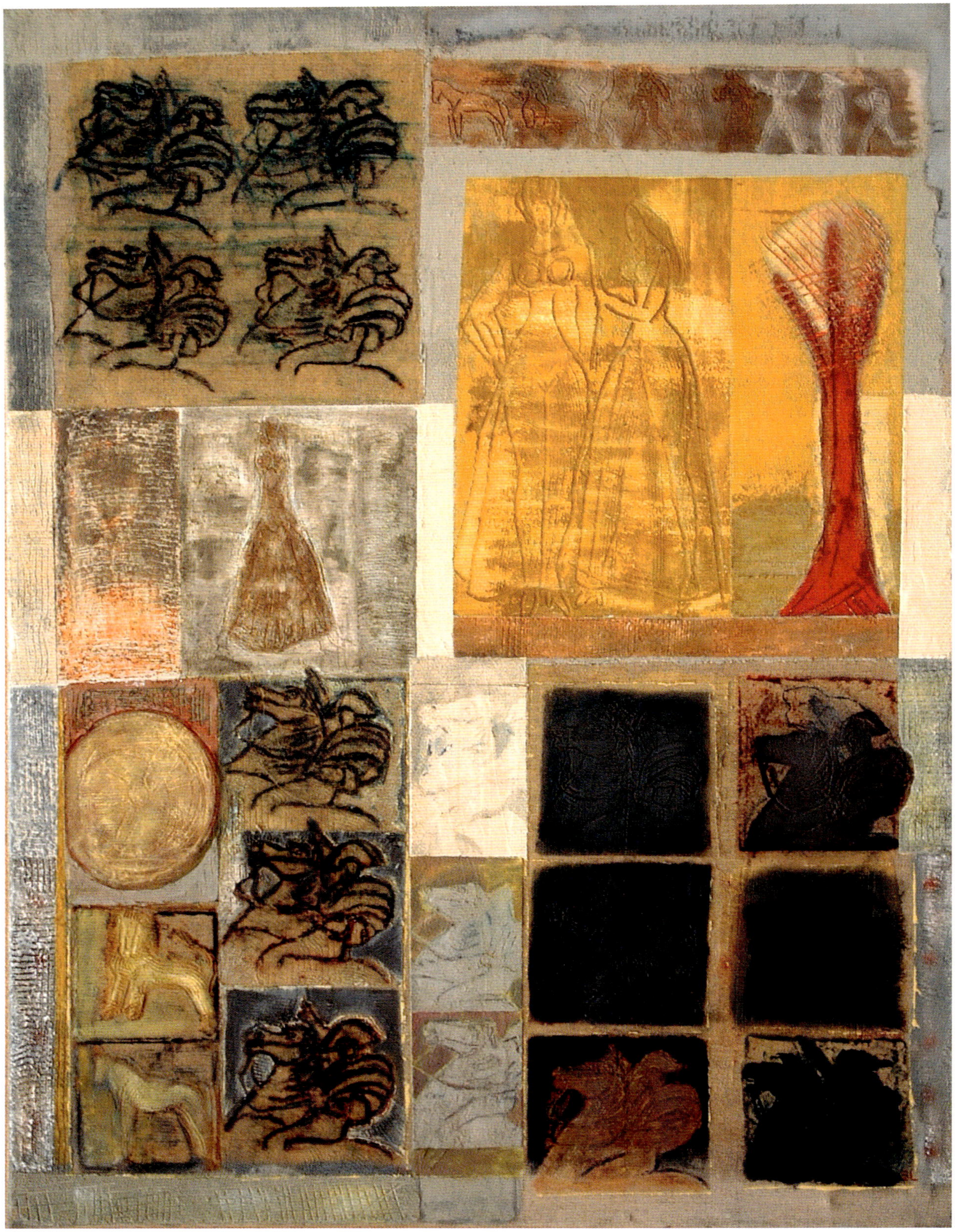

French Connection 2005, oil on canvas, 91 x 71 cm

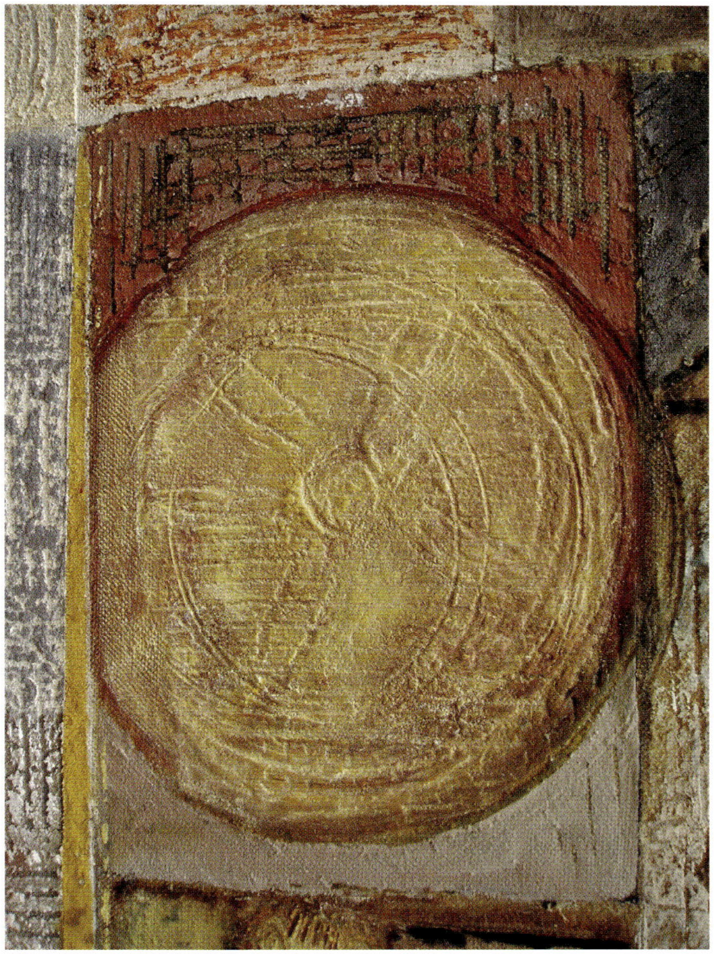

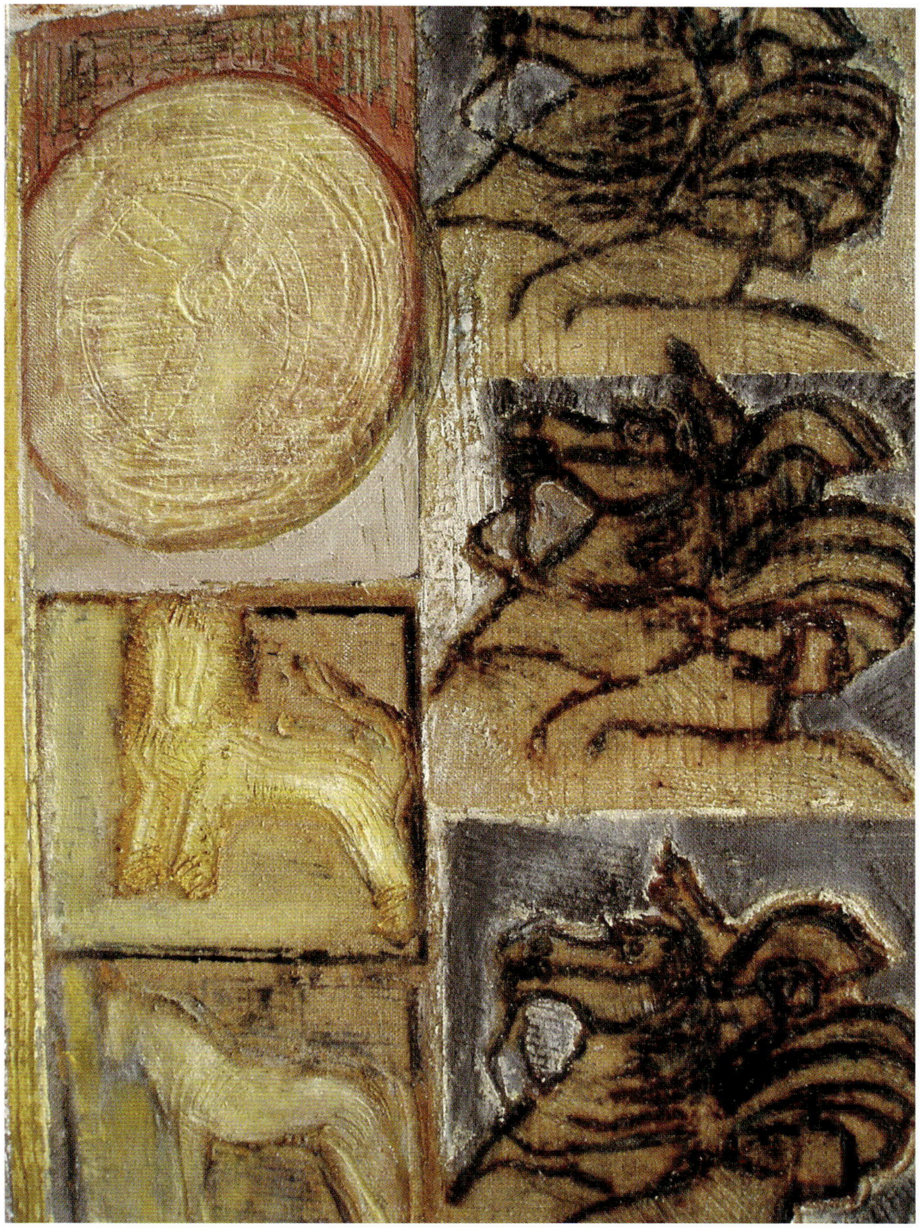

Details from **French Connection**

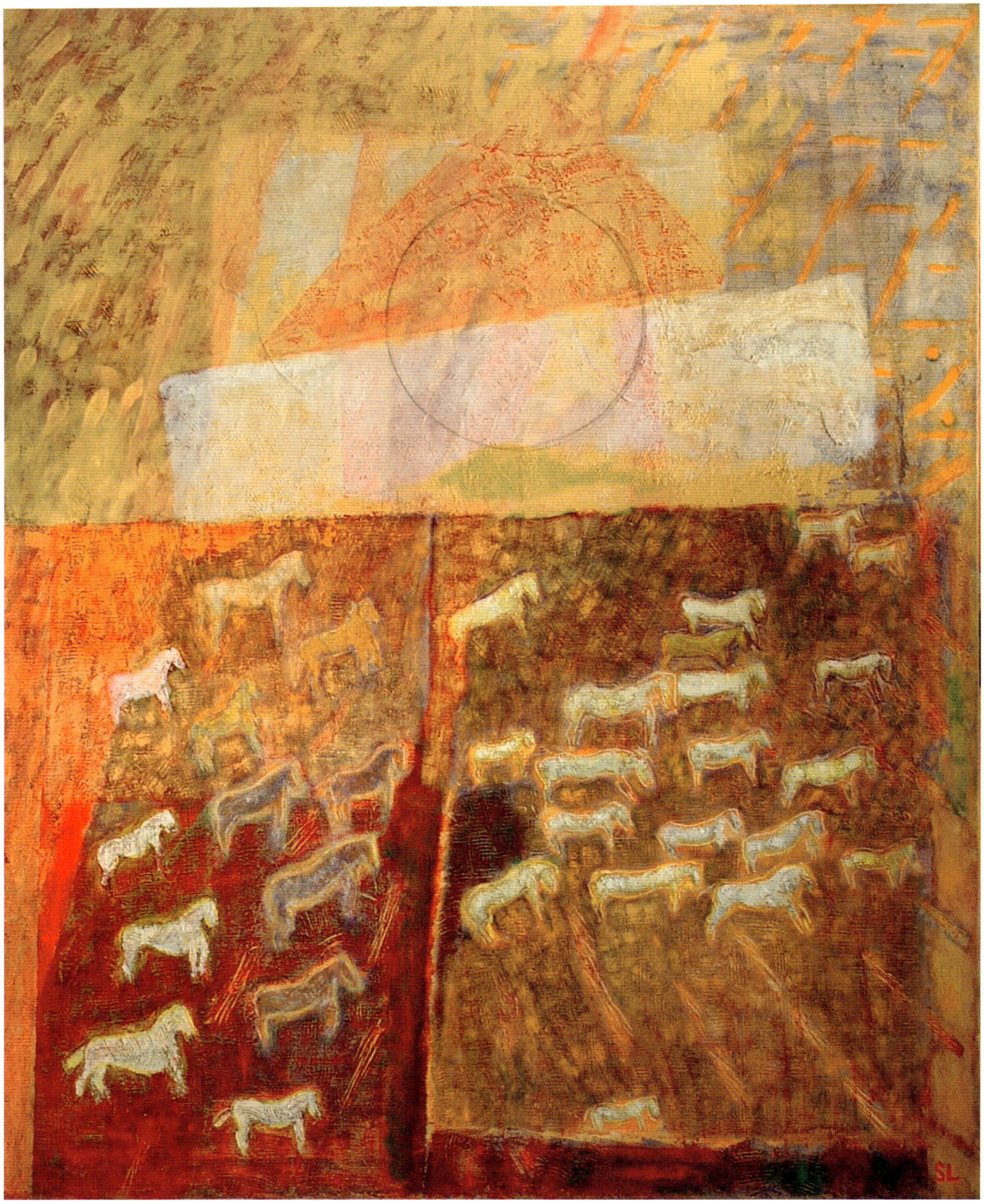

Break of Day 2009, oil on canvas, 119 x 91 cm

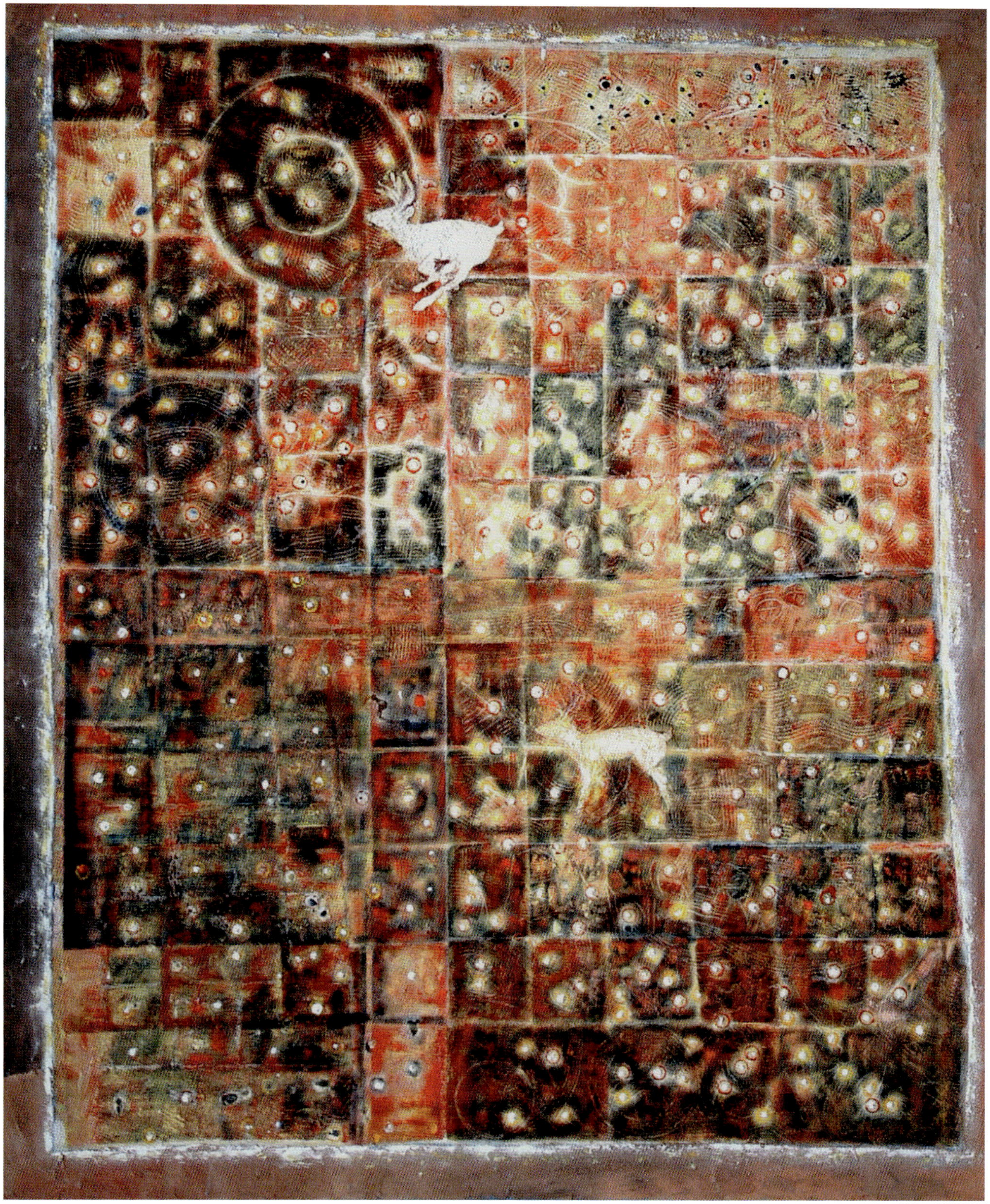

Night Drive 2009, oil on canvas, 119 × 91 cm

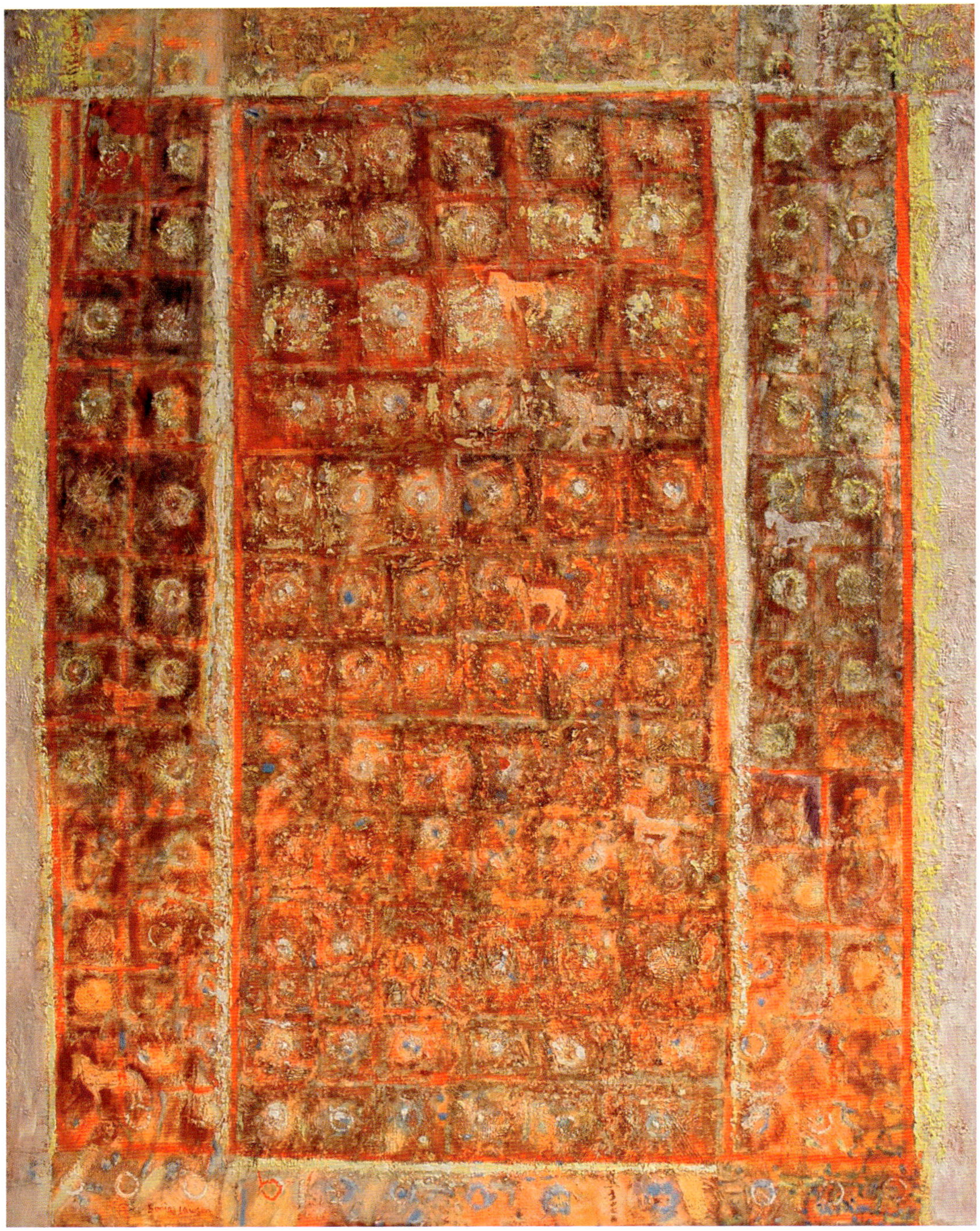

Portal to Shangri-La 2011, oil on canvas, 270 × 100 cm

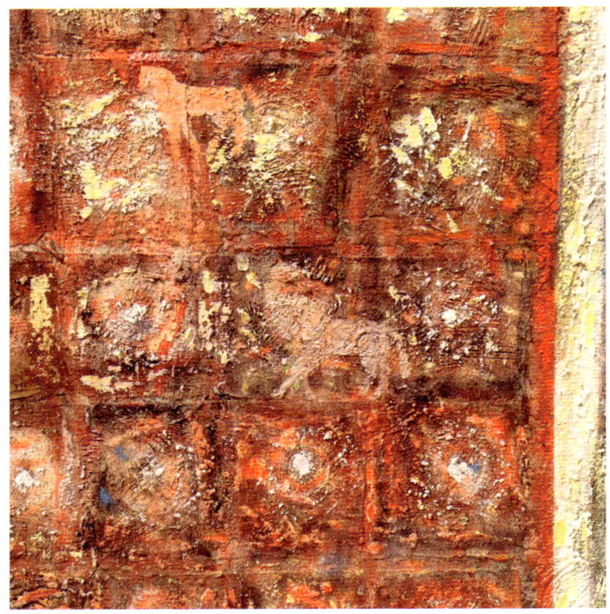

Detail from **Portal to Shangri-Bloody-La**

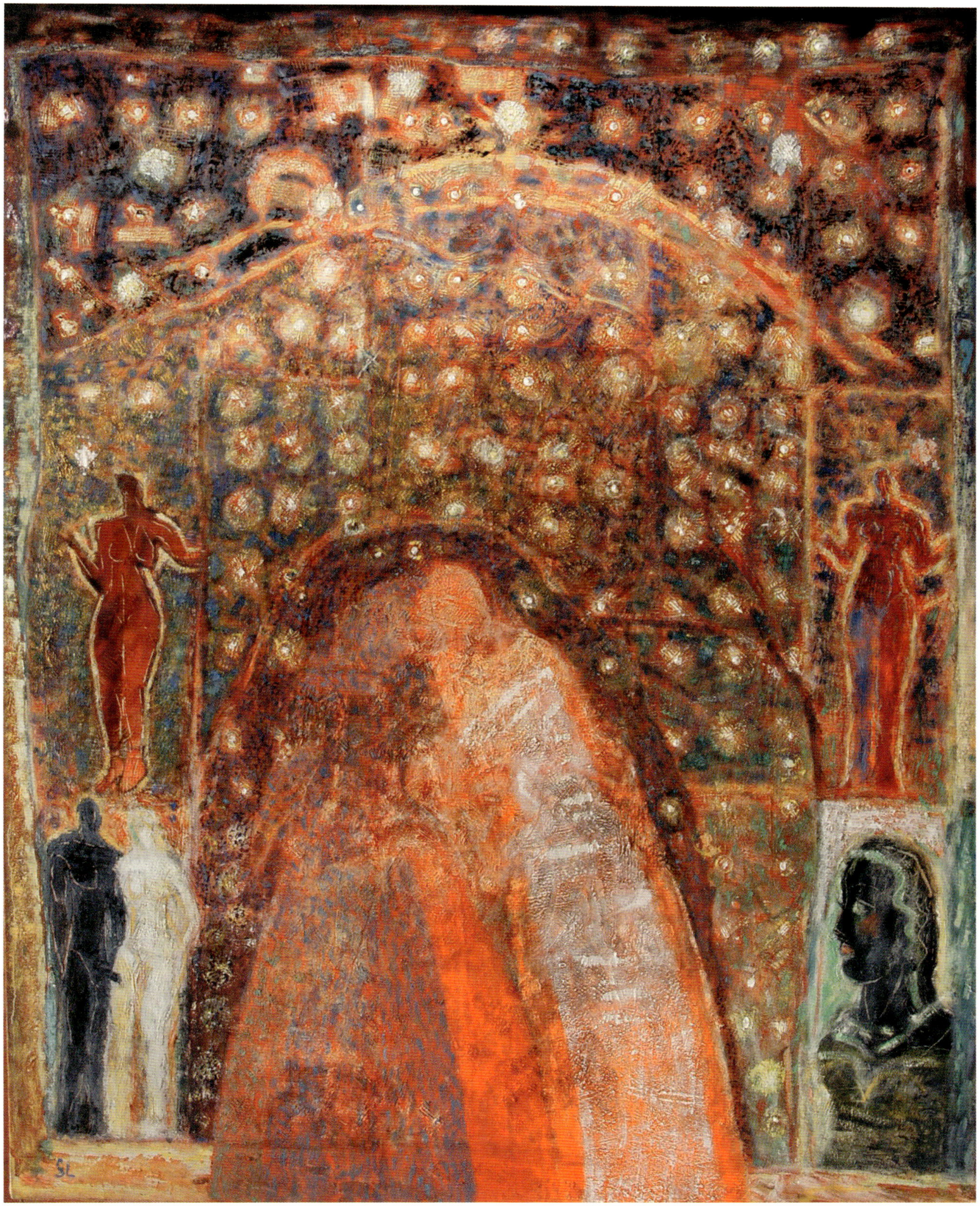

Night in a Private Garden 2010, oil on canvas, 128 × 100 cm

Sketchbooks

Sketchbooks are vital to any artist: the joy of the sketchbook and the freedom it allows invigorates.

One image may be formal, the next playful, then structural, then psychological. It allows unrelated disparate parts to coexist and is telling of the artist's breadth of interest.

I am gladdened by the sketchbook, a distillation of the perceived and imaginary: my liberating tonic.

Sonia Lawson 2014

The following pages of sketchbooks show a selection of images drawn from before Sonia studied at the RCA to the present day.

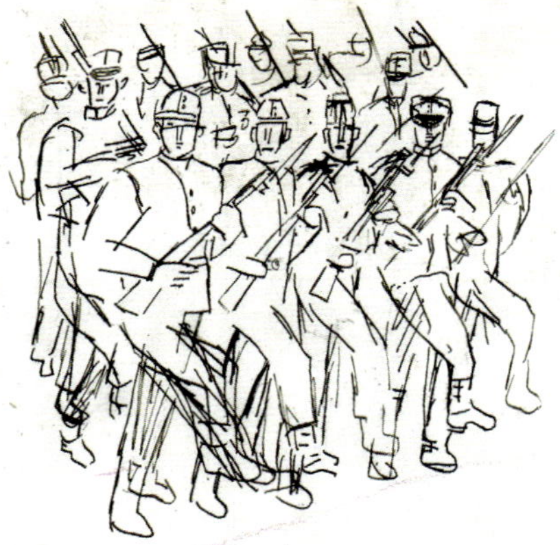

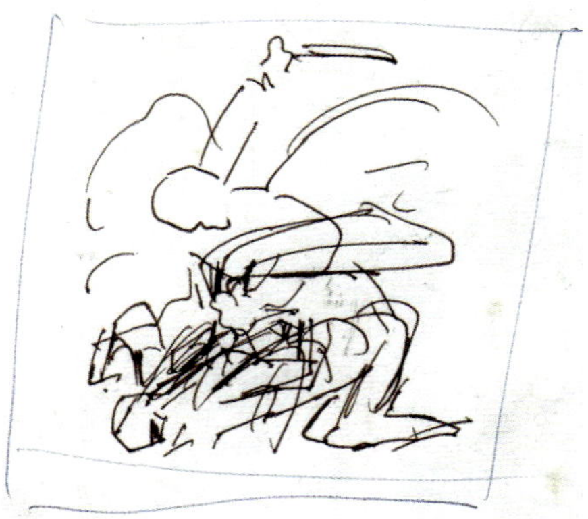

A Beating

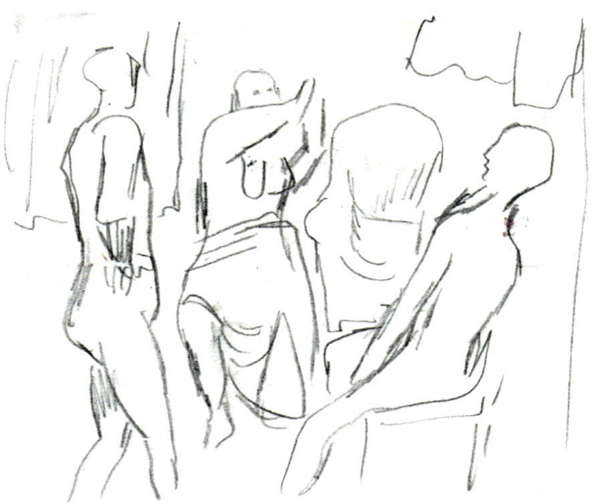

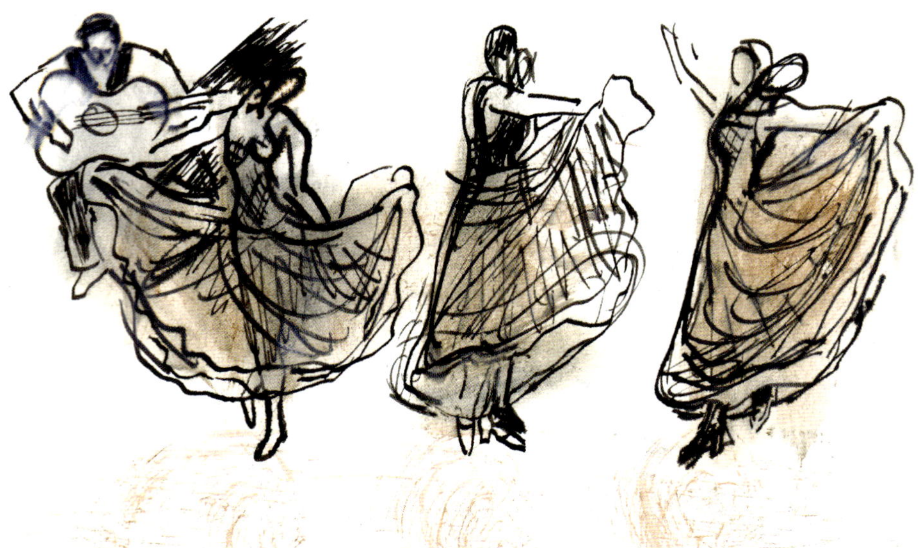

Spanish Dancers

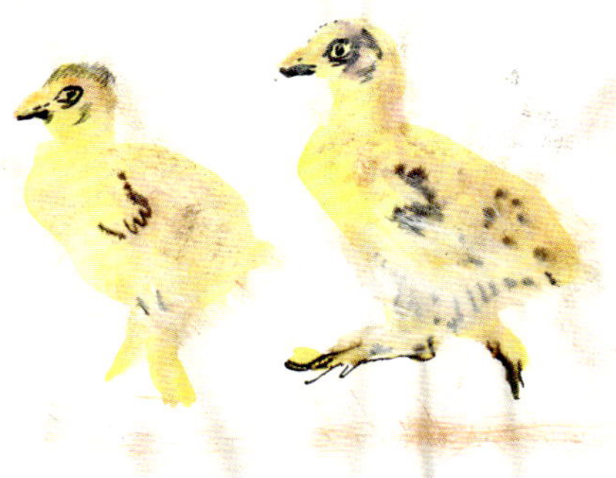

Little Geese

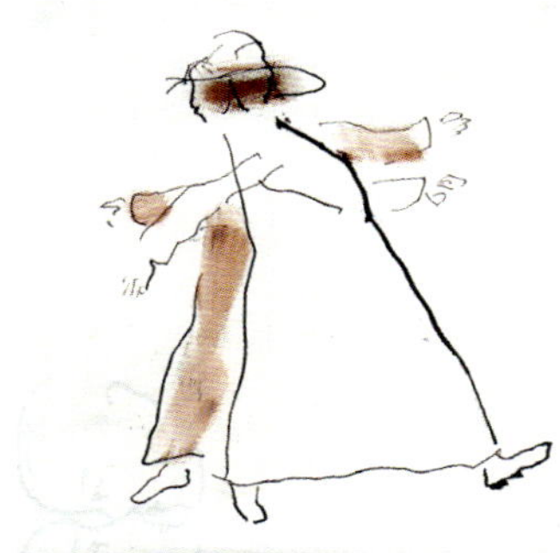

In Two Minds

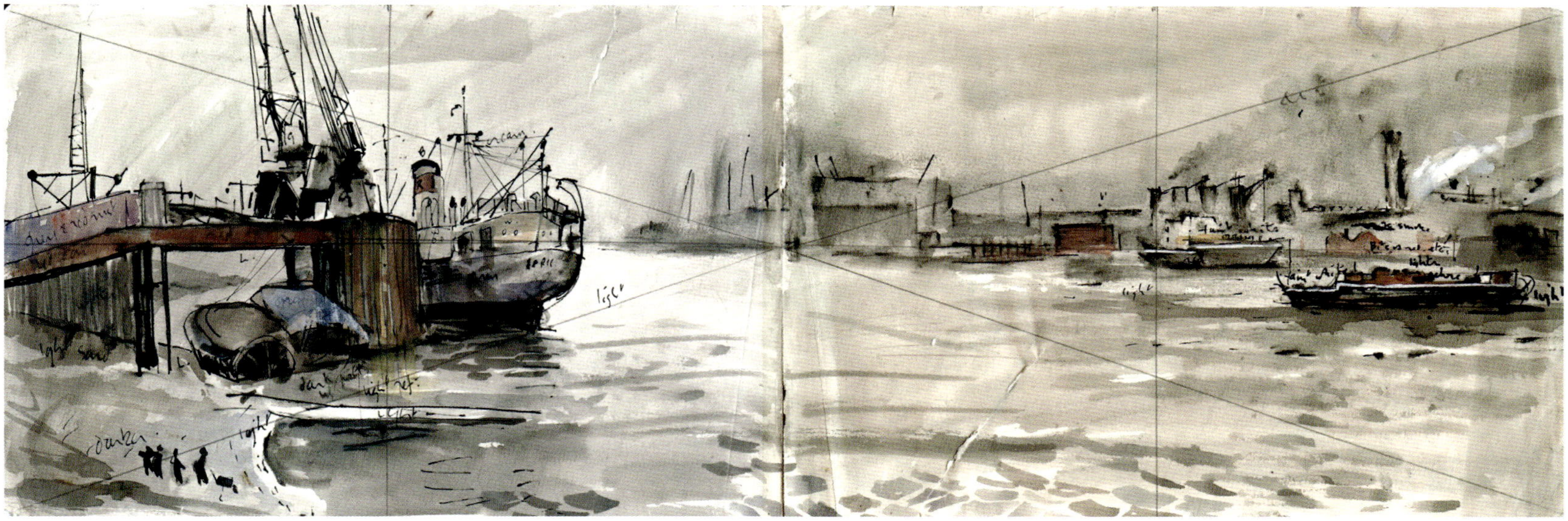

Boats in Harbour 1954–55, watercolour and ink, 18 x 54 cm

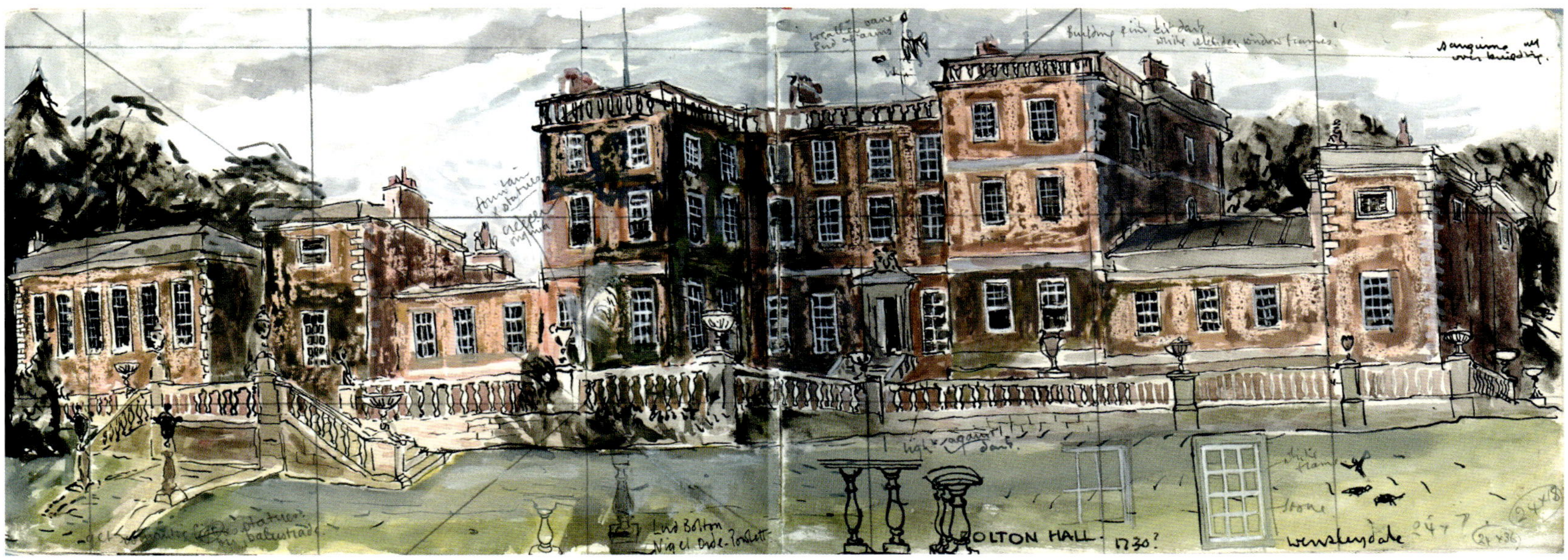

Bolton Hall 1954–55, watercolour and ink, 18 x 54 cm

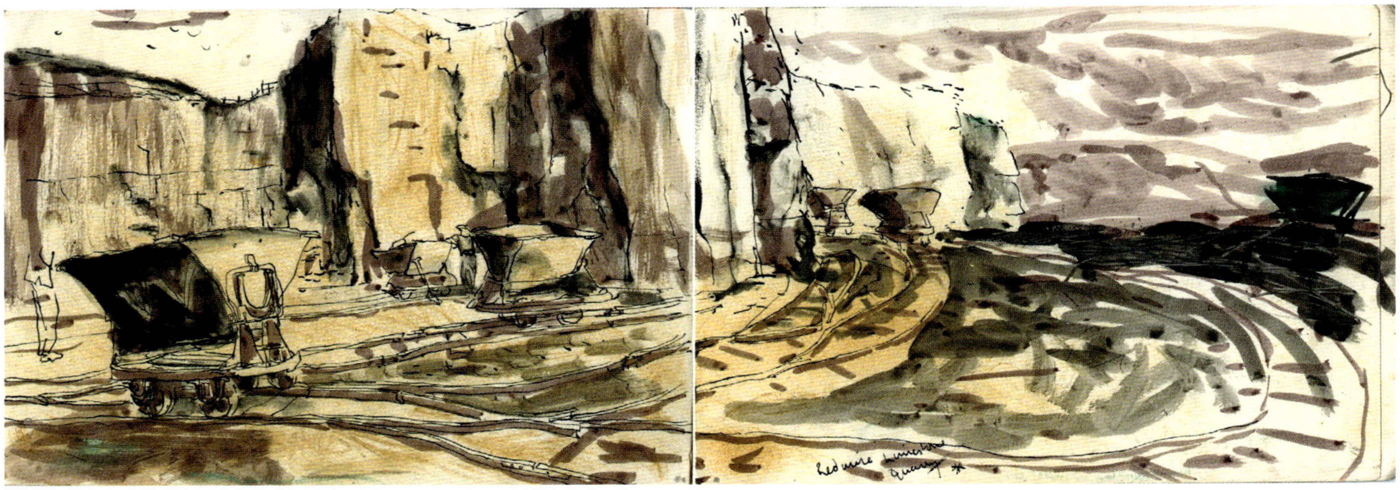

Redmire Quarry sketch, 1954–55, pen and ink with watercolour

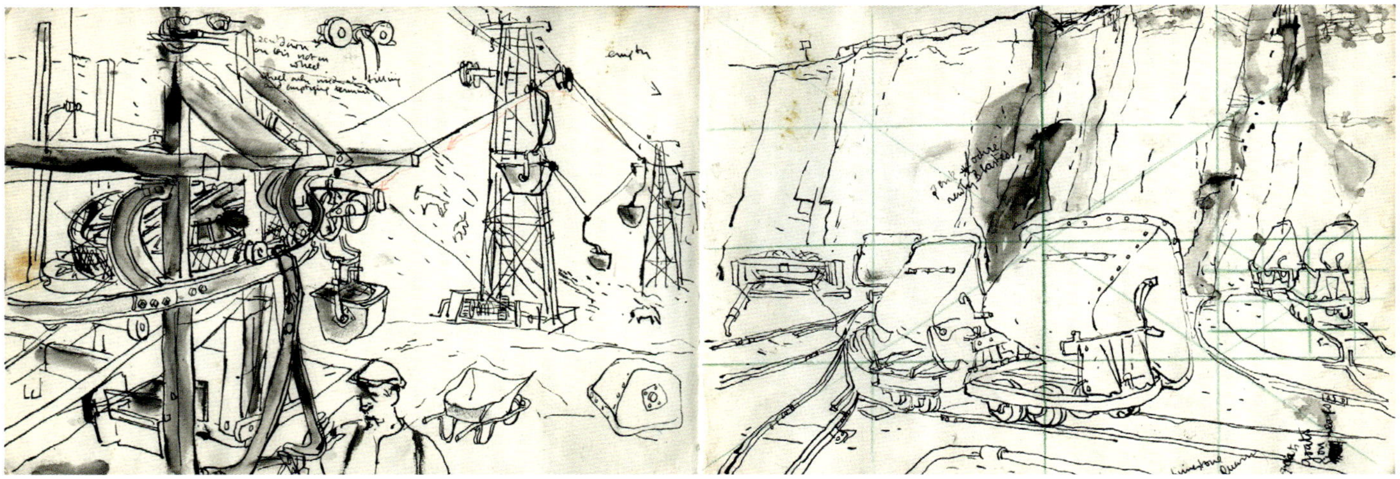

Redmire Quarry sketch, 1954–55, sepia, Indian ink and chalk

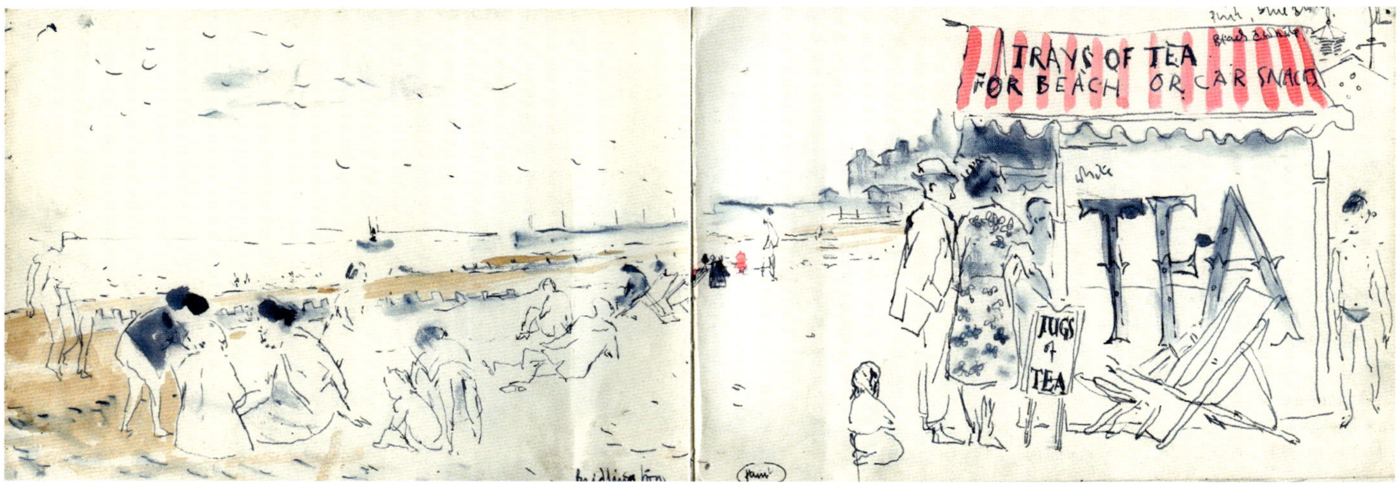

Bridlington Beach 1955, pen, ink and watercolour, 18 x 54 cm

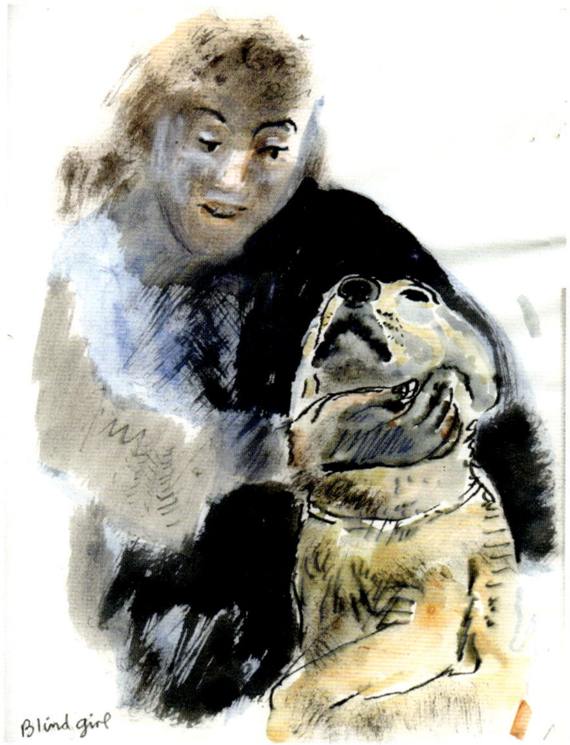

Blind Girl

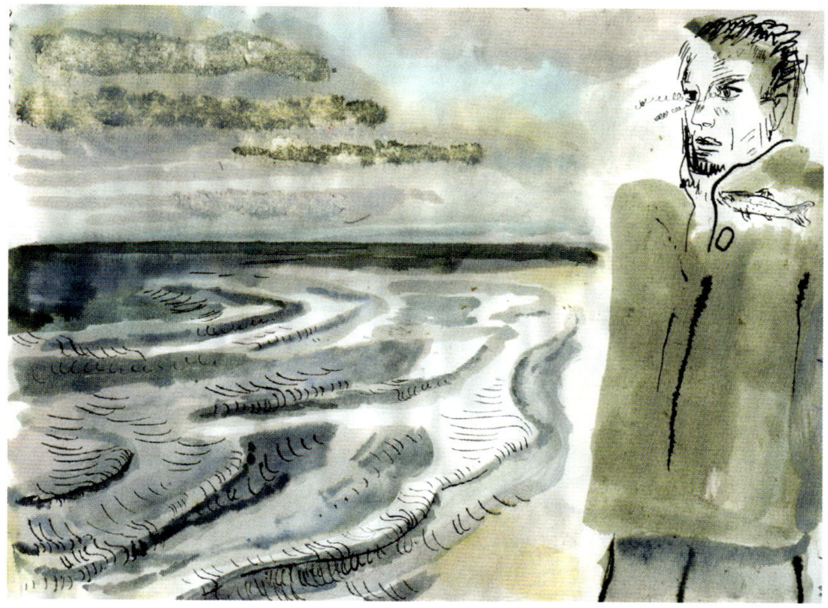

Fear of the Sea

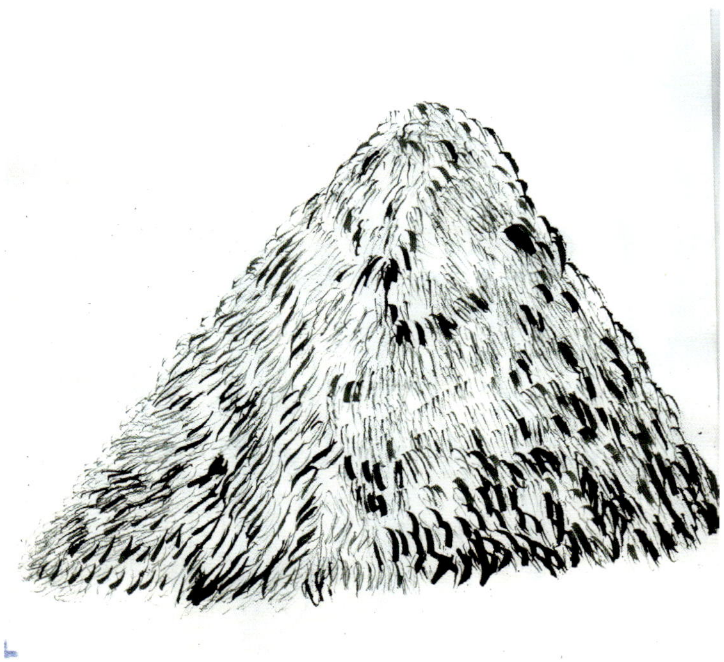

Heap

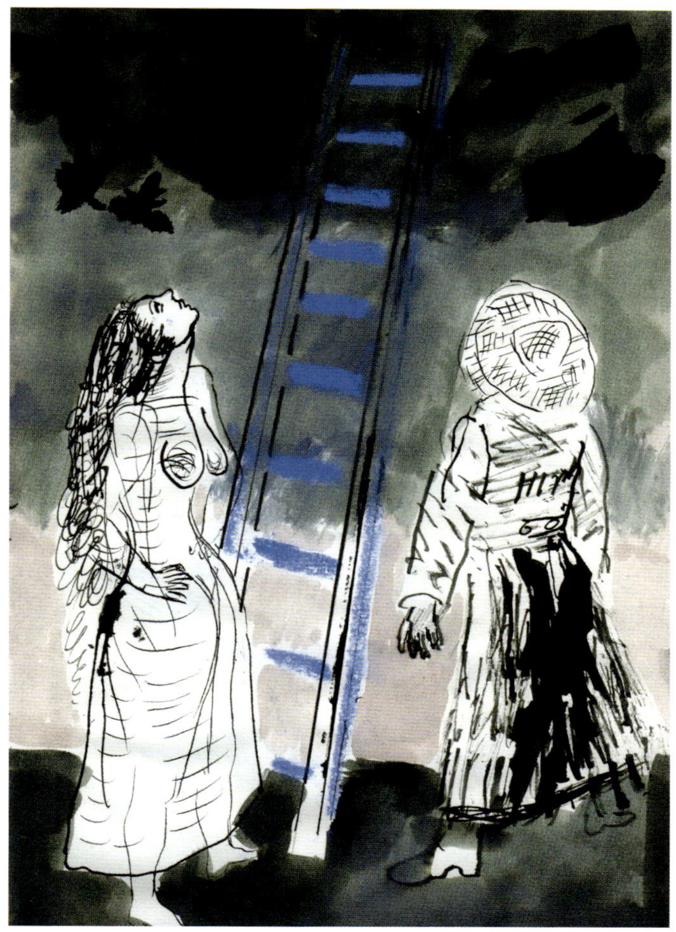

Ad astra

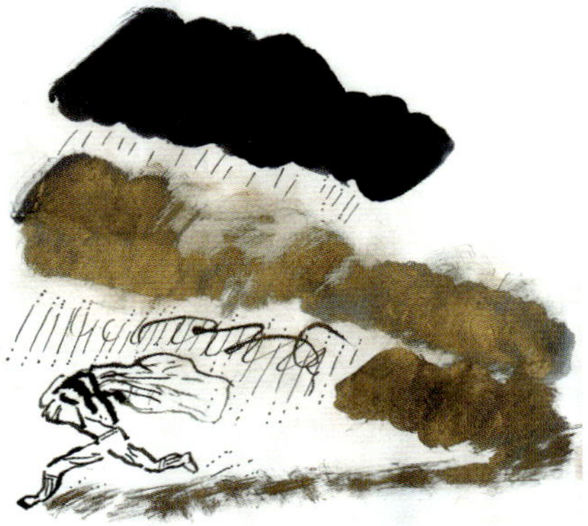

Such is life

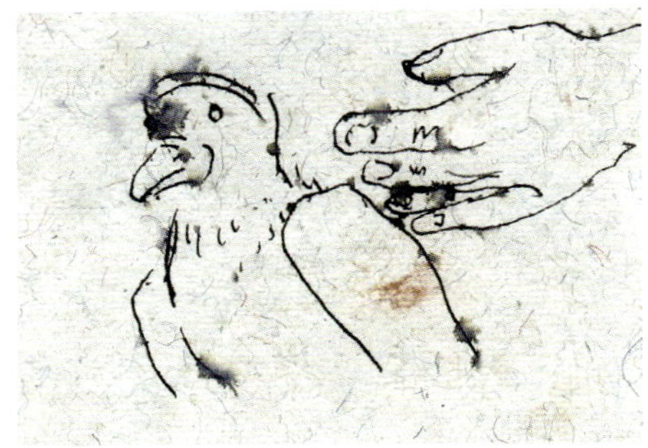

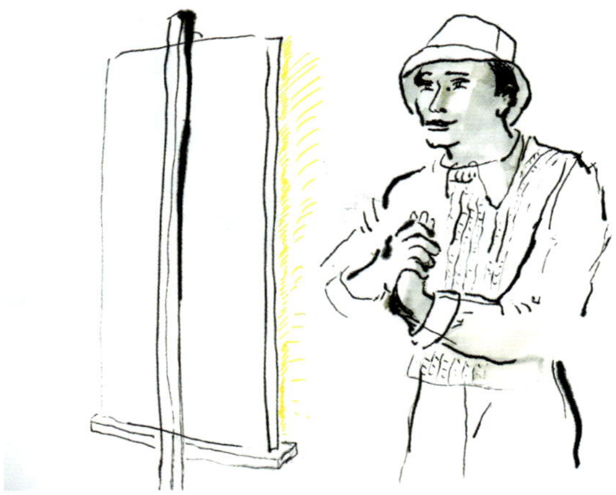

The Sunday Painter

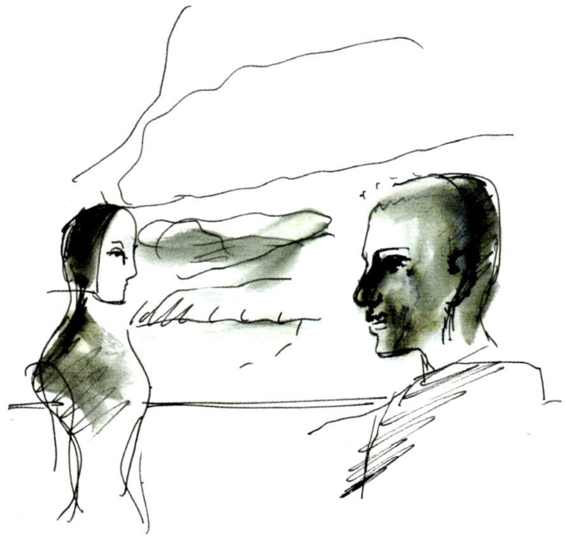

Figures

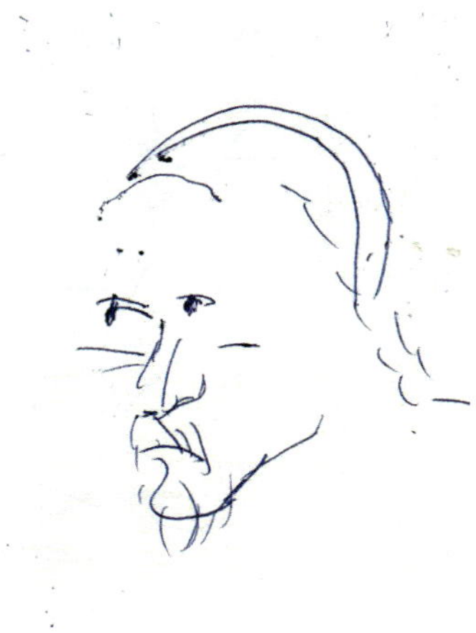

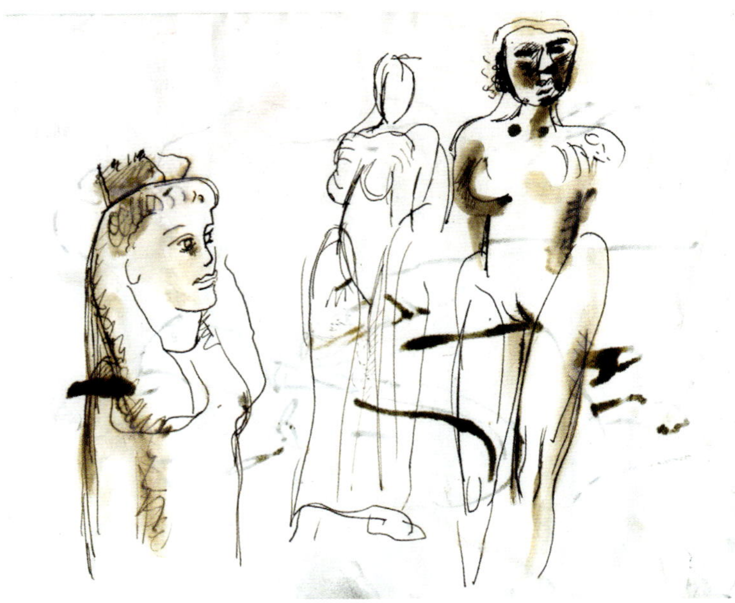

3 figures

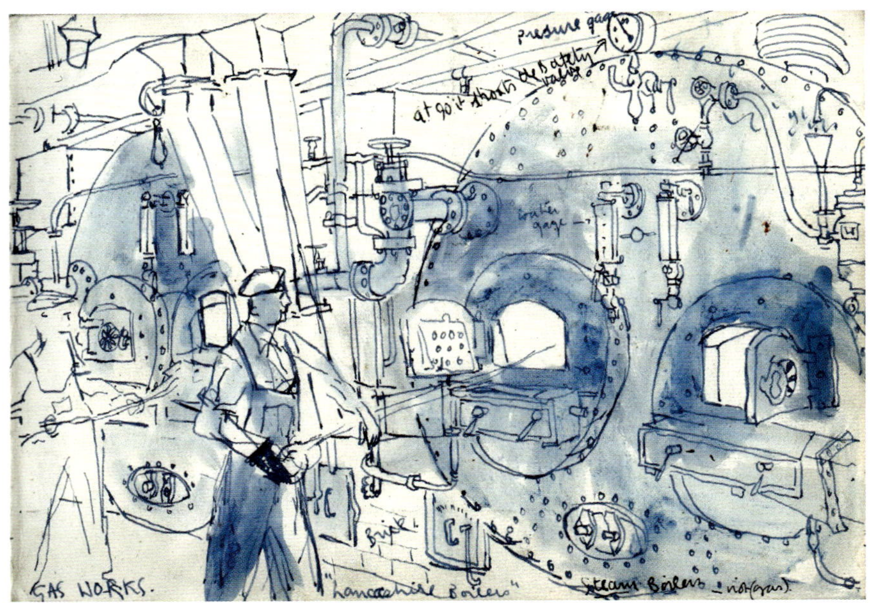

Doncaster Gas Works 1954–55, pen and wash, 18 x 26 cm

Sonia Lawson

Chronology

1954–59 Graduate and postgraduate studies at Royal College of Art
1959–60 Travelling scholarship to France
1960 One of four young artists selected for John Schlesinger's BBC TV *Monitor* documentary 'Private View'
Stratford Upon Avon. 2 paintings commissioned by Richard Buckle to mark the 4th centenary of Shakespeare's birth
1982 Elected Royal Academician
1984 Elected to Royal Watercolour Society
Eastern Arts Drawing Prize
Rowney Drawing Prize
Imperial War Museum commission to record British Army of the Rhine exercise 'Operation Lionheart', Westphalia, Germany
1986–87 Lorne Scholarship, London University
1989 Commissioned by Archbishop of Canterbury to paint the Pope in celebration of ecumenical accord
1990 Eastern Arts Drawing Prize
1993 Commission: Book illustrations to accompany poems by James Kirkup, 'Look at it this way', Rockingham Press.
1994 Commission: University of Birmingham Two Works: *Guardian I & II*
1995 Commission: Drawings published in conjunction with Fay Weldon short story, 'New Years Eve', Clarion Publishing
1999 Cover illustration: *Women's Lives into Print. The Theory, Practice and Writing of Feminist Auto/Biography*, Macmillan Press, edited by Pauline Polkey
2004 Cover illustration: *Ways of Returning*, poems by Linda Saunders, Arrowhead, 2004
2005 Honorary Royal West of England Academician
2008 Open University Lecture: 'Points of Departure'

Works in Public and Private Collections

Arts Council of Great Britain
Bolton Art Gallery
Bradford: Cartwright
Carlisle Art Gallery
Chatsworth Collection
Cranfield College of Technology
Dewsbury Art Gallery
Harrogate: Mercer Art Gallery
Huddersfield Art Gallery
Leeds University
London: Imperial War Museum
London: Royal Academy of Arts
London: Royal College of Art Collection
Middlesborough Art Gallery
Ministry of Works
NHS Trust: Paintings for Hospitals
Nuffield Collection
Oxford: St. Peters College
Rochdale Art Gallery
Royal West of England Academy: Bristol
Sheffield Graves Art Gallery
University of Birmingham
University of Brisbane
USA Canada and Australia
Vatican: Rome
Wakefield Art Gallery
Works in Private Collections: Europe, USA, Canada and Australia

Mixed Exhibitions

1960 London Group
Zwemmer Gallery, London
Royal Academy of Arts, London
Royal Watercolour Society
1962 Cheltenham Art Gallery: 'Six Young Painters'
1963 John Moores, Liverpool
1964 Stratford-upon-Avon, Shakespeare Festival
Leeds City Art Gallery: 'Round About London Galleries'
1970 Trafford Gallery, London
1977 Royal Academy Jubilee: '25 Years of British Art'
1978 Cranfield College, Milton Keynes
1981 Arts Council, 'Fragments Against Ruin'
1982 Midland Group Arts Council, 'The Subjective Eye'
1981–83 Moira Kelly Fine Art, London
1982 London and Edinburgh, Fruit Market Hayward Annual, British Drawing
1982–83 Eastern Arts/Tolly Cobbold 55–86 Touring Exhibition
1983 New York, Britain Salutes New York. '8 in the 80s'
Moira Kelly Fine Art, Green St. SoHo
1984 First Prize 'Drawing for All' Gainsborough House, Eastern Arts Touring
1985 Leeds City Art Gallery, 'Critics Choice'
Bradford Central Library, 'Collectors Choice'
R.C.A. Gallery, 'London Group'
Graves, Sheffield, '"Frail Peace" Personal Visions on War'
London: Arthur Young Industrial Sponsors Exhibition
1986 Leicestershire Invited Artists
Gainsborough House, 'Drawing For All' Eastern Arts Touring
1987 Leeds Polytechnic, 'New Art in Yorkshire'
1988 Royal College of Art, London, 'Exhibition Road' Over 80 eminent painters who studied at the college celebrating the RCA's 150th anniversary
Kingfisher Gallery, Edinburgh
1991–92 John Moores, Liverpool
1992 Gallerie Zur Alten Deutschen Schule, Thun, Switzerland
1993–1999 Boundary Gallery, London
1993–1995 Connaught Brown, London
1993–1999 Lamont Gallery, London
1993 Mercury Gallery, London
1995–1998 Royal Watercolour Society, London
1996 Boundary Gallery, London
1997 Mall Galleries, London, 'Discerning Eye'
1999 Lamont Gallery, London
Royal Watercolour Society, London
2001 Nottingham University, 'Representing Lives'
Featured artist RWS London, Bankside
2004–2005 Royal Academy, London, 'Visual Wit'
2013 RWA, Bristol 'One Hundred Years: One Hundred Works'
2014 Mercer Art Gallery, Harrogate, 'Art and Yorkshire: From Turner to Hockney'

Solo Exhibitions

1963 New Arts Centre, London
1964 Queen Square Gallery, Leeds
1967 Trafford Gallery, London
1973 'Homage to my Friends' (from Giotto to Janis Joplin) Billingham and Middlesbrough
1977 Central Library, Bradford
'British Painting at the Royal Academy' RA 25 years mixed exhibition (1952–1977)
1979 Open University, Milton Keynes
Darlington Art Gallery
Harrogate Art Gallery
1980 Northern Artists' Gallery, Harrogate
1982–83 'Shrines of Life' – retrospective touring to Central Art Gallery, Milton Keynes; Mappin Gallery, Sheffield; Leicester Polytechnic; Cartwright Hall, Bradford; Ferens Art Gallery, Hull; (organiser Edna Read)
1984 West Yorkshire Arts Association, Kirklees
1987 'Midnight Muse', Manchester City Art Gallery
1989 Cartwright Hall, Bradford
1989 Boundary Gallery, London
1994 University of Birmingham
1995 Boundary Gallery, London
1996 Dean Clough Galleries, Halifax Retrospective (30 years)
1998 Boundary Gallery, London
1999 Shire Hall, Stafford
2000 Retrospective Exhibition, Royal West of England Academy, Bristol
Boundary Gallery. London
2001 Carlow Arts Festival, Eire
2002 Vertigo Gallery, London
2003 Boundary Gallery, London
2004 University of Birmingham
2005 Boundary Gallery, London
2006 Aylesbury Museum & Gallery, Points of Departure Retrospective
2008 Wakefield City Art Gallery, West Yorkshire

Credits

The author and publishers thank the following for granting permission to reproduce copyright material:

Pages 8 and 74 'The Remains' and 'The Coming of Light' by Mark Strand. Taken from *New Selected Poems* Copyright © Mark Strand, 2007, used by permission of The Wylie Agency (UK) Limited.

Page 12 'Hay', from *Looking for Luck* by Maxine Kumin. Copyright © 1992 by Maxine Kumin. Used by permission of W.W. Norton & Company, Inc.

Page 87 'Hilton Abstract' by W. S. Graham reproduced by permission of Rosalind Mudaliar, the Estate of W. S. Graham.

Page 110 Lines from *She River* by Linda Saunders are quoted by permission of Vane Women Press.

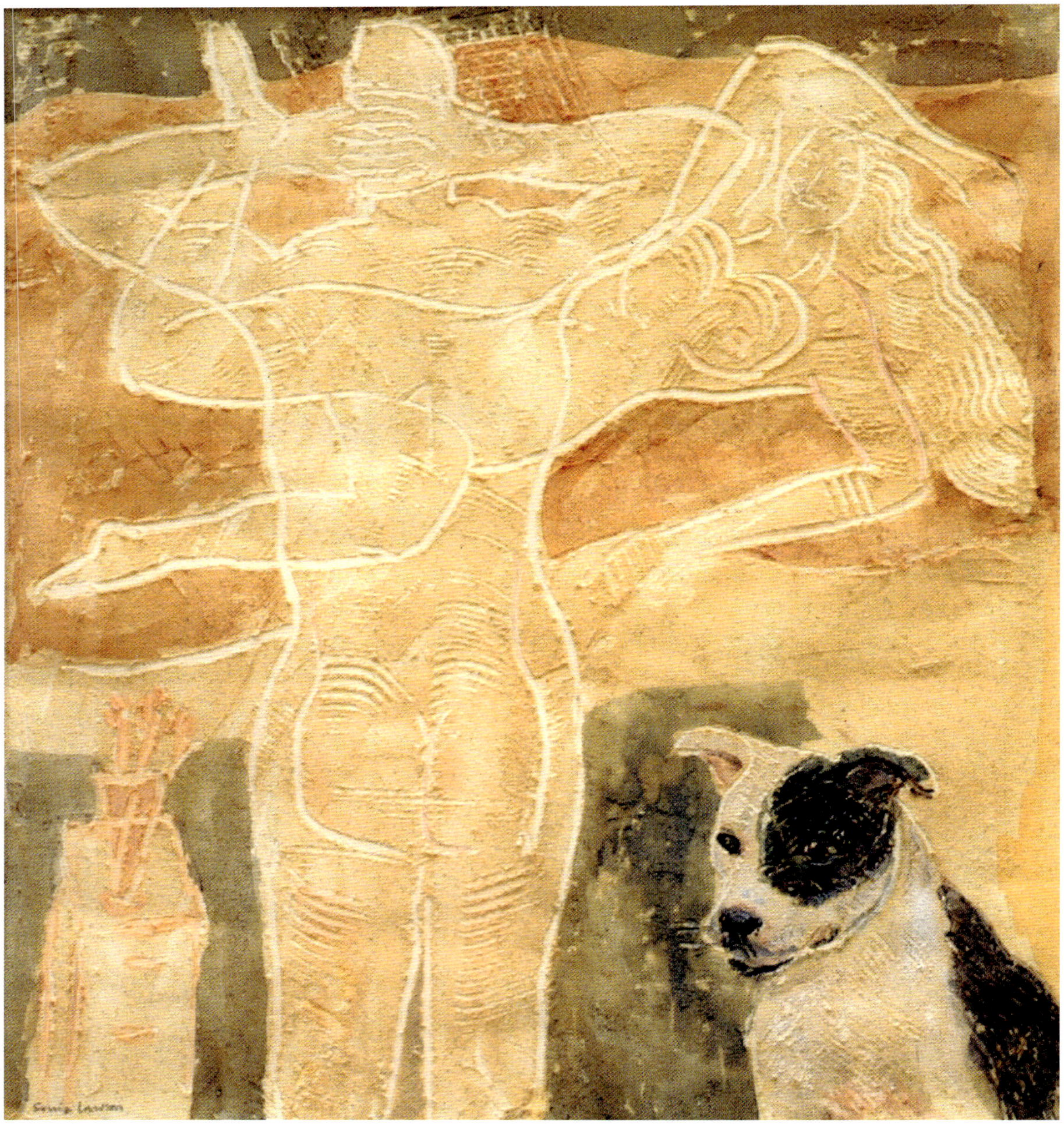

In Your Dreams 2009, watercolour, aquapasto, on paper, 31 x 25 cm